FINDING LOST

SEASON 3

NIKKI STAFFORD

ECW Press

Published by ECW PRESS
2120 Queen Street East, Suite 200
Toronto, Ontario, Canada M4E 1E2
416.694.3348 / info@ecwpress.com

LIBRARY AND ARCHIVES CANADA CATALOGUING IN PUBLICATION

Stafford, Nikki, 1973–
Finding Lost, season three : the unofficial guide / Nikki Stafford.

ISBN 978-1-55022-799-4

1. Lost (Television program). I. Title.

PI992.77.L67S733 2007   791.45'72   C2007-903634-1

Developing editor: Jennifer Hale
Cover and text design: Tania Craan
Typesetting: Gail Nina
Front cover photos: Andrews: Yoram Kahana/Shooting Star; Monaghan: Sue
Schneider/Moonglow Photos; Emerson: Albert L. Ortega; Daniel Dae Kim: Sthanlee
Mirador/Shooting Star; O'Quinn: Yoram Kahana/Shooting Star; Yunjin Kim: Albert L. Ortega;
Fox: Pseudoimage/Shooting Star; Mitchell: Mary Leahy/Agency Photos; Cusick: Mary
Leahy/Agency Photos; Lilly: Yoram Kahana/Shooting Star; Holloway: Sthanlee Mirador/Shooting
Star; de Ravin: Christina Radish/Agency Photos; Garcia: Christina Radish/Agency Photos

Printing: Victor Graphics   3   4   5

PRINTED AND BOUND IN THE UNITED STATES

ECW PRESS
ecwpress.com

Table of Contents

Acknowledgments **v**
How Not to Get Lost **vi**
The Others Are Coming!: Season 3 **1**

SEASON 3
October 2006–May 2007

A Tale of Two Cities (Jack) **6**
    A Tale of Two Cities **12**

The Glass Ballerina (Sun & Jin) **17**
    The Lost Experience **22**

Further Instructions (Locke) **26**

Every Man For Himself (Sawyer) **31**
    Of Mice and Men **35**

The Cost of Living (Eko) **39**
    To Kill a Mockingbird **43**
    Eko's Jesus Stick **46**

I Do (Kate) **48**
    Obsessed With the Numbers: The Season 3 Hiatus **52**

Not in Portland (Juliet) **54**

Flashes Before Your Eyes (Desmond) **60**
    Time Travel **64**
    A Brief History of Time **67**
    David Hume (1711–1776) **72**

Stranger in a Strange Land (Jack) **75**
    The Prisoner **81**

Tricia Tanaka Is Dead (Hurley) **85**

Enter 77 (Sayid) **89**
    Sawyer's Nicknames **95**

Par Avion (Claire) 96

The Man from Tallahassee (Locke) 101
   O Canada 105

Exposé (Nikki & Paulo) 106
   "Exposé" Timeline 110
   The Fountainhead 112
   Rodrigo Santoro (Paulo) 113
   Kiele Sanchez (Nikki Fernandez) 115

Left Behind (Kate) 116
   Pre-Island Relationships 120
   Kate's Aliases 122

One of Us (Juliet) 124
   Elizabeth Mitchell (Juliet Burke) 131
   Carrie 133

Catch-22 (Desmond) 135
   Catch-22 140

D.O.C. (Sun) 144
   Others vs. Losties 147

The Brig (Locke) 152
   Parent Issues 153
   Biblical Names 158

The Man Behind the Curtain (Ben) 161
   Michael Emerson (Benjamin Linus) 169
   The Wonderful Wizard of Oz 171

Greatest Hits (Charlie) 175
   Make Your Own Kind of Music 179

Through the Looking Glass, Parts 1 & 2 (Jack) 183
   Fate vs. Free Will 194
   Through the Looking-Glass, and What Alice Found There 204
   The Others 207

Sources 212

Acknowledgments

Thank you to everyone at ECW Press, especially Jack and David for agreeing to do the book; Crissy for becoming my fellow *Lost* fan and offering tips and advice throughout the writing process; Gail Nina for laying it out; and Simon and Sarah for doing such a great job on the publicity of the previous book.

Thanks to the always awesome Gil Adamson, who once again smoothed out my writing and became another *Lost* fan along the way.

A big, big thank you once again to Ryan Ozawa, Oahu resident and photographer, who provided me with such amazing location photos and addresses. I can't thank you enough.

Thank you to Fionna Boyle, who once again read an early draft of the manuscript and offered feedback, suggestions, and love for Charlie.

Thanks to the *Lost* fans who e-mailed me when the first book came out and encouraged me to write a second one!

A huge thanks to the regular readers and posters on my blog, Nik at Nite. Throughout season 3 they showed up every Thursday morning and agreed or disagreed with my assessments of the previous night's episode (but mostly agreed, right guys? Guys? Hello?) and offered their own insights. A special shout-out to Crissy, Chapati Kid, Colleen/Redeem147, Brian Douglas, Jay Menard, Roland, Michelle, Leor, fb, Kathy Trites, Jeff Heimbuch, Justin Mohareb, Jason Halm, Glenn, TotallyLost, Chris in NF, Maddy, and many, many Anonymouses.

A big thanks to my family and friends, especially Sue for listening to me go on and on about what I was writing on any particular day.

The biggest thanks I reserve for my immediate family — my husband, Robert, who supported me throughout the writing of the book and helped me make the time to write it during evenings and weekends; my fabulous daughter Sydney, who kept my mind sharp with her constant "Why?" questions about absolutely everything (it's a phase, right?); and my son, who had no choice but to accompany me throughout the process and who kept the kicks to a minimum (well, not really, but he kept the writing interesting). And finally, as always, a massive thanks to Jennifer Hale. I'd be truly lost without you.

How Not to Get Lost

Lost is the biggest puzzle on television, and part of the fun of watching it lies in trying to put the puzzle pieces together, which is what my books help you do. Throughout season 3, many "fans" jumped ship. They said they were frustrated that the show's writers weren't providing them with answers. They didn't like the new direction the show was taking. They thought the writers were giving the Others too much attention, and not focusing on season 1 plots like Locke's faith or Jack struggling to be the leader. The problem was, those were *season 1 plots*. The show had moved on from the action/adventure of season 1. By the end of season 2 the show had developed a complicated mythology, and while season 3 had to continue to deal with that mythology, it also moved into new areas.

I welcomed the arrival of the Others. In season 3 I found Ben and Juliet to be as fascinating as many of the Losties on the beach — if not more so. Michael Emerson is rivaling Terry O'Quinn as the best actor on the show. Elizabeth Mitchell plays Juliet so ambiguously that even when we think she's conning the other characters, we love her for it nevertheless. Even the actors portraying more regular characters stepped up their game as well, as if sensing competition. Matthew Fox turns in his best performances of the series, as does Josh Holloway in "The Brig." Terry O'Quinn continues to be fabulous, and Henry Ian Cusick is a welcome and wonderful addition to the regular cast. And Nikki and Paulo give us two characters to hate. *Passionately.*

As I said in the introduction to my previous book, *Finding Lost*, this book is intended to be read alongside the episodes. You can watch the entire season and then read through the book, or you could watch an episode and read the corresponding guide to it. I included my e-mail address in the previous book, and was surprised and pleased to hear how many people had tried the latter approach, and loved it. People told me they got into the habit of reading it while watching the seasons 1 and 2 DVDs, watching an episode, then reading the guide for it, watching the next episode, reading the guide, etc. That is exactly how the book was meant to be read. But with season 3 airing, people felt like they were missing something by not having the book there.

So, throughout the season, I tried my hand at a blog, something I hadn't done before, and I loved it. Because I'm a Canadian, I had the advantage of watching the episodes before they aired in the U.S., so I was able to get a jump on things and offer one of the first analyses on the Net the night of the show. Nik at Nite (nikkistafford.blogspot.com) always gets its highest traffic on Thursday mornings, after an episode has aired. I owe a lot to the regular commenters on that blog who show up day after day to discuss their favorite TV shows.

As I wrote this book, of course, those initial gut-reaction blog entries turned into deeper, more thoughtful entries (with a lot more research behind them). As with my other books, this one will primarily be an episode guide, analyzing the development of characters and plotlines, asking questions along the way, and acting as a companion to viewers. I want you to read the episode guides as if you were discussing the shows with a friend.

Finding Lost is *not*, however, a substitute for watching the show. I will not provide plot summaries or transcripts or anything that would allow a reader to read my book instead of actually watching the show. You must watch the DVDs or the aired episodes. This book will provide a deeper understanding of the characters, the events, and the mysteries, but it will not be a replacement for *Lost* itself. No book could ever hope to do that.

The book proceeds episode by episode. Almost every guide is broken up by some tidbit of information, such as a small sidebar of interest, or a larger chapter on the historical significance of something. Just as life on the island is interrupted by the flashbacks of the characters, so too will the episode guide be broken up by these sections. You can come back to them later and just focus on the guide in the beginning, or read through them to get a better understanding of the references or the actors playing the characters.

The sidebars are usually compilations of small themes or motifs in the episodes. The book summaries provide a more in-depth study of the books referenced on the show. In each of the book summaries, I will give a brief rundown of the plot, and point out the deeper meaning in each book (warning: the book summaries contain spoilers for important plot details), and then some suggestions of the importance the book has on the show, and why it may have been chosen by the writers.

Some of the intermission chapters will touch on historical explanations of allusions on the show, such as the discussion on the show's use of biblical names. Others will take a facet of the episode and explore it more closely than you might have seen on the show, and still others will look outside the show to things like *The Lost Experience* or the 1960s television series *The Prisoner*, which had a huge influence on *Lost*. I will also sometimes refer back to my previous guide to *Lost*, and will call it *FL*.

The guides to the individual episodes will contain some spoilers for that particular episode, so I urge you to watch each episode first. I've been careful not to spoil any episodes beyond what you're reading, so if you watch an episode, and then read the corresponding guide to it, you should be pretty safe from being ruined for any future surprises. The episode guide will feature a one-line summary of the episode and then an analysis. Following each analysis, you'll find special notes of interest, and they require some explanation:

Highlight: A moment in the show that was either really funny, or left an impression on me that I couldn't forget after it ended.

Timeline: In "The Glass Ballerina," one of the characters actually stated that day's date in 2004, and this gave fans an important marker to figure out what the actual dates were for every episode. So I've included a section in the season 3 guide that was not in my original book outlining the in-plot date, according to Lostpedia. I take everything from Wikipedia and Lostpedia with a grain of salt, so this timeline is only a construction by fans, and not necessarily intended by the *Lost* writers. (Wherever I think there might be an error or a wild guess, I say so.)

Did You Notice?: A list of small moments in the episode that you might have missed but are either important clues to later mysteries or were just really cool.

Interesting Facts: These are little tidbits of information that are outside the show's canon, explaining allusions and references, or offering behind-the-scenes material.

Nitpick: Little things in the episode that bugged me. I've put these things in Nitpicks because I couldn't come up with a rational explanation myself. (Maybe you have an explanation, and if so, I'd love to hear it.) What makes the Nitpicks section difficult is that what appears to be an inconsistency now could be a deliberate plot point by the writers that will take on massive significance later. So I'm prepared for several of these to be debunked by the show.

Nikki and Paulo — Why?: This season the writers made a huge mistake in bringing two background characters forward and making them part of the cast. By the time they got their own flashback in episode 14, there were many fans who, to quote Sawyer, thought, "Who the hell are *they*?" This section will document their magnificent annoyingness, right from their first appearance in "Further Instructions."

Oops: These are mistakes that I don't think could be explained away by anything.

4 8 15 16 23 42: In the late season 1 episode, "Numbers," Hurley reveals a set of numbers that have had an impact in his life, and it turns out those numbers have popped up everywhere, on the island and in the characters' lives before the crash. This section will try to catalog them.

It's Just a Flesh Wound: This is a list of all of the wounds incurred by the characters on the show. I've decided to ignore the emotional injuries, as those would take pages to list.

Lost in Translation: Whenever a character speaks in another language that is not translated for us or we see something written that's not immediately decipherable, this section will provide a translation whenever I could find it. Thanks to all of the fans who have provided these to the English speakers like me.

Any Questions?: At the end of each episode, I've provided a list of questions that I think viewers should be asking themselves at that point. For anyone who's already seen the show to the end of season 3, many of the questions have been answered, but I've left them in here to show what questions should be arising at the end of each hour. Many of these questions are still valid and I hope will be resolved in later seasons.

Ashes to Ashes: Whenever a character on the show dies, this section will provide their very brief obituary.

Music/Bands: This is a list of the popular music we hear on the show. In most cases I've provided in italics the name of the CD where you can find the song, but if I haven't, it's because it's a song that is featured on several compilations. I owe most of these findings to LostHatch.com. The analyses of the lyrics are my own.

And there you have it, a guide to the guide. I hope you enjoy the book, and I welcome any corrections, nitpicks, praise (please? just a little?), and discussion at my e-mail address, nikki_stafford@yahoo.com, or come on over to my blog. I cannot stress this strongly enough, however: the opinions in the following pages are completely my own, and if anyone out there has contrary opinions, I respect those. I don't expect everyone to have the same views as I do. What makes *Lost* so much fun to watch and discuss is how many possibilities it presents to us. Ten fans can come away with ten different interpretations of what they just saw, and that's what makes a show great, in my opinion.

Nikki Stafford
nikki_stafford@yahoo.com
nikkistafford.blogspot.com
June 2007

The Others Are Coming!: Season 3

When we last left our castaways, there was much destruction, possible death, and a few kidnappings. The season 2 finale of *Lost* had answered several questions (while, of course, forcing us to ask several more) and introduced us to Desmond via a long-awaited flashback. But it also showed us something more important — that the outside world exists, and someone is looking for the island.

Season 2 had had its share of detractors. Fans were furious with ABC's chaotic schedule — airing an episode, then taking three weeks off, airing two more, taking two weeks off, airing one, taking a whole month off. For a show as complicated as *Lost* is, where fans are asked to remember minutiae from an early episode that will become vitally important later on, ABC was making the viewer analysis a lot more difficult. As such, many fans stopped watching, and some of those who had stayed said season 2 was a huge disappointment after the excitement of season 1.

Of course, not all fans felt like this. *Lost* had become the quintessential show that fans would DVR/TiVo/PVR and watch over and over. Many fans had gone back and watched every episode of the season back-to-back, and those people came into season 3 satisfied with what they'd seen, full of eagerness and anticipation for what was to come.

Season 1 had been about the plane crash on the deserted island. As the castaways got to know one another (and kept their secrets), they were also intent on getting off the island. Sayid worked on trying to send out a radio signal. Michael became obsessed with building a raft. The island itself held danger, with a shapeless monster in the jungle that bellowed and uprooted trees. A woman named Rousseau revealed she'd lived on the island for sixteen years after "the Others" had kidnapped her daughter Alex. Locke struck out on his own as the lone survivor who actually wanted to *stay* on the island, discovering a hatch in the ground and, together with Boone, trying to get it open. The season ended with Boone dying; Locke blowing open the hatch; Jin, Sawyer, Michael, and Walt heading off on a raft; and Walt being kidnapped by the Others before the raft was blown up.

Season 2 was not about escape: it was about learning to live on the island. The Losties discovered there was yet another group of people on the island — those who had been in the tail section of the plane and had landed on another beach. Led by the fierce and angry Ana Lucia, this tribe hadn't fared as well as the Losties. They started off as twenty-three people, and by the time they'd made it to the

Executive Producer Damon Lindelof, one half of the dynamic duo known as "Darlton" among fans. (MARY LEAHY/AGENCY PHOTOS)

other side of the island, they were down to four. Michael spent the season searching for his son, Walt. Jack, Locke, and Kate discovered there was a man, Desmond, who was living in the hatch and pushing a button every 108 minutes to "save the world." After Desmond ran away, Locke took over the button-pushing, despite Jack mocking him for his blind faith. Locke met his theological match in Eko, one of the Tailies, who began building a church with Charlie and who took over pushing the button when Locke lost his faith in the process. The question remained: was the button-pushing merely a psychological experiment and nothing more?

The most significant event of season 2 was when Sayid found Henry Gale, a man claiming to have fallen to the island in a balloon accident that had taken the life of his wife. Sayid didn't believe him, locking him up in the armory and torturing him for information. When the real Henry Gale was discovered in the jungle, this "Henry" had some 'splaining to do. He insisted he was a good person, and gained the trust of Locke, but when Michael returned to the beach and entered the hatch, killing Libby and Ana Lucia and allowing Henry to escape, all bets were off. Michael led Kate, Sawyer, Jack, and Hurley back to the Others' side of the island to deliver them to those people, and in return, the one and only Henry Gale, who had emerged as the apparent leader, gave Michael and Walt a boat to leave the island. Meanwhile, Locke barred Eko from the computer while he and Desmond (who had returned) chose not to press the button. But as the island began to shake violently, Desmond realized the button really was supposed to be pushed, and he ran underneath the station with his fail-safe key, turned it, and presumably obliterated himself and possibly the other people in the hatch.

It was one hell of a finale.

Because of the momentum that had been built up by the final episodes of the season (despite the broadcasting calamity), the producers were looking for something to keep fans occupied throughout the summer, and they came up with the revolutionary online game, *The Lost Experience* (see page 22). This complex maze of clues and hints kept fans going from the final episodes of season 2 to one week before the beginning of season 3, while tying in sponsorships and keeping fans interested enough to keep watching the repeats of the show throughout the summer.

In early July, the Emmy nominations were released, and despite *Lost* winning Best Dramatic Series the year before, it was shut out of all major awards. It still garnered nine nominations — Henry Ian Cusick alone was up for an acting Emmy —

"He writes it, I'm working on *Star Trek*." Executive producers Carlton Cuse and J.J. Abrams. (ALBERT L. ORTEGA)

but won none of them. The cast and crew didn't see it as a major setback, however. "When we started, our big question was, 'Will anybody even watch this show?'" said Evangeline Lilly. "And then when people started watching, we were thrilled. And then when we got recognized critically, we were beside ourselves. So, when we didn't get nominated, all we had to do was remember where we came from." Later in July, *Lost* won a Television Critics Award for Outstanding Achievement in Drama.

After repeated criticisms of the way the network had handled the airing of the show's second season, ABC announced in mid-summer that the show would have no repeats at all. The bad news was, it was going to take a thirteen-week break in the middle of the season. "We really listened to the audience," said ABC Entertainment chief Steve McPherson. He explained that the show would be tailored so that the first six episodes would tell one story, letting us know what happened to Kate, Jack, and Sawyer on the one hand, and to the people involved in the hatch explosion on the other, while the next seventeen would begin in 2007 and have a more extended arc. They had considered skipping the fall premiere and making it a midseason show, but they wanted *Lost* to help launch ABC's new series, *The Nine*, by being a strong lead-in.

Carlton Cuse praised the idea. "We love it. We totally love it, because when *Lost* is on, it's on, and when it's not on, it's not. There's no confusion in the audience, there's no frustration with our repeats. We don't lose the momentum of our storytelling, and it's been really fun to construct a six-episode story arc. It's been really, really enjoyable."

While *The Lost Experience* maintained its hold on online audiences, announcements began trickling out of the ABC offices that new cast members were joining *Lost*. Henry Ian Cusick and Michael Emerson would be joining the main cast. Rodrigo Santoro, a Brazilian actor who was just making his mark on North American audiences, had also been cast in a major role on the show. Said Damon Lindelof, "He's a guy who's perfect for *Lost* because he's a face that the American audience is not familiar with, but he's been in the business long enough, [that he's also] an awesome actor that makes some really interesting choices. And he's certainly not interested in being the hunk on the show, nor are we interested in writing that for him. Although I think when people start to see him and surmise what role he's going to play on the show, that's the place they're going to go to. 'More eye candy for *Lost*!'" (Sadly, that wasn't the reaction audiences had.)

Elizabeth Mitchell, best known for her roles on *ER* and in *The Santa Clause 2*, was announced as joining the cast in August, and early reports suggested she would be a possible love interest for Matthew Fox. Kiele Sanchez was the next announcement, listed as a possible love interest for Santoro's character.

The new season promised to focus on the Others, with the audience following Kate, Jack, and Sawyer to where the Others lived and finding out more about them. Cuse stated, "What you think about the Others now is not the complete story. There's a lot more to know about them and I think you'll have a very different view of them after the end of this season. And certainly, even as the season goes along, the Others are going to change."

This was exciting news for Michael Emerson, who said, "We are going to live with the Others for a lot of time. I think we are going to grow in sympathy for them. We are going to begin to see they are like us. Their hearts can be broken. They have special missions, special habits . . . fashion problems."

Most of the season 3 cast of *Lost*, Others and all: Back row: Michael Emerson, Elizabeth Mitchell, Jorge Garcia, Matthew Fox (dudes, look at the camera!), Daniel Dae Kim, Henry Ian Cusick. Front row: Evangeline Lilly, Josh Holloway, Yunjin Kim, Adewale Akinnouye-Agbaje. (JEAN CUMMINGS/MOONGLOW PHOTOS)

The first six episodes would also divide the action three ways: the Others; what was going on back at the beach; and Sayid, Jin, and Sun squabbling on a boat. But even those characters would all be undergoing major shifts. When asked if Locke would go back to his season 1 self or maintain the season 2 persona, O'Quinn suggested, "I don't think they're going to go back; it's an evolution. Locke and I were frustrated last season. He thought he was seeking the meaning of life, but then found this thing where he had to push this button every few minutes, which wasn't very satisfying. He's got to move on. He's got to find his place in this family. He's looking for someone else to acknowledge him in such a way that will define him to himself." When asked what he would change about his character if he could choose one thing, O'Quinn deadpanned, "More sex."

The season 3 premiere was on October 4, 2006. Everyone involved in the show was excited about the impact the opening moments would have on audiences. "The first five minutes of season 3 we really think is going to blow people's minds," Cuse said. "I think we have come up with something that is compelling and surprising." Reaction to the first episode was mixed, though the opening five minutes, as Cuse predicted, was unanimously praised.

When the show premiered, ratings dipped slightly from its lead-in, but built back up again to make it the #1 show of the night (viewers went away when *The Nine* started, but that show was eventually canceled). Ratings dips would plague the first six episodes, and give the media something to chatter about (see page 52), but despite the griping, those first six episodes were exciting and fresh, and they set up an entirely new dynamic for the show.

SEASON 3 – October 2006–May 2007

Recurring characters: M.C. Gainey (Tom), Tania Raymonde (Alex), Michael Bowen (Danny Pickett), Mira Furlan (Danielle Rousseau), Nestor Carbonell (Richard Alpert), Blake Bashoff (Karl), Andrew Divoff (Mikhail Bakunin), Marsha Thomason (Naomi Dorrit)

3.1   A Tale of Two Cities

Original air date: October 4, 2006
Teleplay by: J.J. Abrams, Damon Lindelof
Story by: Damon Lindelof
Directed by: Jack Bender
Guest cast: Julie Adams (Amelia), Brett Cullen (Goodwin), William Mapother (Ethan), John Terry (Christian Shephard), Julie Bowen (Sarah), Stephen Semel (Adam), Alexandra Morgan (Moderator), Julie Ow (Nurse), Sonya Seng (Receptionist)

Flashbacks: Juliet and Jack

As Jack, Sawyer, and Kate deal with the reality of being kidnapped by the Others, Jack recalls what happened to him after his marriage dissolved.

In season 1, we followed the adventures of a group of people who had crashed on an island and watched as they fought for survival against a mysterious environment, trying to find rescue. By season 2, we'd discovered the Tailies, another group of people who were in the rear section of the plane, and learned about a tribe of "hostiles" the Losties referred to as "the Others." Season 3 will be about how that first group of people learns to cope with the Others — the civilization native to the island — and what happens in a warlike situation. We'll see imprisonment, torture, trickery, and previous alliances falling apart while new ones are made. Season 3 presents us with a very different *Lost* than the one we were watching in 2004. The title of this premiere episode points to the reality of two worlds on the show. We've got the survivors of Oceanic 815 versus the Others. We see, more clearly in this season than any other, how the present and the past come together. But we also see how the time on the island has changed everyone. These characters are very different people than they were when they arrived, and in some cases, they seem to have become the opposite of who they once were.

Jack started out as the only person with a level head in a chaotic situation. He ran around the crash site saving everyone he could, and immediately established himself as the reluctant alpha leader of the group. By the second season, his authority had broken down with the appearance of the hatch, with Locke questioning his philosophical motivations, and with Ana Lucia arriving on the scene as another leader. Now, in season 3, he's angry, belligerent, and has pretty much given up. The island seems to have gotten the better of him. Matthew Fox is brilliant in this episode, featuring the first of many outstanding performances the cast will give this season.

On first viewing, the flashback in this episode seemed contrived, as if it were being shoehorned into an episode that was more island-centric. But it showed that Jack, who until now had seemed to be an honest, good person, had been driven to near madness and to hurt everyone around him when his marriage fell apart. From his perspective, his wife and father were working against him; from their point of view, they were trying to help him. Now, with the Others, circumstances have pushed Jack to that same breaking point. In both cases, he asks all the wrong questions, blames the wrong people, and mistrusts everyone. From his point of view, Jack has no reason to trust any of these people. But as his father told him in the

The police station scenes in "A Tale of Two Cities" were shot at the station located at the corner of Merchant and N. Bethel streets in Honolulu, Oahu, close to other locations used on *Lost*. (RYAN OZAWA)

past, he needs to "let it go" and start asking the right questions. It's not a coincidence that the Communicate button in Jack's cell doesn't work. In this flashback, Jack realizes that maybe the blame no longer rests with his father or with Sarah — maybe he is to blame for the problems he brought upon himself.

We also see a small flashback of Juliet (played by the fabulous Elizabeth Mitchell). The episode opens on Juliet's eye, immediately signaling that this season will focus on the Others. The scene echoes the opening of season 2 — we see a person we don't know, in a place we don't recognize but which seems to be off the island. The person puts on a song from the 1960s that turns out to be ironic. In Desmond's case, he can't make his own kind of music when he's beholden to a computer that forces him to enter a code every 108 minutes. In Juliet's, even though she's alone and life is making her lonely she cannot go downtown, because she's trapped on an island in the middle of nowhere. She can pretend to be somewhere else, holding book clubs and baking her muffins, but in the end, there's a man named Ben who controls Otherville and everyone who lives there.

Yes, the other question answered is that Henry Gale is actually Ben, and it would seem the Others don't like him much more than the Losties did. Michael Emerson continues to be fantastic in the role of "Benry," as fans called him for the first few episodes of season 3.

Meanwhile, Kate and Sawyer are also stuck in cages, but unlike Jack's cage, which is indoors and appears to have been an aquarium at one time, Kate and Sawyer's cages are metal, outdoors, and housed bears. Sawyer is put into his cage immediately, as if the Others don't consider him to be as important as the other two. Kate, on the other hand, is taken down to the beach where she meets with Ben, who warns her that the next two weeks will be very unpleasant for her. When she returns to Sawyer's area, there's something a little different about her. With Sawyer, what you see is what you get, but Kate has spent her entire life playing roles — is she about to play a much bigger one?

Highlight: Sawyer getting a fish biscuit, and how thrilled he is when it happens.
Timeline: The crash we see in the opening happens on September 22, 2004. The rest of the events happen on Day 68, November 28, 2004.
Did You Notice?:
- One of the book club members, Adam, complains about Juliet's book choice, which is Stephen King's *Carrie*, and says Ben wouldn't read the book in the bathroom. In the second season episode, "Maternity Leave," Locke hands "Henry" Dostoevsky's *The Brothers Karamazov*, and Henry replies, "Dostoevsky? You don't have any Stephen King?"
- When Ben sends off Goodwin and Ethan to go to the two camps, he tells them he wants lists in three days, which finally explains who was ordering the lists, though we still don't know why they chose the people they did. (Goodwin was the man that Ana Lucia impaled with a spear.)
- In the first flashback where Jack is sitting in the car watching Sarah, he's listening to Glenn Miller's "Moonlight Serenade," which is the same song Hurley and Sayid picked up through the radio when they were sitting on the beach at the end of "The Long Con" in season 2.
- Jack is working on a crossword puzzle in the car, and the words he's filled in all have something to do with the island: "raft," "necessary evils," "prenatal," "ensemble," "essential facts," "heroes," "area," etc., yet if you look at the words reading down, they don't make any sense at all, as if he was just filling in words that fit without paying any attention to the clues. (The bridge game underneath the crossword puzzle was identified by one online fan as being from the July 31, 2006, issue of the *Los Angeles Times*.)
- In the scene where Christian is talking to Jack in his office, you can see several books on a bookshelf behind Jack. Aside from the expected medical textbooks, dictionaries, and encyclopedias are: *Skinny Dip* by Carl Hiaasen, *Dark Horse* by Tami Hoag, *Pale Horse Coming* by Stephen Hunter,

Nighttime is My Time and *No Place Like Home* by Mary Higgins Clark, *Valhalla Rising* by Clive Cussler, *Domes of Fire* by David Eddings, *Harry Potter and the Prisoner of Azkaban* by J.K. Rowling, *Easy Prey* by John Sandford, *The Scottish Bride* and *The Eleventh Hour* by Catherine Coulter, *The Greatest Generation* by Tom Brokaw, *The Power of Beauty* by Nancy Friday, *Redemption* by Leon Uris, *Two Dollar Bill* and *Dirty Work* by Stuart Woods, and — surprise surprise — *Hearts in Atlantis* by Stephen King.

- When Jack gets out of jail in the flashback, he walks past a Wanted poster on the wall and the guy on it looks a lot like Hurley.

Interesting Facts: Sawyer's cage is a reference to an experiment established by B.F. Skinner, where a rat in a cage was trained to learn that it would receive food after pushing a lever, and worked to figure out how many times it would have to push the lever to make something happen.

As I explain in more detail on page 187 of the original *Finding Lost* book, Skinner believed in positive reinforcement, that if a rat believed something good would come of its efforts, it would learn how to achieve the reward. Where Pavlov believed in electrocuting the rat when it hit the lever a certain number of times — thus making the animal scared of continuing — Skinner instead focused on experiments where the rat would work toward something. It would seem the Others have combined the thoughts of the two scientists, but the experiment ultimately proves Skinner's theory, that humans could also be trained to do something over and over if they thought there was a reward at the end of it.

The sign on the door of Christian's meeting, which reads "Friends of Bill W.," is a common sign on the door of AA meetings. Bill W. is Bill Wilson, the founder of Alcoholics Anonymous.

Julie Adams plays Amelia, the older lady who comes to Juliet's book club at the beginning of the episode. Adams has dozens of film acting credits to her name, but she will always be remembered best as Kay Lawrence in 1954's *Creature from the Black Lagoon.*

Juliet's favorite book is Stephen King's *Carrie*. This book will take on more significance as the season progresses (see page 133).

Jack's cell is in the Hydra Station. In Greek mythology, the Hydra is a many-headed water beast with poisonous breath that guarded the water entrance to the Underworld. Heracles killed the Hydra as the second of his Twelve Labors.

Nitpicks: Jack goes through all of Sarah's cell phone bills and is shocked when he dials a number and his father's phone rings. Wouldn't he know his father's cell number, especially considering how closely he works with him and probably contacts him that way?

Oops: The CD case that Juliet opens is Talking Heads' *Speaking in Tongues*, but she puts in a Petula Clark CD. The writers admitted that they changed the song at the last minute, and didn't have time to switch the CD case prop.

4 8 15 16 23 42: Juliet was making a dozen muffins (4 + 8) and 4 of them rolled onto the floor. When Jack is waiting outside the school, he looks down at his pager and it says 7:15:23. Kate's dress was hanging in locker 811. When Juliet brings Jack the grilled cheese sandwich, she's cut it into 4 pieces. Christian has been sober for 50 days (42 + 8). When Jack leaves the jail cell, there's a 64 on a box behind him (8 x 8). When Sarah leaves Jack standing on the street and returns to the car, we can only see the first two letters of the plate, which is 2F (F is the sixth letter of the alphabet, so 2 + 6 = **8**).

It's Just a Flesh Wound: Sawyer is electrocuted by the button in his cage, and then hit with a dart. Kate's wrists are severely chafed by the handcuffs. Jack and Kate have been injected with something. Jack tackles Juliet, and Juliet punches him. Karl is beaten by the Others.

Any Questions?:
- Where did they get so many copies of *Carrie* for the book club? Is there an island Barnes & Noble we haven't yet seen?
- How long has Otherville been established? How did they get all the amenities onto the island (stoves, furniture, CD players, etc.)? How do they have working plumbing and electricity?
- When Jack and Kate wake up there's a Band-Aid on each of them. What did the Others inject them with? Why didn't they inject Sawyer?
- Karl, the kid in the cage across from Sawyer's, warns Sawyer not to hit the button a third time. Who is Karl? Has he been in the cage before, and why? Why does he ask about their camp and how long it would take to get there?
- What did Tom mean when he said Kate wasn't his type? Is he gay?
- All of the shampoo products have big Dharma symbols on them. Are the Others somehow affiliated with Dharma?
- Why are there chains hanging from the ceiling of Jack's aquarium cell? Did they keep sharks for experiments and the chains held them in place?
- Ben tells Kate that the next two weeks will be very unpleasant. What does he mean?
- Have the Others put Kate up to something?

- Was Jack just hallucinating when he heard Christian saying, "Let it go, Jack," through the communication device, or are the Others somehow manipulating him? Could Christian be alive?
- Jack clearly decides he's not going to make Juliet's interrogation easy on her, but of all the jobs to choose, why did he say he was a repo man?
- Juliet tells Jack he can trust her. Can he?
- When Jack sees his father laughing while talking on a cell phone in the hallway, the nurse that is with him is the same woman who was Locke's nurse in "Deus Ex Machina." Was Locke at the same hospital where Jack works?
- Juliet punches Jack and knocks him unconscious. Does she have some sort of superstrength like Ethan, or is Jack just extremely weak right now?
- Tom tells Sawyer the bears figured out how to get a fish biscuit in two hours. Is he referring to the polar bears?
- When Jack's cage was used as an aquarium, was his side filled with water and the other side was the observatory room? How could they have fit large creatures through the door to get them in?
- How did the Others get Jack's file? How did they get Christian's autopsy report when Jack didn't have it to get onto the plane? Do the Others have similar files on Kate and Sawyer?
- Is Juliet a willing participant in the Others' plan, or is she acting against her will?

Music/Bands: In the opening scene, Juliet listens to Petula Clark's "Downtown" (available on any Clark greatest hits compilation). Jack listens to the Glenn Miller Orchestra's "Moonlight Serenade." When Sawyer scores a fish biscuit, the loudspeaker plays John Philip Sousa's "The Thunderer."

A Tale of Two Cities by Charles Dickens (1859)

The book opens with one of the most famous lines in English literature, and one can't help but think of *Lost* when reading it: "It was the best of times, it was the worst of times, it was the age of wisdom, it was the age of foolishness, it was the epoch of belief, it was the epoch of incredulity, it was the season of Light, it was the season of Darkness, it was the spring of hope, it was the winter of despair, we had everything before us, we had nothing before us, we were all going direct to Heaven, we were all going direct the other way. . . ." The passage points to the eternal struggles of good and evil, light and darkness, hope and despair, all of which do battle on the island every day.

The story opens in 1775 with Jarvis Lorry traveling by mail coach when the coach is stopped by a messenger telling him to wait at Dover for a woman. Lorry responds with an enigmatic "Recalled to Life" and sends the messenger on his way. When Lorry arrives at Dover and meets with Lucie Manette, the person who had sent him the message, he reveals to her that her father — believed to have been dead for many years — has been found alive, and he will take her to him.

The book's setting shifts to Paris, where Dickens illustrates a city full of hungry peasants who are desperate for social change. Lucie and Lorry enter a wine shop, where they overhear men referring to each other as "Jacques" (the code name for revolutionaries, and the French version of Jack), whispering about a rebellion. The wine shop is owned by Monsieur and Madame Defarge, and the former, who refers to himself as Jacques, takes Lucie and Lorry up to a room where her father, Doctor Manette, is sitting. He has clearly gone mad, his clothes in tatters, his voice quiet and feeble from years of disuse, his hair white, and he is busily making shoes. When asked his name, he replies, "One Hundred and Five, North Tower." Lucie insists that they move him back to London, and Lorry at first disagrees, worried about Manette's health, but gives in when Lucie argues that he'd be safer traveling home than staying where he is.

The book jumps five years ahead to the trial of Charles Darnay, who is being charged with treason for allegedly tipping off the King of France to the British Army's intention to send troops to the American colonies. The lawyers for the prosecution parade several witnesses to the stand to see if any of them remembers seeing Darnay on a boat ride from Paris to London five years earlier. Among the witnesses are Lucie and her father. Lucie recalls having a conversation with Darnay, but Dr. Manette says he was too ill to remember the man. Midway through the trial, Darnay's attorney Stryver calls attention to Sydney Carton, his assistant, and his uncanny resemblance to Darnay. The witness on the stand realizes the two men look so much alike it would be difficult to ascertain that Darnay was in fact the man on the ship, and the jury returns with a verdict of not guilty. The group leaves the courtroom, with Lucie expressing her compassion for Darnay, and Carton rudely showing his contempt for the man by arguing with him the entire time. Despite Darnay and Lucie being set up as the upright heroes of the story, Carton is a far more memorable character in the book because of his flaws and inward goodness. As Carton and Stryver return to the latter's apartment, Stryver comments on the fact that Carton has so much potential, but is throwing it away, instead remaining mired in his own depression. Stryver has his suspicions that Carton is in love with Lucie.

In Paris, we're introduced to Marquis Evrémonde, the epitome of the disgustingly rich. The Marquis rides through the streets of Paris in his carriage, full speed, watching the peasants leaping out of the way and laughing the whole time. When the carriage runs over a young boy, killing him, the Marquis throws some coins at the boy's father, Gaspard, who is being comforted by Monsieur Defarge of the wine shop. The Marquis continues on his way to his country home, where he is met by his nephew — Darnay — asking to be removed from the will so he doesn't become heir to everything the Marquis has, which he believes is corrupt and tainted. Darnay now wants to live in England and separate himself from the family and the legacy. The Marquis asks him if he has found refuge with a doctor who has a daughter, perhaps. The following morning, the Marquis is discovered dead, stabbed through the heart. On the knife's hilt is a brief note: "Drive him fast to his tomb. This, from Jacques."

A year passes, and suddenly Lucie has many suitors that surround her without her knowing it. Darnay comes to Dr. Manette, telling him he's in love with Lucie, and he confesses that his real name isn't Darnay. Before he can tell Manette what his name is, however, Manette stops him, and tells him to wait until the wedding day. The confession is clearly enough to unnerve Manette, however, because when Darnay leaves, he sits down and begins madly making shoes again, much to his daughter's shock. Stryver tells Carton that he's in love with Lucie as well. Carton visits Lucie, opening up to her that he could have been more important, and she listens with compassion, telling him she'll help save him. Carton's spirits are lifted for the first time in a long time, and he vows that he would give his life to save hers.

Back in Paris, we witness more of the revolutionary planning that the Defarges are involved in. M. Defarge meets with several men named "Jacques" to discuss the downfall of the aristocracy. Mme. Defarge knits all the while, and we find out that she's actually knitting a registry of names of the accused, the ones who will die when the Revolution begins. The Defarges hear that a spy, John Barsad, will be coming to town, and when Barsad arrives he tells the Defarges that Lucie will be marrying Charles Darnay, who is actually the nephew of the

Marquis. Mme. Defarge adds Darnay's name to her registry, but M. Defarge is unsettled because he'd been loyal to Dr. Manette for so many years.

The night before Lucie's wedding, her father finally begins talking about his time in the Bastille, and says she has been his salvation. The next morning, Darnay and Manette go into a room together, and when they come out, Manette looks pale and upset, and after the wedding, begins a manic shoemaking frenzy that Miss Pross (Lucie's nanny) and Lorry worry will prevent him from joining the Darnays on their honeymoon, as they'd all planned. After nine days, however, Manette suddenly stops and says he doesn't know what happened, that something traumatic must have triggered the response in him.

Years pass in the novel. Lucie has a little girl, also named Lucie, and a little boy who dies young. Lorry comes to the Darnays to tell them that a large number of French are sending their possessions to England. In 1789, the Defarges lead the storming of the Bastille, and once inside, M. Defarge insists on being taken to 105 North Tower. He rejoins the mob, who murders the governor who had defended the jail. Then the Marquis' castle is set on fire, and Gabelle, the local tax collector, is almost killed by an angry mob until he escapes to the roof of his house.

Three years later, Lorry receives an urgent letter addressed to the nephew of the Marquis, but he cannot find him. Darnay takes the letter, reassuring Lorry that he knows the man and will get it to him. The letter is from Gabelle, saying the locals have imprisoned him, and he needs Darnay to come and save him. Darnay decides to do so, writing a goodbye letter to Lucie and her father.

Once in Paris, Darnay is captured and thrown into a prison called La Force. He is put into solitary confinement in a tiny cell. Lucie and Manette come to Paris searching for Darnay, and go to see Lorry, who is working at the Paris branch of his bank to keep things under control. Manette insists that because he used to be a prisoner at the Bastille, he could help save Darnay. Lorry instead takes him to a window and shows him the revolutionaries outside, sharpening their weapons, and reveals they are going to kill the prisoners. While Manette runs into the crowd to beg for mercy, Lorry takes Lucie, Miss Pross, and Lucie's daughter to a nearby place. Defarge and his wife go to see Lucie with a message from Darnay, and when she begs for his life, Mme. Defarge says they cannot play favorites when it comes to a revolution. After being imprisoned for fifteen months, Darnay's trial date is set.

At Darnay's trial, the court hears evidence that Darnay had given up his title because of his disgust for the Evrémonde family's ways, and he is quickly acquitted. Only one day later, however, he is arrested again, and the soldiers reveal the charges are from Defarge, his wife, and one unnamed person. Meanwhile, Miss Pross is reunited with her scoundrel brother Solomon (whom she worships, for some reason). Jerry Cruncher, a man who works for Lorry and has played small roles throughout the novel, recognizes Solomon as the man who'd originally fingered Darnay as a traitor so many years earlier. Sydney Carton suddenly appears (the coincidence has been critiqued by many over the years) and reveals Solomon's real name is John Barsad. Carton threatens to reveal Barsad's true identity to the revolutionaries (who have his name on the register) unless he helps him with a plan, and Barsad reluctantly agrees. Carton leaves and buys some liquid at a shop.

The following day, the third accuser is announced: Manette. Manette acts with shock and horror, but the Defarges step forward and reveal the letter they'd found in 105 North Tower. In it Manette says he was caring for a sick peasant girl who had been raped by Darnay's uncle, who had then killed her husband and brother. The girl died, and Darnay's mother — with good intentions — approached Manette telling him the girl's sister was hidden somewhere, but he was captured and put into the Bastille before he could help her find the girl and keep her safe. The jury, shocked to hear the contents of the letter, reverses the earlier decision and sentences Darnay to death as retribution. Darnay tells Manette that he doesn't blame him for what is happening.

At the wine-shop, Carton overhears Mme. Defarge revealing herself as the sister of the peasant girl who had been raped by the Marquis, and she says that when Darnay is dead, she will not rest until Lucie and her daughter are both dead also, because all descendants of the Marquis must pay a price. Back at the house, Carton calms Manette and tells him to take Lucie and the child and leave with their papers. He also hands over his own papers. He tells them to leave the following day.

The next day, Carton goes to visit Darnay in his cell, and convinces him to switch clothing with him. He then drugs him with the mysterious liquid he'd purchased earlier, and has Barsad carry Darnay out of the cell. Carton stays behind, clearly ready to sacrifice himself in place of Darnay, with whom he shares such a strong resemblance. Darnay and his family flee Paris. Meanwhile, as the executions are about to begin, Mme. Defarge goes to Lucie's house and finds Miss Pross, who refuses to give up Lucie's whereabouts. In the ensuing struggle, Miss Pross accidentally shoots Mme. Defarge before escaping. Back at the prison, Carton is led to his death, and before being executed, he thinks of how Paris will someday be beautiful again, how Lucie and Darnay might name a child after him, and in the famous final lines of the novel, he realizes: "It is a far, far better thing that I do, than I have ever done; it is a far, far better rest that I go to than I have ever known."

A Tale of Two Cities is a novel about redemption, resurrection, mob mentality, and the power of love, much like Dickens' other book mentioned on *Lost* — *Our Mutual Friend*. The episode of the same name concerns Jack, Kate, and Sawyer, and if you put them into the spots of Darnay, Lucie, and Carton, it makes you wonder what mysteries these characters still hold. Sawyer believes no one loves him — "I'm not a good man," he told Charlie — and that he doesn't love anyone else, but we know he cares about Kate more than he lets on. Jack seems to be the good guy, just as Darnay appears to be a good person when he meets up with Lucie, but like Darnay, who has dark secrets in his past, we've seen several secrets of Jack's cropping up in the flashbacks. Will Sawyer ultimately sacrifice himself the way Carton did? Or will it be the other way around — will Jack turn out to be Carton, and Sawyer will be Darnay, getting the girl and leaving Jack behind to take the fall?

The book explores the French Revolution from all sides — the bourgeoisie and the peasantry — and shows how both sides turned it into a horrific event where no one was the winner. It was all about perspective. Similarly, what is happening on the island is all about perspective. The Others believe they are right and the Losties are wrong. They don't act like they see anything wrong with what they're doing or how they're treating Sawyer and Kate and Jack. They've kidnapped children and adults, but apparently it was for "good," just as the French revolutionaries believed they were doing the right thing. Throughout this season our loyalties will shift back and forth between the Losties and the Others, and by the end of season 3 we'll be asking, is either side right?

3.2   The Glass Ballerina

Original air date: October 11, 2006
Written by: Jeff Pinkner, Drew Goddard
Directed by: Paul Edwards
Guest cast: Tony Lee (Jae Lee), Byron Chung (Mr. Paik), Paula Malcomson (Colleen), Joah Buley (Luke), Sophie Kim (Young Sun), Tomiko Okhee Lee (Mrs. Lee), Teddy Wells (Other)

Flashbacks: Sun and Jin

As Sun remembers what happened to Jae Lee, Sayid devises a plan to trap the Others.

"The Glass Ballerina" is an episode about how we can never truly know another person. In Sun's flashback, we see that even though she seems to be one of the most honest people on the island, since childhood she has known how to manipulate a situation for her own means. We see her as a little girl, lying to her father and getting someone else in trouble, knowing that by doing so, she will save herself and condemn them. In the present, she's lied to Jin about her affair with Jae Lee, and her continual lying about that affair leads to something much worse happening just before she and Jin get onto Oceanic Flight 815. Just as the shattered ballerina represents Sun's deceitfulness as a child, the similarly shattered Jae Lee shows us the repercussions of her lying as an adult. And the confirmation that she did, in fact, have an affair with Jae Lee leads us to the obvious question: Is her baby Jin's? The answer to that question just might destroy more lives in the near future.

The Others pride themselves on knowing everything that is going on, and Colleen confronts Sun with that same arrogance they've shown to Jack, Sawyer, and Kate, explaining that they know Sun, and they know what she's capable of. However, Colleen quickly finds out that Sun is not the person that she (or we) thought she was.

The irony of Sayid's plan — to trap two of the Others, so that the rest will be forced to cooperate — is that the Others have done exactly the same thing. By putting Kate and Sawyer together, all they have to do is threaten Kate, and Sawyer stays in line. By extension, even by this second episode, it appears that they really want Jack, and they've only brought along Kate and Sawyer to keep Jack behaving well.

The end of this episode was amazing (and shows once again that Matthew Fox has seriously stepped up his acting chops this season), when suddenly, Colleen isn't the only one caught by surprise. Ben begins rattling off things that have happened in the outside world since the plane went down, and when Jack hears that the Boston Red Sox have won the World Series, he laughs out loud. In the season 1 episode, "Outlaws," Jack explains to Sawyer that his father always used the phrase, "That's why the Red Sox will never win the World Series," and it was his comment on fate and destiny. Jack tells Sawyer, "Some people are just supposed to suffer," and Christian believed the Red Sox were among those people. As long as the Red Sox continued to lose no matter what, Christian would continue to believe in fate over free will. Jack refused to accept his father's

Daniel Dae Kim and Yunjin Kim joke around off the set. (ALBERT L. ORTEGA)

claim, but some part of him clearly believed that what Christian was saying was true. For when Ben rolls the television out and shows Jack the championship moment, we see Jack's smile disappear, and he just stares. His entire worldview has changed in that one brief moment, and now there's nothing he can be sure of.

Highlight: Sawyer smirking when Danny suggests to Kate she could take her dress off to work in the heat, and then when he sees Kate's face, suddenly saying to Danny, "How dare you??"

Timeline: The events on the boat and in the Other cages happen on Day 69,

November 29, 2004, according to Ben. It's clear they're running concurrently, though there's a suggestion that Jin, Sun, and Sayid have been floating around for two or three days waiting for Jack et al to come back.

Did You Notice?:

- Fire played a big role in this episode: the glass ballerina falls in front of a fire; Paik "fires" the maid; Jin says to Sayid that it's been over a day since the fire was lit; Sayid builds an even bigger fire to bring the Others over; in Sun's flashback when Jin comes home after Paik gives him his "mission," her hands shake as she tries to light a candle; Sun is trying to light a fire on the gas stove when the Others board the boat.
- The inside of the Paiks' house looks a lot like Walt's house in Australia.
- When Juliet hears that the Losties have a boat, she reassures Ben that they'll just sail in circles around the island, as if she knew about what happened to Desmond and that they can't leave.
- Sawyer calls Danny "Boss," as if he's been in prison before and is used to work detail.
- It seems rather nearsighted of Sayid to leave Sun on the boat, considering the Others killed Steve by approaching the beach by water.
- Jin looks unsure of himself in the flashback as he waits in the car, unable to go inside. Then he sees Jae Lee talking to a doorman, and suddenly remembers the way Lee's father had shamed him, and that's when he gets out of the car.

Interesting Facts: The line, "You taste like strawberries," is taken from the season 6 episode of *Buffy the Vampire Slayer*, "Wrecked." Willow is a Wiccan who develops a taste for dark magicks, and she goes to visit a "magic dealer" named Rack, who uses magic to tour around inside her soul to see what she's made of, and when he's finished tells Willow she tastes of strawberries. One of the writers of this episode of *Lost*, Drew Goddard, was a writer on *Buffy* in that same season.

To put the episode into a real-world context: President Bush was reelected on November 3, 2004; Christopher Reeve died on October 10, 2004; and the Boston Red Sox won the World Series on October 27, 2004.

Ben's last name is Linus. In Greek mythology, Linus was the name of three sons of Apollo, all of whom met gruesome deaths: one was killed by his own father, one was torn apart by dogs, one was killed with his own lyre by Heracles. Linus Pauling was a pioneer in the study of quantum mechanics. He won the Nobel Prize in 1954 for chemistry, and won the Nobel Peace Prize in 1962 for his work campaigning against nuclear testing.

Several fans speculated that maybe Sun killed Jae Lee, but Damon and Carlton confirmed on their podcast for this episode that she was definitely *not* the killer.

Nitpicks: The relationship between Jin and Sun is inconsistent. When they first arrived on the island, he was a domineering husband, even though he wasn't very dominant in their relationship before they got on the plane (his behavior shift is easily chalked up to what happened in the bathroom before they got onto the flight). Then he and Sun separated on the island for a while when he realized she'd betrayed him by learning English, but by the season 2 episode, "The Whole Truth," Jin realized Sun wasn't easily pushed around, and the two of them came to an understanding that their relationship required mutual respect. Now, he's talking down to her the way he did when they first came to the island, and she's being the subservient wife. What happened?

Oops: When Jin gets off the elevator to go and pay Jae Lee a visit, you can see the number outside the elevator is 2, indicating he's on the second floor. But Jae Lee's hotel room number is 1516, which would be on the 15th floor. Not to mention, if Jae Lee had jumped (or been pushed) from a second storey window, it wouldn't have done much damage. Also, watch after Sun comes out of the water and Jin is trying to warm her up. She holds his hand in hers, and you can see she has a perfect French manicure. For someone who toils in a garden and has been on an island for 69 days, it seems highly unlikely that her fingernails would be that impeccable. Is someone running an aesthetics salon on the beach somewhere?

4 8 15 16 23 42: When Sun is playing piano as a little girl, the metronome is set at 120 (**108** + **8** + **4**). When Danny shocks Sawyer with a taser, he says it's set at a 1/4 charge. Jae Lee is staying in room **1516**. Ben tells Jack that the Sox were down three games to none in the playoffs, and they won **8** straight games to win the Series.

It's Just a Flesh Wound: Sawyer is zapped by Pickett twice with a taser and hit with the butt of Danny's gun. Sawyer punches Danny repeatedly and hits another man. Colleen is shot by Sun.

Any Questions?:
- Who is the father of Sun's unborn baby?
- Why did Colleen look so jealous when she saw Juliet and Ben talking together?
- How did Ben not know about Desmond's boat?
- What is the purpose of having people breaking rocks? Are the Others

building something? Or was the whole "chain gang" thing staged just to put Kate and Sawyer into a tension-filled situation?

- Is Alex somehow involved with Karl? What does she mean when she says Kate isn't supposed to be in the cage? Is Alex in on what the Others are up to, or is she a victim, too? Why is she hiding in the bushes like she is? Has there been some sort of social experiment where they tried to push Alex and Karl together in the same way they appear to be pushing Kate and Sawyer together?
- How much English does Jin understand?
- Did Jin know that Sun slept with Jae Lee? Did he suspect it's why Papa Paik wanted Jae Lee dead? He says on the beach that he knows Sun betrayed him — in what way does he mean that?
- Who killed Jae Lee? Did he commit suicide? Did Mr. Paik pay him a visit after Jin left? Did someone else do it?
- If Ben just wanted the boat, why didn't Colleen let Sun leave the boat like Sun asked?
- We see that Ben has cameras on Jack's cell, Kate's cage, Sawyer's cage, the hallway outside Jack's cell, in the jungle, and the last one is obscured by Ben's head. Is the jungle nearby, and what is on the sixth monitor?
- How do the Others get a television feed? How have they stayed attuned to the outside world all this time? Can Ben really take Jack home? Why do the Others need Jack so badly?
- Ben says he's always lived on the island. Is that true?

The Lost Experience

In the summer of 2006, the writers of *Lost* came up with an ingenious way to keep fans interested in the show (and watching the summer reruns) by creating an interactive online game that paralleled the events of the show, while being an alternative reality to the series. It also was a brilliant tactic to use with advertisers, as the clues were often hidden in the commercial breaks, forcing fans with PVRs and TiVos to watch the fake ads if they wanted to keep up with the game. Not to mention many of the clues that fans followed online fed into more ads for products such as Sprite (which made this writer feel like Ralphie in *A Christmas Story*, excitedly filling out the clues from his decoder ring only to discover an ad for Ovaltine), and there were also sponsorships from Jeep, Verizon, and Monster.com.

The game began in the U.S. on May 3rd, during the commercial break for the episode, "Two for the Road," in which a phony commercial for the Hanso Foundation flashed a telephone number. Viewers who called the number were then directed to the Hanso Foundation Web site, where hacker Persephone provided them with a password to help hack into the site. The clues continued, as fans were able to delve deeper and deeper into the site, seeing internal documents, videos, and photos that were not meant for public consumption. Along the way, a story line unfolded about the mysterious Persephone.

At the same time, *Bad Twin* (a bad novel) by Gary Troup was released, and reports and interviews with the fictional author (who disappeared on Oceanic Flight 815) began surfacing to coincide with Persephone's clues. The book was supposed to contain clues to the game, but the link was never completely clear. A press release went out written by Hanso communications director Hugh McIntyre (who later made several other appearances in the game), stating that the material in *Bad Twin* was not to be believed. He appeared on *Jimmy Kimmel Live!* in character, pleading with people not to buy the book and not to buy into the hype surrounding the online game.

In the second stage of the game, hansofoundation.org was shut down due to Persephone's hacking, and she was revealed to be Rachel Blake, who then became the main protagonist of the game. Over several months, players discovered that Rachel had been raised by a single mother, but had received a premium education, and was wondering how her mother could have afforded it. She got a job at Widmore Corporation when she was barely out of school, and discovered that there had been a trust fund set up by the Hanso Foundation that had covered her schooling. She began investigating the company, hacking into their site to discover confidential information, and soon set up a video blog so fans could tune in to watch her daily updates. She discovered that Thomas Mittelwerk, an executive at Hanso, had been doing research into islands. (Mittelwerk was the name of the factory where thousands of prisoners were worked to death by the Nazis building weapons for WWII.)

After confronting Mittelwerk, Rachel learns about a secret Valenzetti Equation (apparently Troup's previous — no doubt equally unreadable — novel had been about this equation, but the book was now "unavailable"). Rachel travels to Italy, where she is tailed by Hanso executives, and is tipped off to travel to Paris. When she arrives, the contact is not there, but she discovers the contact had been Hugh McIntyre's mistress, Darla Taft. A man who works for Mittelwerk, Malik, saves Rachel when she is attacked in her hotel room, and gives her the key to Hugh and Darla's apartment, where she discovers maps and videos about the "Spider Protocol." She books a flight to Sri Lanka to get to the bottom of things.

To begin the next stage of the game, the actress portraying Rachel (Jamie Silberhartz) made a live appearance at ComicCon in character, and attacked Lindelof and Cuse for upholding Hanso as a philanthropic organization, urging fans in the audience to go to HansoExposed.com. That site chronicled her adventures in Sri Lanka, where fans got snippets of a film that Rachel had hidden on the site. We see footage of Mittelwerk and Alvar Hanso discussing the Valenzetti Equation, which they'd been running over and over to try to come up with the answer, but all they kept coming up with were six mysterious numbers: 4, 8, 15, 16, 23, and 42. They have unleashed a retrovirus on a small town in Sri Lanka where they're hoping for a 30 percent mortality rate, and they intend to do research on the victims. They discover Rachel listening, but she escapes.

Rachel's next site is whereisalvarhanso.org. The Apollo candy bars that we saw throughout season 2 were handed out at various comic book stores in the U.S., U.K. and Australia, and fans who acquired a bar were then supposed to log onto this site and post a photo of themselves holding the candy bar. When 100 percent of the bars were accounted for, Rachel called these new people her army who would back her in her fight against Hanso. She then announced it was time to reveal the truth about the Hanso Foundation.

The final stage in the game started with a DJ Dan podcast. DJ Dan (played by *Lost* writer Javier Grillo-Marxuach) was supporting Rachel in her quest to take down Hanso, and would release podcasts containing more clues for fans. But the key moment happened on September 24, 2006, when Rachel released her final video. She finally comes face to face with Alvar Hanso, who reveals that he is her father, and that Thomas Mittelwerk had been behind everything, and had done all of the bad things.

The game revealed some key information that fans of the actual television series had been wanting for a long time. DHARMA stood for Department of Heuristics And Research on Material Applications. The Black Rock had been a slave ship owned by Alvar's grandfather, Magnus Hanso (on the blast door map, we see a marker where Magnus Hanso is buried). Most importantly, the numbers in the Valenzetti Equation, when manipulated a certain way, revealed the date that the human race was going to die out. The Hanso Foundation, in creating the Dharma Initiative, were actually trying to find a way to change all of those numbers, so the human race could live longer, and as such, their experiments *were* philanthropic, because they were trying to save the human race from extinction. The reason they were killing people in Sri Lanka with a retrovirus was to change one of the numbers in the equation, which showed the human race becoming extinct through overpopulation. They believed if they killed off 30 percent of the human race, then 70 percent would still live. The experiments on the *Lost* island are solely to work on this equation, and there are six stations on the island, each assigned to a different number. The six numbers (and therefore six stations) were concerned with one of the following: mathematical forecasting; wellness/disease prevention; mental health; electromagnetic research; genomic advancement; and life extension.

By the end of the game, it was unclear whether these revelations were actually meant to be part of the show, or separate from it; in other words, would the revelations made in the game have any impact on the *Lost* story line, or was the game just a fun "what if" for the diehard fans? Because of the immense amount of information revealed, it would seem *The Lost Experience* was just a stand-alone game. How disappointed would television fans who had not participated in the game be if the answers to the Hanso Foundation and Hurley's numbers were actually revealed in some online game, and not on the show itself? And why reveal them two or three years before the end of the series, while maintaining on the show that the numbers are still a mystery?

The jury is still out on the writers' intentions. Carlton Cuse and Damon Lindelof told Buddy TV that the answers revealed in *The Lost Experience* actually *were* canon, and were meant to be part of the show, which would be very disappointing indeed.

"I would say in terms of all the . . . background that we did, in terms of the Valenzetti Equation and explaining the formation of the Hanso Foundation and doing the other films . . . we'd consider that stuff canon to the show," said Lindelof. He said that obviously where it doesn't work was where Rachel was in the world, actually accusing the producers of *Lost* of using their show to promote Hanso (i.e. the show can't actually be part of itself). "But we can say that all the factoids that she was uncovering were vetted, in fact many of them were written by us personally, so they are canon."

Will Hurley's numbers really be an equation that reveals the end of the human race? Is the Dharma Initiative a division of Hanso that's trying to avert the catastrophe? Does Sprite really allow us to obey our thirst?

3.3   Further Instructions

Original air date: October 18, 2006
Written by: Carlton Cuse, Elizabeth Sarnoff
Directed by: Stephen Williams
Guest cast: Chris Mulkey (Mike), Virginia Morris (Jan), Justin Chatwin (Eddie), Joel Himelhoch (Sheriff), Dion Donahue (Kim)

Flashback: Locke

Locke receives a vision telling him to help Eko, and he sets off with Charlie to find him.

The character whose flashbacks always intrigue me more than anyone else's is John Locke. He's been in a wheelchair, he was conned by his father again and again, he attended anger management classes, and he fell in love only to lose the girl because of his father.

This episode doesn't feature any revelations that are jaw-dropping, but it's a good episode nonetheless. After losing Helen, Locke ends up at a commune with a group of hippies who teach him to defuse his anger naturally, and he brings in a new recruit. But as we've seen time and time again, Locke is easily fooled, and his mistake will affect not only him, but the people he cares about the most. The flashback comes on the heels of the hatch explosion, where he became so convinced of something that it threatened to kill everyone. Like Jack in "A Tale of Two Cities," Locke realizes that he's made a mistake, and he needs to fix it. With the pressure of all his past mistakes resting on his shoulders, Locke is looking to the island to help him help others, rather than hurt them, and this flashback shows how he'd done it once before and screwed up. Is he about to mess up again?

After two episodes of knowing nothing about what happened to the people in the hatch, it's great to see they're not dead. Locke has lost his ability to speak (which forces him to listen for a change), Charlie has some sort of tinnitus that is affecting his hearing, Desmond is naked (thank you, writers!), and Eko has been dragged away by a polar bear. But for the first time this season, the humor was back. Hurley's reaction to finding Desmond running around in the buff is priceless, and Charlie was likable in a way he wasn't most of last season. In season 2, Charlie devolved from the funny little Brit into a dark, cruel, mean-spirited character. This season we'll see more of the season 1 Charlie, without forgetting any of the lessons that Charlie has learned along the way. While he wasn't exactly nice to Locke in this episode — "You're not taking drugs, are you John? I only ask because of the strict zero tolerance policy you've enacted, and I wouldn't want you to have to start punching yourself in the face" — his comments to Locke are funny without being vicious. And, after the events of the second half of the last season, Locke kind of deserves a few verbal jabs. (Of course, this episode also featured the first appearance of two — how shall I put this nicely — *loathsome* characters, but more on them later.)

The most important scene in this episode was Locke's hallucination scene, where "Boone" takes him through the airport. The relationships he sees in the airport are from his own mind, and it's how he sees everyone: he is stuck in a wheelchair, unable to walk; Claire, Charlie, and Aaron are all together as if they're a family; Jin and Sun are arguing, but Jin is speaking English and Sun is speaking Korean, and Sayid is trying to calm them down; Hurley is the ticket agent, helping everyone to get onto the plane; Desmond is the pilot; Kate and Sawyer are together and acting intimately toward one another; Jack stands alone in the lineup; Ben is working airport security. For each of these people, Locke wonders if they are the ones he should be helping, and Boone's response to each is very interesting. He says Claire, Charlie, and Aaron will be fine, but adds, "for a while," as if they won't be for long. Boone says "I think Sayid's got it," suggesting he can handle Jin and Sun's argument. He says "Not Hurley" quite definitively, as if Hurley will always be fine. For Desmond, the pilot (an indication that Locke sees Desmond as a man who is completely in control of himself or of others and their fate), Boone says, "Forget it . . . he's helping himself," which is a curious response. Boone says there's nothing Locke can do to help Kate, Sawyer, and Jack, then adds, "Not yet."

Eventually Boone stands at the top of an escalator, covered in blood, and he tells Locke to come up. The scene evokes the story of Jacob's ladder in the Book of Genesis. Jacob falls asleep and dreams of a ladder extending to Heaven, and God tells Jacob that he will have many descendents and that He will protect him, and when Jacob awakes he realizes the ladder must have gone to the gates of Heaven. Locke ascends the escalator, where he finds Eko's Jesus stick covered

For Locke's flashback, the crew filmed on a lychee farm deep inside Mililani Mauka. (RYAN OZAWA)

in blood, confirming the religious imagery.

The ultimate consequences of the hatch explosion will become clear in the next episode. Eko reassures Locke that he's a hunter, even if his flashback shows him in a weak moment. For, while Sun shocked everyone the previous week by doing something someone else insisted she would never do, Locke couldn't go through with it, and lived down to the person his psych profile said he was. Eko's message to Locke suggests there will be a shift in Locke's character at this point. Will his weakness prevail or will he really become a hunter?

Highlight: The entire first scene with Hurley and Desmond, including Hurley's response to Desmond telling him he woke up in the jungle naked: "So . . . like, the hatch . . . blew off your underwear?"

Timeline: This episode runs concurrently with "The Glass Ballerina," so the date is also November 29, 2004.

Did You Notice?:

- The episode title comes from the season 2 episode "?" where Eko told Locke to make camp, go to sleep, and "wait for further instruction."
- Locke mentions Eureka and Bridgeville, so the commune is in Humboldt County in Northern California.
- When Boone is standing at the top of the escalator, it's hard not to remember the last time we saw him in one of Locke's hallucinations in "Deus Ex Machina," where he was also covered in blood and saying, "Theresa falls up the stairs, Theresa falls down the stairs."
- When Locke hallucinates seeing Ben in the airport, the name tag reads "Henry Gale." That makes sense, since that's the only name Locke knows him by.

- The band on Eddie's shirt is Geronimo Jackson, the psychedelic band whose record Hurley and Charlie found in the hatch, and neither one of them knew who the band was. (The in-joke would have been much funnier if the writers hadn't had Eddie point it out.)
- Locke's first name is actually Johnathan.
- Locke tells Charlie not to hang around him, because "Bad things happen to people who hang around with me." That's the same thing Hurley thinks about himself.
- Someone in the commune is named Adam, just like one of the Others. (In fact, the commune seemed a little Otherville-like.)
- Eddie and Locke refer to a girl in the commune named "Lizzy." Variations on Elizabeth are common in the Lostverse: we had Libby; Desmond's boat was the *Elizabeth*; Kate has a friend named Beth; Christian has a patient die in "All the Best Cowboys" who was named Beth; Michael's wife Susan hires a lawyer named Lizzy to fight for sole custody of Walt.
- When Mike and Jan find Eddie's police file, they say he's a rookie fresh out of college, yet if you look closely at the file, it says he graduated college in 1991, and has been on the division since 1994. There's a 1995 date in the file as well, so he's been out of college for at least four years, and that would place this flashback as being somewhere around 1995.

Nitpicks: Ian Somerhalder has grown out his hair for other roles, but Locke would have hallucinated him looking like the Boone he last saw, with short hair. Locke finding little tufts of polar bear on the leaves seemed very contrived, as did finding Eko's tiny cross in that giant jungle. And finally, Jan seems incredibly hostile toward Locke, considering she, too, welcomed Eddie with open arms.

Nikki and Paulo — Why?: While I'll reserve my nastier remarks for the future episodes, Nikki and Paulo were hated by fans the moment they appeared on the island, and for good reason. The first time we see Nikki she's hostile to Hurley. Hurley has just returned to the camp, and the first thing he tells everyone is that Jack's been kidnapped by the Others, and Nikki shouts back, "And when were you going to tell us this, Hurley??" as if he should have somehow transmitted a message to them from the other side of the island. Maybe she could have said "Hello" first?

Oops: When Locke holds up the one sign to Charlie, he spells guard "gaurd." Locke's a pretty smart guy, and wouldn't have made that mistake. At one point, we see Locke's gun registration and it says his birthday is November 11, 1946. But in

"Deus Ex Machina," his mother's papers indicate she was born in 1940, making his birth date impossible. (It's also hard to believe he's almost 60.)

4 8 15 16 23 42: Locke's address is 2**5164** Franklin St. His height is 5'10" (5 + 10 = **15**). Eddie's officer number is **84023**. Eddie says to Locke that he's been at the farm for 6 weeks, which would be **42** days. On Eko's Jesus stick, instead of a Bible verse in one spot he's written out the numbers like a verse, but we can only see **4:8:15:16**.

It's Just a Flesh Wound: Locke wakes up with blood on one side of his head, Desmond's right arm is bloody. Charlie has scratches on his face. Eko's head and body are covered in blood, from both the detonation and the bear.

Lost in Translation: In the airport hallucination scene, Jin and Sun are arguing over something, but it's not clear what they're saying. Fans who attempted to translate the scene came up with Jin telling Sun that he'd asked her to deal with the luggage (or baggage, or something she's carrying, which could be the baby) many times, and she responds angrily, asking why she always has to be responsible for it.

Any Questions?:
- At the beginning of the episode, when Claire is talking to Charlie, he acts like he can't hear her. Later when he's with Locke, he constantly asks Locke to repeat himself. Has he suffered some hearing loss, or is it a temporary ringing in his ears from the explosion?
- Why did Locke choose Charlie to help him over everyone else? Is it because Charlie is the person he's wronged the most (of those who are still alive)?
- What was in the crazy paste that Locke ate? Was it the same stuff that he gave to Boone to make him hallucinate Shannon's death in "Hearts and Minds"? In that episode, Boone didn't eat it, Locke put it on his head wound.
- What did Boone mean when he told Locke he's here to help him bring the family back together?
- Did the hatch implode, like Locke said it did, or did it explode? If it had imploded, how could everyone have been thrown from it?
- Charlie mentions that polar bears are the Einsteins of the bear community. Is that why Dharma chose to bring them to the island to experiment on?
- Did Eko really speak to Locke, or was that paste Locke ate earlier still in his system and he imagined it?
- Can Desmond really see the future? What happened to him? Why were his clothes missing?

Music/Bands: When Locke picks up Eddie, the song playing on the radio is "I Feel Like Going Home" by Muddy Waters. The song is about how he woke up and everything he had was gone, and in it he mentions the ocean.

3.4 Every Man For Himself

Original air date: October 25, 2006
Written by: Edward Kitsis, Adam Horowitz
Directed by: Stephen Williams
Guest cast: Kim Dickens (Cassidy Phillips), Ian Gomez (Munson), Paula Malcomson (Colleen), Bill Duke (Warden Harris), Dorian Burns (Corrections Officer), Dustin Geiger (Matthew), Ariston Green (Jason), Hunter Quinn (Prison Tough #1), Peter Rudicco (Agent Freedman), Christina Simpkins (Munson's Wife)

Flashback: Sawyer
When Colleen returns to the Others suffering from a gunshot wound inflicted by Sun, it's up to Jack to try to save her life. Meanwhile, Ben conducts his own "operation" on Sawyer to keep him in line.

The title of this episode comes from the season 1 episode "White Rabbit," in what is quickly becoming the most repeated dialogue of the series. After Jack finds the cave, he returns to the beach and addresses everyone, telling them, "Every man for himself is not going to work." He insists that they need to work together to find supplies and water and the basics for survival, and finishes with the now-famous line, "if we can't live together, we're going to die alone" (which Kate repeats again in this episode). Sawyer has always been a loner, from before he stepped onto the plane to his life on the beach. But he's also kidding himself when he thinks that he doesn't care about anyone else. Ben decides to test him by seeing if Sawyer will stay in line to save someone other than himself.

All of Sawyer's flashbacks have been about cons. We've seen short cons, long cons, even mini-cons on the island. This episode is rife with them. We see the way Sawyer conned a man when he was in prison. Ben cons Sawyer into believing there's a pacemaker in his chest. Sawyer's explanation of a long con in the season 2 episode of the same name has set us up for what appears to be a long con perpetrated by the Others. Ben conned everyone in season 2 by pretending to be Henry Gale, so he's completely untrustworthy.

All of those cons are obvious. But the most important line in the episode is Ben's, when he tells Sawyer at the end that the only way to gain a con man's respect is to con him, and adds, "you're pretty good, Sawyer, but we're better." Sawyer's pride in his abilities to pull the wool over everyone else's eyes backfires — he lets his own guard down, because he never expects anyone to try it on him. Thus, while he's so fixated on being a great con man himself, he's not realizing that he's probably the easiest person to con. So who is conning Sawyer in this episode? Obviously Ben makes him believe he's killed a defenseless bunny, inserted a pacemaker into his chest that could make his heart explode, and will do the same to Kate, but what else is going on?

Was Cassidy conning him in the backstory? Back in "The Long Con," Cassidy may have been conning Sawyer just as much as he was conning her. Perhaps she was on to him early and knew what she was doing the entire time he thought he was conning her. So did she *really* have a daughter by him or does she know exactly what buttons to push? After all, a man who grew up without parents is going to be sensitive to the thought of his own child growing up without his help. Did she pull a long con of her own, to gain his trust, let him take her money, get him caught by the police (where she probably recovered most of her money) and then get even more money out of him by pretending to have a daughter by him?

Meanwhile, Jack discovers an X-ray that could be the answer to why he's been kidnapped and brought over to this island. Maybe the Others *do* sincerely need Jack's help, but if they do, why are they taking such drastic measures to get it? Wouldn't it have been simpler just to show up on the beach, introduce themselves as longtime inhabitants of the island, and explain they have a seriously ill individual who needs Jack's help? Something much bigger is going on.

By the end of this episode, we discover that even Sawyer's belief that they're on the same *island* has all been a con. The idea of two islands is an interesting one, and brings us back to the title of the premiere episode of the season, "A Tale of Two Cities." We now have the idea of two very separate worlds, but it also opens up a lot of questions. If Ben was pointing to the north side of the Losties' island, and we know the Losties have been on the south side, then it would explain why they've never seen the island on the horizon. However, when Sayid, Jin, and Sun traveled to the other side of the island in the boat, why didn't they see this other island? Why didn't Desmond see it when he was traveling on the boat? Why didn't Sawyer, Michael, Jin, and Walt see it when they were traveling on the raft (since they were also traveling north)? Do the Others live on this island or do they live on the larger island and only use this for experiments? While the idea of another island is intriguing, it illuminates a lot of inconsistencies.

"Every Man for Himself" was a good episode, but not as strong as the rest of the first part of season 3.

The dashing con man himself, Josh Holloway. Would you trust this face?

(MARY LEAHY/AGENCY PHOTOS)

Highlight: Sawyer's pulse increasing as Kate gets undressed.

Timeline: November 30 and December 1, 2004.

Did You Notice?:

- We see Ben's superstrength again, just like we did when he was Henry Gale.
- Ben says he hates needles, which is interesting considering how often he seems to administer them.
- When the Others are about to put the needle into Sawyer, one of them says, "You have to put it in the sternum, like in the movie," which is an obvious reference to *Pulp Fiction*, where a group of drug addicts has to put an adrenaline shot into a character's heart through the sternum because she has overdosed.
- Desmond predicted the rain the same way Locke did in season 1.
- The federal officer in the prison is named Agent Freedman (freed man).

Interesting Facts: The cartoon that Jack was watching at the beginning of the episode was the Looney Tunes' *The Blue Danube*. The scene we see features three ducklings being chased by a vulture (suggesting Kate, Jack, and Sawyer have fallen prey to the Others? Or that Colleen has fallen prey to Sayid, Sun, and Jin?). The cartoon is a version of *The Ugly Duckling*, where a mother duck rejects one of her offspring as the ugly duckling, choosing to favor her other three. When a vulture swoops in to kill the ducklings, even he rejects the ugly duckling, who puts a sign around his neck with "Rejected 4F" written on it. Eventually the ugly duckling saves his siblings by killing the vulture, and the mother accepts him into the fold.

While Ben's rabbit clearly has an **8** on its back as a nod to Hurley's numbers, it's also a reference to Stephen King's 2000 memoir, *On Writing*, in which he talks about how writing can achieve both time travel and telepathy. He writes, "Look — here's a table covered with a red cloth. On it is a cage the size of a small fish aquarium. In the cage is a white rabbit with a pink nose and pink-rimmed eyes. In its front paws is a carrot-stub upon which it is contentedly munching. On its back, clearly marked in blue ink, is the numeral 8." He continues by saying all of his readers are picturing that image — the rabbit with the number on its back, the tablecloth, etc. — and therefore he's just achieved telepathy, by transmitting an image into our heads. And because our imaginations are in the future (he's writing the book in 1999 to publish it in 2000), he's also achieved time travel.

The name "Clementine" means merciful, mild, and gentle. More aptly, the children's song "My Darling Clementine" is about a miner and his daughter Clementine. She gets too close to the water and falls in and drowns because her father can't swim to save her. The father sings the song and laments her death, but oddly, at the end of the song, says he kissed her little sister and promptly forgot about his Clementine.

Nitpicks: Why isn't Hurley a little more sullen than he is? In the last couple of days he's lost his girlfriend and then found out a friend of his was the murderer, was almost kidnapped, and then let go as if he wasn't as important as the rest of them. Now he's just making fruit salads and cracking jokes as if nothing had happened to him. Also, Ben bases Sawyer's heart rate on his age and weight, which isn't an accurate measurement. He could have a normal weight but be completely out of shape, thus putting his resting heart rate much higher.

Nikki and Paulo — Why?: Last week was our first taste of Nikki, who ripped into Hurley the moment she saw him on the beach. This week we're introduced to the ever-pleasant Paulo, who, aside from having a terrible golf swing, tells Desmond he can take his 5-iron, a club he doesn't really use, so when Desmond dies in the jungle, Paulo won't have to go looking for him. Both such gentle souls.

4 8 15 16 23 42: Munson's prisoner number is 248, and Sawyer's is 840. Sawyer lies and says he's 32 (a reverse **23**). His real age is 35, which is **16** + **15** + **4**. He says his weight is about 180, which is divisible by **15** and **4**. The rabbit in the cage that Ben pulls out has an **8** on its back. Ben says if Sawyer gets within **15** beats of his danger zone, his watch will beep. When Colleen dies, the last pulse reading we see on the monitor is **16**. Sawyer tells the Warden that the money will be found off highway **44**1 (4 + 4 = 8) and inside unit **23**C. The last pulse we see on Sawyer's watch before Ben tells him it's fake is 135, which is divisible by **15**.

It's Just a Flesh Wound: Sawyer twists Ben's arm. Ben and Danny beat Sawyer, the Others give him an injection and make an incision in him. Sawyer punches Ben in the mouth.

Any Questions?:
- If Juliet is a trustworthy person, which she seems to be, how do we take her comment to Jack that she and Ben make the decisions equally around there, which we know to be untrue?
- Juliet tells Jack she was a fertility doctor. Will she later have something to do with Jin and Sun?
- Whose X-rays did Jack see? Are they Locke's? Ben's? One of the Others'?
- Why does Danny hate Sawyer in particular, and not Jack or Kate?
- Kate tells Sawyer that she lied about loving him. Is she telling the truth?

Ashes to Ashes: Colleen, one of the Others, died from the effects of a gun-shot fired by Sun Kwon. Little is known about her, other than the fact she was married to Danny Pickett, and seemed to harbor some affection for Ben Linus.

 ## *Of Mice and Men* by John Steinbeck (1937)

John Steinbeck's books are always full of desperate circumstances, hard-working characters (mostly men), and femmes fatales who threaten to bring them down. *Of Mice and Men* is one of Steinbeck's greatest, and is often considered one of the best books of the twentieth century. The book centers on two men — George and Lennie. George is as big, lumbering, and slow-witted as Lennie is small, cautious, and smart. It opens with the two men stopping in the woods and discussing their new placement at a ranch where they'll be helping out with the harvest. They were run off from their last place after Lennie grabbed a woman by her dress, wanting to feel the texture, and wouldn't let go when she told him to. She eventually wrested herself free, but told the authorities that he'd raped her.

George has some affection for Lennie, despite him being a burden to him, and keeps up Lennie's spirits by telling him about the little house they'll both own some day from the money saved up. The house will have a picket fence, no one will tell them what to do, and Lennie will take care of rabbits in cages. As George prepares Lennie for their new placement, telling him to keep his mouth shut, don't talk to anyone or touch anyone, and keep his head down, he realizes Lennie has a mouse in his pocket that he'd caught and accidentally crushed. He throws it away and tells Lennie to be more careful and not to touch things that are smaller than him, or he could break them. He instructs Lennie to memorize the spot they're standing in, and to come here and hide if anything bad happens so George can come and get him.

At the ranch, we're introduced to Slim, the head guy at the ranch who becomes a sympathetic ear to George (coincidentally, in the 1992 film version, John Terry, who plays Christian Shephard, plays Slim); Candy, the aging handyman with only one hand and an old, decrepit dog, who worries that he'll be kicked out soon for being too old; Curley, the malicious son of the ranch owner, who is small but tries to make up for his size by being loud and threatening; Crooks, the African-American stable hand with the crooked back who sleeps in the stables away from the others; and Carlson and Whit, two ranch hands. Soon after their arrival, Carlson tells Candy that his dog smells and is useless, and eventually convinces him to let him take the dog outside away from the house and shoot him. Candy hears the shot, and regrets that he didn't have the courage to do it himself. The only thing that pulls him out of his funk is overhearing George and Lennie talking about their future little house with the rabbits, and he offers his life savings to come in on the deal, which would allow them to purchase the house within the year.

George begins to worry about Lennie when Curley's wife (who is never given a name) begins showing up at the door of the bunkhouse and flirting with the guys. He immediately recognizes her as trouble, and worries that Lennie might fall for her wiles and get them all into trouble again. He orders Lennie to stay away from her no matter what.

Slim's dog has had a litter of puppies, and he tells Lennie he can have one of them, but only when they're old enough to be taken from their mother. Lennie begins sleeping in the stable with the puppies, and George tells him not to pull them out of their box or he could hurt them, because he doesn't know his own strength. George laments to Slim that he used to be mean to Lennie, and to this day Lennie will do whatever he tells him to do. Curley comes into the bunkhouse one night and threatens Lennie and begins slapping him to show off to everyone else that he's a tough guy. Lennie refuses to fight back because George told him not to. George, unable to control his anger, suddenly tells Lennie to make Curley stop. Lennie grabs one of Curley's hands and squeezes, breaking most of the bones in Curley's hand. George tells Curley that he can't repeat what happened to anyone, and Curley agrees.

One night, George accompanies the guys to a brothel in town, while Lennie stays behind. He goes out to the stable to be with his puppies, and encounters Crooks, who seems to take a shine to Lennie. Candy joins them, and he and Lennie begin talking about the house and the rabbits, despite George's insistence that they don't tell anyone about it. Crooks tells them it's a pipe dream, but then says that he'd be able to help out if he could come and live with them. Suddenly Curley's wife shows up and flirts with Lennie, asking him if he's the one who damaged her husband's hand. He says no, and while the other men tell her to back off, she keeps talking to Lennie, but eventually she leaves.

The next morning, Lennie is sitting in the barn, stroking one of the puppies that he's accidentally killed. Terrified that George won't let him tend the rabbits if he finds out that he broke the puppy's neck, he begins to bury it, when Curley's wife comes in. She tells him she doesn't even like Curley, and had dreamed of going to Hollywood to make it as an actress, but was stuck in this life instead. Lennie tells her about the rabbits that he and George are going to have some day, and tells her he likes rabbits because they're soft, like velvet. She tells him that her hair feels like velvet, and encourages him to touch it. He leans over to do so, and then holds on. When she tells him to let go, he holds on tighter, just as he'd done with the woman in the red dress. She begins to struggle and call out, so Lennie clamps his other hand over her mouth to get her to stop yelling, and, not knowing his strength, snaps her neck. When he realizes what he's done, Lennie mutters that he's "done another bad thing," hastily throws some hay over her body, and runs out of the barn, heading for the spot George had shown him at the beginning of the book.

Candy comes into the barn to tell Lennie about some ideas he has for the house. He finds Curley's wife's body, and immediately runs outside to bring George in. George sees the body, instantly knows that Lennie has done it, and realizes Lennie has to be caught and locked away. He says that he should have known this was going to happen. Candy, however, tells him that Curley is capable of nasty things, and if Lennie is caught, he won't merely be put away. Then he looks at George and says, "You an' me can get that little place, can't we, George?"

But the look on George's face tells him that Crooks was right — it was never a life that was going to happen. Just as Curley's wife had been trapped in a life she'd never wanted, so were they all. George asks Candy to give him a few minutes to get back to the bunkhouse so the guys don't think he had something to do with it, and vows he won't let them touch Lennie.

Candy waits a few moments and then calls out to the rest of them, who all come running. Curley vows revenge. George stands by with Slim, who says quietly to George that maybe it was like that time with the woman in the red dress. Carlson comes running out of the bunkhouse, shouting that Lennie has taken his Luger, the gun he'd used to shoot Candy's dog. They all head out to find Lennie.

Lennie, meanwhile, is hiding in the spot where George told him to. He has visions of his Aunt Clara, a woman who had raised him, and she reprimands him for being such a burden on George. He apologizes to her, telling her he'll go away and stop being such a nuisance to George. Suddenly George appears, looking sad and quiet. Lennie is surprised that George isn't here to chastise him, and he asks him to tell him about the rabbits again. George can hear twigs snapping in the distance, and knows the others are coming. He tells Lennie to look across the pond so he can imagine the story as George tells it. As Lennie does so and continues to talk to George about their dream house, George pulls out Carlson's Luger and holds it up to the back of Lennie's head. He hesitates, but when he hears the men getting closer, pulls the trigger. The guys emerge from the bush and see George standing over Lennie's body. Slim is the only one who knows exactly what just happened, and tells him, "Never you mind. A guy got to sometimes."

Of Mice and Men is a short, heartbreaking novel about two men longing for a life they can't have. It's about loneliness and reaching out to those around you for someone to talk to. George tells Lennie, "Guys like us, that work on ranches, are the loneliest guys in the world. They got no family. They don't belong no place. . . ." But he explains that it's different with them, because they stick together. Only by sticking together they survive, pool their collective resources, and buy the house they want. Everyone in the book seems to be lonely.

The book also explores the idea of the survival of the fittest. The mouse, puppy, and Curley's wife all die because they are weaker than Lennie. But Lennie dies because his mind is weaker than everyone else's. He cannot survive in this world, and George recognizes that and kills Lennie before the rest of them can get to him. He knows Lennie is going to die, so he gives him the quick death that

Carlson had given Candy's dog, rather than the long, tortured one that Curley would no doubt dish out.

It's easy to see why Sawyer would enjoy *Of Mice and Men* and be intrigued by it. As a loner, he can understand that being out in the world on your own is a difficult thing when you can't make friends or put down roots. He also understands the world is full of cruelty, and that one must rely on strength and brains to get through everything. When Ben is taking Sawyer on his walk and tells him he wants to show him something, Sawyer replies, "That little place you always wanted, George?" He clearly identifies with Lennie, and not just because he believes Ben is taking him somewhere to kill him. Like Lennie, he often causes trouble wherever he goes, makes mistakes, and has to run out of town before he's caught.

Ben counters a few moments later with a quotation from the book, said by Crooks after he's stopped toying with Lennie, and explains how important it is for the two of them to be together and how difficult it is being the guy stuck in the barn, all alone, night after night: "A guy goes nuts if he ain't got nobody. Don't make no difference who the guy is, long's he's with you. I tell ya . . . I tell ya, a guy gets too lonely an' he gets sick." Just as Crooks was trying to explain to Lenny the importance of being with George, so does Ben tell Sawyer that he isn't alone — he's got Kate. As long as Kate is in that cage across from him, he has someone to care for, someone to live for, and someone he will sacrifice himself to save. Ben's comment might seem like he's trying to insult Sawyer, but he's actually showing him that his life is richer than he might think. Just as long as he doesn't mess up so badly that Kate is forced to hold a gun to the back of his head.

3.5   The Cost of Living

Original air date: November 1, 2006
Written by: Alison Schapker, Monica Owusu-Breen
Directed by: Jack Bender
Guest cast: Adetokumboh M'Cormack (Yemi), Hakeem Kae-Kazim (Emeka), Muna Otaru (Amina), Aisha Hinds (Nigerian Nun), Jermain "Scooter" Smith (Daniel), Lawrence Jones (Soldier), Michael Robinson (Trader), Ariston Green (Jason), Kolawole Obileye Jr. (Young Eko), Olekan Obileye (Young Yemi)

Flashback: Eko

When Eko is visited by a vision of his brother, Yemi, he follows him into the jungle and is told to confess his sins.

"The Cost of Living" is a stunning episode, a fascinating exploration of religion and whether it's our salvation or a weight upon our shoulders. Like all Eko flashback episodes, this one focuses on his religious beliefs and how they have strengthened since landing on the island. But the end of the episode caused most fans' jaws to drop.

Eko is forced once again to look back on his life and assess whether or not he was a good man or a bad one. Eko stole food — and yes, from the church — when his brother was hungry. Is that the same as stealing something out of greed? As young Eko walks to confession he must be wondering how a benevolent God could punish a child for preventing his brother from starving. In "The 23rd Psalm" we saw how Eko damned his own soul to keep his brother's pure. But, as if fate were canceling out the good deed he did for his brother, Eko's actions ultimately killed Yemi.

From that point on, Eko was a changed man. He took on the role his brother had left behind, but it didn't last for long before he slaughtered the militiamen inside his brother's very church. Were Eko's actions wrong? Or were they a more violent form of stealing bread to feed the hungry? The deaths of these monsters could save countless lives (before more militiamen show up to replace them, of course), but the parishioners don't see it that way. Eko did a lot of things wrong in his life, but while religion tries to separate things into good and evil, Eko sees a gray area, and most of his life has existed within that area.

The Others also show themselves to be religious beings. The funeral for Colleen has an eastern feel to it. In India, white is the color of mourning, hence the white flowing outfits (or kurtas) that we see them wearing in this scene. In a Hindu funeral the body would be burned until it's nothing but ashes, which would then be thrown into the Ganges, but in this case they set Colleen's body alight and set her off on a funeral pyre into the ocean, where her body will eventually burn into ashes and blow into the waters.

Later, as Jack and Ben discuss Ben's spinal tumor — for the X-rays were his — Ben turns it into a religious discussion, asking Jack point blank if he believes in God. When Jack turns the question around, Ben responds, "Two days after I found out I had a fatal tumor on my spine, a spinal surgeon fell out of the sky. And if that's not proof of God, I don't know what is." As with everything that comes out of Ben's mouth, it's not clear if he's just saying this because it sounds

Eko shows his brother Yemi (Adetokumboh M'Cormack) the cross that he holds sacred, but Yemi has an unfortunate surprise in store for his brother.

(MARIO PEREZ/© ABC/COURTESY EVERETT COLLECTION)

poetic or if he actually believes it, but there's definitely something about this island that is spiritual, as Locke has pointed out repeatedly. Is Ben a religious person because he's supposedly spent a lifetime on this island? As we saw in Juliet's flashback at the beginning of "A Tale of Two Cities," Ben looked as surprised as anyone to see that plane break apart in the air. If he had nothing to do with it, maybe he really does believe that a miracle happened, and that God made it happen.

Whether or not Ben believes in God, we know Eko does. By the end of this episode, Eko meets Yemi in a reenactment of the New Testament. Jesus was buried in a tomb. Yemi was put into a plane that was burned. On the third day, an angel rolled a stone away from the entrance to the tomb. Eko rolls stones away from the entrance to the plane. Mary Magdelene entered the tomb and found that Jesus was gone. When Eko enters the plane, there's a Virgin Mary statue still in there (it's a different Mary, but the two women are often mistaken for each other or conflated in the stories). Mary saw Christ's shroud lying on a slab, but Christ was not there. Eko finds a bunch of sheets lying in the plane, and Yemi is gone. Mary finds Jesus in a nearby garden, and He brings her news of everlasting life. Eko also finds Yemi in a lush green area with bright flowers all around him.

But Yemi doesn't have the message that Christ gave to Mary. Instead, Eko comes face to face with his own Judgment Day, and refuses to admit that he did anything wrong. When given the opportunity to confess his sins, Eko says he has none — "I did not ask for the life I was given, but it was given nonetheless. And with it, I did my best." What happens next is shocking, as Yemi disappears, replaced by the smoke monster. What exactly the monster is remains a mystery, but when it comes to Eko, it seems to represent fear. In "The 23rd Psalm" the monster showed up, got in Eko's face, and he stared it down, forcing it to retreat. Earlier in this episode, the smoke monster approaches Eko as he's drinking from a river, but when he sits up and instantly turns in its direction, it retreats once again. This time, it catches him off guard, and for the first time, Eko looks scared in the face of it. As if the monster senses his vulnerability at that moment, it attacks.

The death of Eko was shocking. (Was it necessary to kill off *all* the Tailies but Bernard? Speaking of which, where *is* Bernard?) His final words to Locke are foreboding, suggesting they all have something to fear on the island. But what made the scene work is that final flash before Eko's eyes of him and his brother Yemi, together again as children, before the incident that so violently tore them apart. It's as if everything that happened in his life was simply reduced to a "what if?" scenario that never actually played out, and that somewhere, Yemi and Eko are just two brothers playing soccer together. Knowing that Eko has finally found some peace shows that *something* on that island has some mercy.

Highlight: That final scene. I don't think I'll ever watch it with a dry eye.
Timeline: Colleen's funeral happens on the evening of December 1, and the rest of the episode takes place on December 2.
Did You Notice?:

- How did Jack figure out those X-rays were Ben's? He's not the only guy on the island who is in his early 40s.
- When Locke tells Desmond, "Don't mistake coincidence for fate," he's repeating the line that Eko had said to him in the season 2 episode, "What Kate Did."
- Jack suddenly seems far more at ease with Juliet, as if his guard is breaking down and he's beginning to trust her.
- Locke's explanation that he saw a blinding light in "Walkabout" is the first time we hear what he saw in the jungle, though we still don't know what

To Kill a Mockingbird by Harper Lee (1960)

When Juliet does her cue card act for Jack, she says ahead of time that she's going to put on *To Kill a Mockingbird*, and says that Jack will like it. The book and movie are about racism, judgment, and hatred. The story is mainly about Jem and Scout Finch, the two children of lawyer Atticus Finch. They become obsessed with an old house on their street in which lives the mysterious Boo Radley, whom they think is the town bogeyman. Atticus scolds the children for being silly, and tells them they need to be more tolerant of different people and not assume that they're enemies. Atticus takes on the case of an African-American man who's been accused of raping a white woman, and the Finches are ostracized as a result, but Atticus perseveres, proving in court that the man was set up by the woman and her hateful father. It's all for naught, however; the all-white jury convicts the man without a second thought, and he's killed while trying to escape the jail. Despite everything, the woman's father vows revenge and tries to hurt the Finch children, but Boo Radley saves them and fatally stabs the man. Scout realizes that Boo is a human being, just as the man her father was defending wasn't the monster everyone said he was, and she knows she was quick to judge and vows to change.

The title of the book is integral to its overall themes. Atticus gives the children air rifles for Christmas, and tells them they can shoot blue jays, who are loud, obnoxious creatures, but they must never kill a mockingbird. A mockingbird does no harm to anyone, and therefore, if you kill one, it's a sin.

Why does Juliet choose that film for Jack? A season 1 episode about Jack was entitled "Do No Harm," and these words are integral to medical training and the Hippocratic oath. But the message is probably something much deeper. The Losties have judged the Others and have declared them their enemy, even though they don't know them. Most of the people on the island have made judgments on others without fully understanding who those other people are. Much of *Lost* has been about understanding our fellow human beings on a fundamental level before judging, and that's what the book's message is. Of course, Juliet doesn't actually *show* this film, but instead pretends to and has Jack tell her to shut it off, which would signal to Ben (if Ben is watching) that he has no interest in learning to be tolerant of others.

scared him at the end of the season.

- Juliet's little charade with her cue cards is borrowed from Bob Dylan's "Subterranean Homesick Blues."
- Now we know why Eko was building a church on the island.
- When the smoke monster kills Eko, it does so by making an inverted cross, picking him up and going side to side, up and down, which is an inversion of the usual head, heart, shoulder, shoulder action.

Interesting Fact: After "The 23rd Psalm," Akinnuoye-Agbaje was so convinced that that character had been tightly written that he felt no need for him to stick around longer than a season. He approached the writers and asked to be killed off at the end of season 2, but they were able to convince him to stick around for the first part of season 3. "There was an ongoing dialogue [when he signed on] about what the longevity of the character would be," Lindelof told *Entertainment Weekly*. "And we all decided the shocking and emotional death would be the best way to go."

Nitpicks: For some reason the writers chose to give Jin and Sun the second flashback of the season, yet since then they've played absolutely no role in the show. Sayid is on the beach, which means they've all returned to no fanfare, which is strange. And Hurley's comment to Eko was *so* obvious, I was shocked it was written by anyone on this particular writing staff: "Stay alive, dude, okay?" Note to writers: "Stay away from the bad foreshadowing, okay?"

Finally, just before the hatch explosion, Locke and Desmond locked Eko outside of the computer room, forcing Eko to try to explode the door open, which knocked him unconscious. Then the electromagnetic pulse blew everyone sky-high. When Eko finally regains consciousness, Locke is sitting right there talking to him like nothing had happened. Why isn't Eko a little angrier about everything that has happened? And in the bigger picture, why isn't Locke more torn up at the havoc that he has caused? His mistake led to Eko being seriously injured, Charlie suffering from hearing loss, and Desmond having his clothes blown off (okay, not all of the repercussions were negative ones). Why hasn't anyone attacked him for almost killing them all?

Nikki and Paulo — Why?: By this third episode where we've had to suffer Nikki and Paulo, they've become intolerable. The writers use them for cheesy exposition: "Oh, see, this plane, here, Paulo, *this* is the plane that had Eko's brother in it! And *he's dead now*. So Eko burned the plane, so that's why it's all black and stuff." What makes them especially irritating in this episode is what happens in the Pearl station. Nikki sits in a chair staring at the televisions and makes the genius comment that maybe the televisions are all patched into various hatches. Listen to the way Terry O'Quinn delivers the next line — "Well, I'm certainly feeling very stupid" — and you'll see that even he was unimpressed with the fact that the writers had some nobody like Nikki make this revelation while somehow it never occurred to Sayid or Locke. Come *on*. If I were O'Quinn, I'd have been asking the writers to kill my character off next. And apparently Paulo's only use so far is to show us that the hatches have working bathrooms. And that he doesn't wash his hands after using one.

4 8 15 16 23 42: There are **16** people at Colleen's funeral. There are **4** militiamen in Eko's flashback. Before his death, Eko begins reciting Psalm **23**.

It's Just a Flesh Wound: Eko's most significant wounds are on his right arm, chest, and left hand and he has scratches on the right side of his face. Eko is beaten to death by Old Smokey.

Lost in Translation: When Locke first bends down to hear him, Eko whispers, "I will guide you. I'm going soon."

Any Questions?:

- If Sun, Sayid, and Jin are back, where is the boat?
- Yemi kept a photo of Eko inside his bible. Is it to remember what has been lost, or an acknowledgment that his own salvation was wrapped up in Eko's corruption?
- How did Juliet manage to make Jack a cheeseburger? Where are these people getting their food supplies?
- Is Ben telling the truth when he tells Jack about their plan, or is he just continuing the con?
- Ben says to Jack, "I want you to *want* to save my life." Why are they going through all of this? What's with this entire game, when his tumor was so severe?
- How did Ben (pretending to be Henry Gale) survive all of the beatings and fight back as violently as he did when he was suffering from such a painful tumor?
- Where did Yemi's body go?
- Who is the guy with the patch over one eye in the hatch? Does he have anything to do with the glass eye that Eko found back in "The Other 48 Days" when they discovered the trunk in the Arrow station? Also, on the mural, there's a drawing of a man with an X over one eye: is that a reference to Patchy as well?
- Can we trust Juliet? Or was Ben behind her little cue card movie?
- When Juliet's cue card show begins, the first card says, "Ignore everything I'm saying," yet among the things she says is "Free will is all we've really got" and "You can trust me." Did she intentionally tell Jack to ignore those things or was that a mistake?
- Will Jack go against his Hippocratic oath and kill Ben?
- Was Yemi really so hardhearted to Eko, or does Eko just remember him that way and he's created this Old Testament version of Yemi in his head?

- What did Eko mean when he said, "You're next"? What is going to happen?
- Locke interprets Eko's meaning as "*We're* next," but how did he know Eko meant the plural "you"? Maybe he was pointing at Locke directly.

Ashes to Ashes: Mr. Eko, a man who was destined to be good, but forced to become a "bad man," was killed by the island's smoke monster. In recent years he suffered the loss of his brother, but found faith in his new role as a priest. He is survived by no one.

Music/Bands: During Colleen's funeral, we hear Brenda Lee's "I Wonder," from the CD *By Request*. When Eko goes to the black market dealer and tells him he has some vaccines to sell, we can hear the song "Eko Lagos" by Femi Kuti (*Fight to Win*). In the liner notes to the song, we are told that Eko is the name the natives called Lagos, an area in Nigeria, before the colonialists renamed it. Kuti sings in the song that he dreams of Eko, a place where there is no more violence and suffering, and everyone lives in peace. He wakes up to realize that Eko doesn't exist, and that Lagos is still ensconced in violence, but he dreams of a day when a peaceful Eko will exist.

Eko's Jesus Stick

Last season, Eko began carrying a stick on which he would carve various bible citations (Charlie disparagingly referred to it as his "Jesus stick"). He walked around for most of the season with the same passages on it (see *FL*, page 235, for the list), but in the frenzy surrounding the hatch explosion, he seems to have added several more to it.

Romans 6:12

Paul's Letter to the Romans states how people must find salvation through Christ and God. In this passage, he explains the importance of baptism, and how it makes us one with Christ, and how because Christ was crucified, Christians have been washed of their sins. Paul asks if that means we should continue to sin, and concludes that we shouldn't. In this particular passage, he states, "Sin must no longer rule in your mortal bodies, so that you obey the desires of your natural self."

John 3:05

In this section of the Gospel of John, a Jewish leader named Nicodemus asks Jesus what he means by being born again. "'I am telling you the truth,' replied Jesus, 'that no one can enter the Kingdom of God unless he is born of water and the Spirit.'" He goes on to explain that birth from one's mother is a physical birth only, but baptism brings about a spiritual birth.

Hab[akkuk] 1:3

The book of Habakkuk contains the words of the prophet of the same name who implores God to answer why he is allowing the Babylonians to rule in fear and terror, when the righteous people are suffering, and God isn't doing anything to save them. God replies that he will save them in time, and that ultimately the unrighteous people will suffer, while the righteous will be rewarded. The verse on Eko's stick is where Habakkuk questions God: "Why do you make me see such trouble? How can you stand to look on such wrongdoing? Destruction and violence are all around me, and there is fighting and quarreling everywhere."

Genesis 13:14

Abram and Lot leave their home with their family, animals, and all possessions, because God has told Abram that he will show him the land where he and his descendents will live. When they get to the southern part of Canaan, they begin quarreling because there isn't enough land for both of their animals to graze, so Abram tells Lot to choose an area and go there, and he and his family can have that land, and Abram will go in the other direction. Lot chooses the whole of the Jordan Valley and he heads off. God speaks to Abram in this passage: "And the LORD said unto Abram, after Lot was separated from him, Lift up now thine eyes, and look from the place where thou art northward, and southward, and eastward, and westward."

4:8:15:16

One could argue that Eko etched this last passage after he became obsessed with the numbers and entered them into the computer to serve the island's purpose, as if he were adopting Locke's accepted religion. We only see the first four of the six numbers on the stick, etched near the rope that Eko holds to carry it. However, it also leads us to a passage in the Bible. The fourth book of the New Testament, the Gospel of John, chapter 8, verses 15-16, sums up Eko's character perfectly: "You make judgments in a purely human way; I pass judgment on no one. But if I were to do so, my judgment would be true, because I am not alone in this; the Father who sent me is with me."

3.6   I Do

Original air date: November 8, 2006
Written by: Damon Lindelof, Carlton Cuse
Directed by: Tucker Gates
Guest cast: Nathan Fillion (Kevin), Fredric Lane (Marshal Edward Mars), Ariston Green (Jason), Eden-Lee Murray (Suzanne), Mark Dillen Stitham (Minister), Michael Vendrell (Big Guy), Teddy Wells (Ivan)

Flashback: Kate

When Jack refuses to do the surgery that will save Ben's life, Danny threatens to kill Sawyer, and Kate must try to stop him.

This was a great episode. A Kate flashback is never as exciting to me as a Locke one, but afterward I always feel like I know so much more about her, which shows how private Kate is with her fellow Losties — she's more of an enigma than anyone else on the island. The events in this episode had been alluded to in the season 1 episode, "Outlaws," when Kate and Sawyer played a round of "I Never." Sawyer said he'd never been married, and Kate took a quick sip, then said, "It didn't last long." Later she drank again when Sawyer asked her if she'd ever been in love.

As with all Kate flashbacks, this episode was all about her being someone else. We see that Kate married someone she really was in love with (played by Nathan Fillion, the man Joss Whedon fans love to love), but even then couldn't bring herself to reveal her real name to the man. Kevin mistakenly thinks he can trust her, and ironically the minister says at their wedding that Kevin likes "Monica's" honesty, and "what you see is what you get." The marshal, on the other hand, knows another side of Kate, and despite her insistence that she's finally found happiness and wants to stay put, he knows she was "born to run," and there is no stopping point for her (except, maybe, an island in the Pacific). The scene of her looking at the negative pregnancy test is a sad one. Clearly Kate has made a pact with herself: if the test is positive, she'll stay. If not, she goes.

On the island, the main story seems to be the fulfillment of many fans' dreams. Danny says he's going to kill Sawyer (no, not that part), and Jack is refusing to do Ben's surgery (just bear with me for a second) and after Kate is unsuccessful in convincing Jack to do the surgery to save Sawyer's life, she finally climbs into Sawyer's cage and sleeps with him (there you go). Sawyer/Kate fans all over rejoiced . . . but did we see what we thought we saw? In the flashback Kate told someone she loved him while conning him the entire time. In the end, she left him, which was the most painful thing she could do, but she did it to save him the embarrassment of being caught harboring a fugitive. In the present, she's led down a hallway to Jack's cage, and begs him to do the surgery. He sends

Wisecracking Nathan Fillion does a superb job as Kate's former husband, Kevin.
(STHANLEE MIRADOR/SHOOTING STAR)

her away. But could something have happened between seeing Jack and returning to Sawyer's cage? Did the Others tell her she needed to sleep with Sawyer in order to convince Jack, and if she didn't do it, they'd kill Jack? She slept with Sawyer, then refused to tell him that she loved him even when he asked, and the next thing you know, Jack's cage door is wide open, allowing him to see the monitors and become a willing surgeon. He believes that he's alone and Kate and Sawyer are together, so now he's going to bargain his way out of here for his own reasons, "friends" be damned. And that's exactly what the Others wanted him to do. Or Kate could be simply acting on instinct, one that Ben had already predicted.

Sawyer, Hurley, Ana Lucia, Jack, Locke, Eko, Sun, Jin, Libby, Desmond, Charlie, Sayid, Kate — has *anyone* on this island truly revealed who they are? The most genuine person is Rose, and even she hasn't told anyone she doesn't want to leave (where *is* Rose this season, by the way?) How are the Losties any different from the Others? Just as the Others pretend to be people they're not, as they refuse to reveal the facts about who they are and what they're doing, so too do the crash survivors. The difference is, the Others are conning the Losties, while the Losties are conning each other.

Highlight: Ben says he's disappointed in Jack's choice to not try to save his life, and Jack cruelly retorts, "At least you won't have to be disappointed for very long." Ouch!

Timeline: Most of the episode happens on December 2, and Pickett storms outside early in the morning of December 3.

Did You Notice?:

- Sarah's fiancé (the one who left her when he thought she was paralyzed in the accident) was also named Kevin.
- The plane tickets that Kevin gives to Kate are on Oceanic Airlines.
- Kevin's last name is Callis, and he's with the Miami Police Department.
- Jack tells Ben he wants to get the hell off this island, and Ben says, "Done." Ben is smart: he could be telling the truth, just not what Jack thinks, because he could simply take him to the other island.
- When doing the eulogy, Locke says the hatch *ex*ploded, but in "Further Instructions," he'd said it *im*ploded.
- Kate's pregnancy test is a Widmore product, the same as Sun's was in "The Whole Truth." However, the actual pregnancy stick is different.
- Before Ben is put under, he says, "See you on the other side," which is exactly what Anthony Cooper said to Locke right before their kidney surgery.
- At the end of the episode, Kate tells Jack she can't run, and he thinks she means she can't leave without him, but she means she literally *can't*, seeing as they're on another island.

Interesting Fact: When Kate calls Marshal Mars, he mentions that it's the Feast of the Ascension. This holy day in Catholicism is celebrated 40 days after Easter Sunday, so it is always held on a Thursday. It celebrates the day when Christ ascended into Heaven 40 days after his resurrection. In Roman Catholicism the day is marked by the extinguishing of a candle that represents Christ's presence leaving that of the disciples. It's not clear why the writers reference this day in particular, other than to suggest that in many ways Kevin was Kate's savior, but this phone call to Mars has confirmed her worst suspicions — that she's going to have to leave him, and his presence in her life is about to be extinguished.

Nitpicks: Kate tells Kevin that she has to hold her breath to fit into her wedding dress. What did she buy, size minus 2?

Nikki and Paulo — Why?: Notice that Paulo was at Eko's funeral, but never uttered a word? That's the best use of the character yet.

Oops: Kate tells Sawyer that he breaks the rocks, and she hauls them, but when we've seen them working, it's the other way around.

4 8 15 16 23 42: Kevin's mother says she has 4 sons.

It's Just a Flesh Wound: Alex hits two Others with rocks. Sawyer punches Jason. Jack knocks one of the surgical assistants unconscious.

Any Questions?:

- The minister who marries Kate and Kevin is played by the same actor who was the head doctor in "All the Best Cowboys Have Daddy Issues." Is it supposed to be the same man, or did they just use the same actor?
- When she's breaking rocks, Kate overhears Danny saying to Juliet that it was supposed to be two weeks. What is he talking about?
- Alex shows up and asks about Karl. What *have* they done with Karl?
- Who was communicating with Jack through the com device on the wall?
- Why does Ben ask Juliet about Alex? Why does Juliet lie? Where is the "home" that Juliet mentions they've taken Alex to?
- When Danny storms outside to kill Sawyer, he growls at Tom, "Shephard wasn't even on Jacob's list." Who is Jacob? Is *he* the real head honcho around there? Could he be Ben's father?
- When Jack makes the incision in Ben's kidney, everyone begins doing whatever Jack says to appease him so he'll save Ben's life. So does that make Juliet a liar, since she said everyone wants Ben dead?
- Would Jack really kill Ben?
- Will Kate become pregnant after being with Sawyer? Or has he discovered that if you hit the button 42 times, a prophylactic comes out?

Music/Bands: At the beginning of the episode, as Kate is walking down the hotel corridor, we hear Ann-Margret's "Slowly" (*Let Me Entertain You*).

Obsessed With the Numbers: The Season 3 Hiatus

Following *Lost*'s sixth season 3 episode on November 8, 2006, the show went on hiatus for three months. The network had decided to split the season into two, with the main course running from February to May 2007, and an appetizer showing for six weeks in the previous fall, to avoid the unnecessary repeats of season 2. But for the show's creators, Damon Lindelof and Carlton Cuse, the hiatus was spent warding off criticisms of the first six-pack and media speculation that the show's ratings were plummeting and *Lost* was losing it.

Many fans were disappointed by the first six episodes. They complained that there were too few beach scenes, that the show was too focused on Kate, Jack, and Sawyer, and they didn't like the emphasis on the Others. The major criticism lobbed at the show was that the writers hadn't provided enough answers: there was no explanation in the first six episodes of who the Others were, why they were on the island, why they'd kidnapped people, and how everyone was going to get home.

It was a criticism that didn't make a lot of sense. Viewers who actually liked the first six episodes scratched their heads in confusion, wondering why disgruntled former fans wanted every answer up front. Were they hoping the show would start down a new path? Did they really think that the writers would provide them with every answer at the beginning of season 3, with possibly two or three more seasons to go?

The media, for the most part, agreed with the departing fans. Several journalists backed up the criticisms, saying that the show's failing ratings were proof that *Lost* no longer had it. One reporter wrote, "the most likely reason [for the ratings dip] is that fans are dissatisfied with the drama's dragging plotlines. Message boards are full of complaints about producers' failure to tie up almost any of the mysteries on the show, instead adding new ones as well as new characters."

Yet many of the questions *had* been answered in those early episodes because Lindelof and Cuse were well aware of the need to keep fans sated. "I think the lesson we learned from *Twin Peaks* is you have to provide answers along the way," said Cuse, "and so we've tried to answer questions along the way. If you look over the course of last season, we did answer a lot of questions and we really paid a lot of attention to that at the finale. . . . At the same time, if you don't have new questions, the show is over. If you solved your mysteries, the audience loses its compulsion to watch — so it's a daily dilemma."

Writer Jon Lachonis (a.k.a. DocArzt), writing for the online site Buddy TV, agreed, saying that *Lost* was better than ever, and it didn't make sense to him that fans would want to know everything up front. "[I]f *Lost* is planned to end in season four or five," he said, "then we are roughly in the second third of the story. What book worth a read gives up its secrets at this early stage?"

The season premiere garnered about 15 million viewers, down 20 percent from the season 2 premiere. By the second episode, they'd lost 2 million viewers. By the third episode, the papers were trumpeting in bold headlines that *Criminal Minds* was getting more viewers. What they left out was that when they said "more," they meant a mere 30,000 more viewers. Not millions, just thousands. As well, reporters were quick to point out that *Lost* was in a ratings slump, even though that week the ratings had jumped higher than for the premiere, around 16 million. Depending on where you looked the season premiere was down by a million, or 20 percent, or 50 percent, or 5 million . . . it's still unclear by how much the ratings *were* down, since the numbers appeared to have been plucked from the air for the most part.

One of the most common comparisons the show received was to *Heroes*, the new NBC sci-fi show. *Heroes* had borrowed many of its themes and formatting from *Lost*, which creator Tim Kring admitted. This excellent new show was answering questions every week, rather than building up one big mystery and forcing fans to speculate. Fans were quick to compare the two shows in their 2006–2007 seasons, ignoring the unbalance of comparing one show's freshman effort to another's third season. Despite the media saying the show was killing *Lost* in the ratings, it began the year with about two million fewer viewers than *Lost* had, and lost more as the season wore on. *Heroes* is a fascinating show, but *Lost* had an arguably more compelling first season, and it still remains to be seen if *Heroes* will be as good in season 3 as it is in season 1.

One of the culprits affecting the ratings was the increasing use of DVRs and TiVos. *Lost* was the sort of show that fans recorded and watched over and over. But if they watched the episode even an hour after it aired, it wouldn't count in the Nielsen ratings. In the days following each broadcast, upwards of 2 million people were downloading the episodes from iTunes, meaning that whatever ratings numbers Nielsen was reporting, it could have been up to 5 million higher.

In December it was announced that *Lost* would move to 10 p.m. to avoid competing with Fox's *American Idol*. Shockingly, reporters were quick to point out that ratings would drop further because *Lost*'s younger demographic wouldn't stay up until 11 p.m. to watch the show. However, while 10 p.m. was rather late, the "younger demographic" would certainly stay up that late — *Lost* wasn't exactly a show for preschoolers. (Canadian broadcaster CTV aired the show at 8 p.m. to avoid clashing with *American Idol*, and ABC might have been better off doing the same.)

In January, Cuse and Lindelof said they were in talks with ABC about when to end the series, sparking all sorts of opinions and debates about how much longer the show could go on, keeping in mind that despite what the media was saying, the ratings were still high enough that ABC would not let it go quietly. Lindelof stated that they had always envisioned the show lasting between 90 and 100 episodes, so fans speculated it would end after season 4, since the season 4 finale would put it at episode 93. However, months later, in May, the negotiations came to an end, with *Lost* scheduled to end in 2010 (!) at the end of its sixth season. Seasons 4 through 6 would air from February to May, and would be only 16 episodes each.

The fans who decided to stick with *Lost* through the hiatus and into February were hugely rewarded. After seeing a copy of the return episode, "Not in Portland," *Entertainment Weekly* reviewer Daniel Fierman raved, "I'm not going to screw around. It's good. Really good. Like season-one, stuff-gets-answered, can't-wait-for-the-next-episode good."

And it would only get better.

3.7   Not in Portland

Original air date: February 7, 2007
Written by: Carlton Cuse, Jeff Pinkner
Directed by: Stephen Williams
Guest cast: Zeljko Ivanek (Edmund Burke), William Mapother (Ethan), Robin Weigert (Rachel), Rob McElhenny (Aldo), Kimberly Estrada (Sherry), Ariston Green (Jason), Steve Labrash (Morgue Employee), Teddy Wells (Ivan)

Flashback: Juliet
Jack makes a potentially dangerous incision in Ben, saying he won't close it up until the Others allow Kate and Sawyer to leave.

"Not in Portland" is the first episode to feature a flashback of an Other, not counting the very brief Juliet flashback we saw in "A Tale of Two Cities." The background into Juliet portrays her as a gentle, brilliant woman who cared more about people than research, but who was kept a prisoner long before she came to the island. Juliet's ex-husband Edmund Burke, played by the always loathsome Zeljko Ivanek (best known as the governor from the HBO series *Oz*), holds her back through a quiet reign of abuse, and when she's recruited to work for an up-and-coming research firm that could change her life, she can't do it. So the firm decides to take matters into their own hands, it would seem. Juliet's research — which has a positive, life-changing effect on her sister, Rachel, who appears to be dying of cancer — seems to be coveted by the firm courting her, and their recruiting department consists of none other than . . . Others.

For Edmund Burke's lab building, the *Lost* crew used the new John A. Burns School of Medicine in Kakaako, Oahu. (RYAN OZAWA)

Meanwhile, Kate and Sawyer are trying to escape, and they run into Alex, who asks them to help rescue her boyfriend Karl and if they do she'll give them a boat to leave the island. When they find Karl, the state of him is shocking. It's like a scene right out of *A Clockwork Orange*. Where Malcolm McDowell's eyes in that film were held open by clamps while an assistant constantly squirted liquid into them, Karl is wearing goggles that flash a fluorescent light into his eyes and keep him awake. Harsh, bombastic music blasts in the room so loudly it puts your teeth on edge just tolerating it for a minute. An IV drips into Karl's arm, while his body is strapped to a chair so he can't move. As strobe lights flash constantly throughout the room in various colors, a movie screen in front of him flashes strange iconic images with equally strange messages. It's like a deranged Fruitopia ad used as terrorist warfare.

Is Karl being brainwashed? If so, are they telling him to have sex or *not* to have sex? If Karl and Alex were caught together by the Others, one would assume the punishment would be to make him not have sex with her. But consider the messages that flash before Karl's eyes: "Plant a good seed and you will joyfully gather fruit"; "Everything changes"; "We are the causes of our own suffering"; "God loves you as he loved Jacob"; "Think about your life." The first one especially seems to be promoting sex, not condemning it. And if the Others value children so much (and are perhaps infertile, as many fans have speculated) one would think they would encourage everyone of childbearing age to be doing it.

Except, of course, if that child is one of theirs. For it's revealed at the end of this episode that Alex is Ben's child (Juliet refers to Ben as Alex's father). Is he really her father? Did he have any contact with Rousseau? Or is it safer to assume that he has raised her as his daughter after kidnapping her from her real mother, Rousseau, right after she gave birth to her in the jungle? Does Alex know that Ben is her adoptive father only? *Is* he her adoptive father? So perhaps Ben is a hypocrite, wanting the Others to bear children, as long as his Alex isn't one of the bearers.

By the end of this episode, we understand Juliet a bit better, and she seems just as genuine to us as she was in the opening of the season premiere. Juliet was lied to, told that she would be taken to a facility just outside of Portland, and that she would be given freedom. What the Others did, instead, was kidnap her and strip her of her freedom. But then again, now that we've seen the hold her ex-husband had over her, was Juliet ever free?

Highlight: Edmund Burke talking on his cell phone: "Because you're insufferable and you're mean. Well, you asked me for the truth, Mom."

Timeline: December 3

Did You Notice?:

- When Juliet pulls back the curtain in Rachel's room, an Oceanic airplane is in the sky.
- There's a copy of Stephen King's *Carrie* on Rachel's bedside table.
- The Others refer to the Losties by their last names when talking about them. (They call them by their first names when talking directly to them.)
- Alex has hiding places and trapdoors throughout the jungle, just like her mom.
- Jack says to Juliet, "You have three minutes," with Ben, which is exactly how much time Miss Klugh gave Michael to see Walt.
- Juliet is recruited by Mittelos Bioscience. Mittelos is an anagram for Lost Time.
- Juliet protests that she's not what Mittelos is looking for, saying that she's not a leader, she's a mess. She just said the magic words: the Others don't want leaders, they want followers.

- One of Karl's messages, "God loves you as he loved Jacob," is important because in the previous episode, Danny refers to "Jacob's list," as if there's an important man on the island named Jacob.
- When Rachel shows Juliet the pregnancy test, you can see it's the same Widmore brand pregnancy test that Sun and Kate used.
- When Burke is hit by the bus, there's an ad on the side of the bus for Apollo chocolate bars.
- Tom says he doesn't like the sight of blood, which is like Hurley, who similarly had to help Jack with serious surgery (though Tom ends up being a bigger help because Hurley fainted).

Elizabeth Mitchell and Zeljko Ivanek rehearse a volatile scene from "Not in Portland." (RYAN OZAWA)

- It seems that, while the Others and the Dharma Initiative are two different organizations, the Others are recruiting scientists to come and work on a deserted island on research that will change lives for the better, the very mandate of the Hanso Foundation and Dharma Initiative. Is there some connection?

Interesting Facts: Edmund Burke was a British Enlightenment thinker, during the same era as John Locke, Jean-Jacques Rousseau, and David Hume (at least one of the writers on this show majored in eighteenth century philosophy). He supported the American colonies in their revolution against King George III, yet disagreed with the French Revolution. As a member of the British Whig party, his conservative views were adopted in the American colonies and influenced the political thought there. His first published essay was the first-ever defense of anarchism, though later, when looking to gain political office, Burke claimed it was satire. When he became a member of the British Parliament in 1765, he argued strongly against the king having complete power, and said political parties should have more say, which is the beginning of his influence on the colonies. So it came as a shock when he denounced the French Revolution and its similar aims, and Thomas Jefferson, who had previously upheld Burke's philosophies, now condemned him as an enemy of democracy. In 1794 Burke's son died suddenly, and Burke never recovered from the blow, dying three years later.

There were two different references to the online *Lost Experience* in this episode. In the online story, Thomas Mittelwerk was the president of the Hanso Foundation, and in this episode, Mr. Alpert, the man recruiting Juliet, claims to work for Mittelos Bioscience (mittelos is German for penniless or indigent). Secondly, the main character in the *Lost Experience* was named Rachel, which is the same name as Juliet's sister.

Sawyer tells Aldo that he fell for the old Wookie prisoner trick. He's referring to a scene in *Star Wars* where Han Solo and Luke Skywalker dress up as stormtroopers escorting Chewbacca to prison, and they make it on board the Death Star using the ruse.

Robin Weigert, who plays Rachel, is virtually unrecognizable from her best-known role as Calamity Jane on HBO's *Deadwood*.

Nitpicks: If Juliet was breaking into the research facility to steal medicine, and her cell phone went off accidentally out in the hallway, wouldn't that remind her that it's on and she should turn it off? Also, the bus crash sequence was badly done. Not only were the special effects lousy, but the actual logic of the crash didn't make any sense. Why would Edmund step out into the road and just stand there talking? It wasn't a parking lane; it was a two-lane road. Secondly, we see the bus at a full stop only moments earlier, so it couldn't have been going very fast when it hit him. Presumably the bus was being operated by a "Mittelos" person, but even then, how the bus could get from 0 to 60 in a few yards is perplexing. And even if it *was* being driven by a Mittelos person, how did they know Burke would just step out into the street like an idiot? Also, why didn't Alex, Sawyer, or Kate stop Aldo before he radioed Danny? Finally, the fact that Ben's serious spinal surgery appeared to take Jack about 45 minutes to complete was annoying.

Oops: The surgical assistant that Jack knocked unconscious in the previous episode is suddenly standing next to him like nothing happened, and Juliet sends him out to find Danny. Also, Jack is talking to Tom and saying Ben has 40 minutes left to live, when Ben suddenly wakes up and starts talking. The scene cuts away, but when we come back to the scene, presumably immediately following what we just saw, Ben explains he's been able to hear them for several minutes and wants three minutes with Juliet, which isn't a lot to ask if he only has 27 left. How did 13 minutes go by between Jack's sentence and Ben's reply?

4 8 15 16 23 42: The vial number on the compound Juliet injects into Rachel is A4983 (4 + 9 + 8 + 3 = 24, a reverse **42**). The research lab is A-4. Ben says he only has 27 minutes left (**23** + **4**). Karl was being held in Room **23**. Jack tells Tom that in 40 minutes, Juliet will get her wish. When Jack nicks an artery, Ben's pulse drops to 120 (**108 + 8 + 4**). Just as Jack tells Kate not to return for him, Ben's pulse drops to **108** (the sum of all the numbers). Juliet says that she's been on the island for 3 years, 2 months, and 28 days (3 + 2 + 2 + 8 = **15**).

It's Just a Flesh Wound: Sawyer beats up Danny and electrocutes him. Kate kicks Jason unconscious. Alex hits Jason in the head with a rock. Kate knocks Aldo unconscious after Sawyer hits him. Karl's clearly been beaten. Juliet shoots Danny.

Though it's a blur during the episode, if you pause the screen when the bus zooms by Juliet, you'll see the prominent ad for Apollo Bars. (RYAN OZAWA)

Any Questions?:

- Juliet turns on Jack in this episode when he tells Tom about her cue card messages, and later tells him to save Ben's life. Was it all an experiment to see what Jack would do, or did she really want Ben dead? Was she really working alone, and had to save her own skin so she refuted Jack's statements to do so?

- Tom tells Jack that Juliet and Ben have history. What kind of history? Were they romantically involved?

- Mr. Alpert shows Juliet an ultrasound of a womb that she believes is taken from a woman who is 70, and he says no, the woman is 26. Who does the ultrasound belong to, someone on the island? What happened to her?

- How did the Others find Juliet to recruit her? Why was it so important to have a fertility scientist on the island? Are the Others infertile? What is the significance of them asking her if she'd impregnated a male mouse? Are they looking to impregnate the males on the island?

- What was the purpose of the film Karl was watching? How did they film it or get access to it? At one point, if you watch closely, you'll see Gerald de Groot, the founder of the Dharma Initiative. Did they take the film from Dharma, or are they part of Dharma somehow? Will Karl survive the "treatment" or will he be emotionally and mentally damaged?

- Why didn't Juliet tell Danny to radio Tom to confirm that Ben really wanted them to let Sawyer and Kate go? Is it possible she's not telling the truth?

- Jack asks Tom why they didn't take Ben to the mainland for surgery, and Tom says, "Ever since the sky turned purple, we haven't . . ." but doesn't finish his sentence. What was he going to say? That they haven't had communications since then? That doesn't answer the question of why they didn't take Ben to the mainland in the 62 days prior to the sky turning purple.
- Did the Others kill Edmund Burke?

Ashes to Ashes: Danny Pickett, one of Ben's faithful but most brutal soldiers, died at the hands of Juliet Burke. He had suffered the loss of his wife (by the same method) only four days earlier.

3.8   Flashes Before Your Eyes

Original air date: February 14, 2007
Written by: Damon Lindelof, Drew Goddard
Directed by: Jack Bender
Guest cast: Sonya Walger (Penelope), Alan Dale (Widmore), Shishir Kurup (Donovan), Fionnula Flanagan (Ms. Hawking), Jeremy Colvin (Delivery Man), David Cordell (Jimmy Lennon), Katie Doyle (Receptionist), Michael Titterton (Bartender), Stephen Quinn (Photographer)

Flashback: Desmond
When Charlie demands to know how Desmond can see the future, we find out what happened to Desmond during the hatch explosion.

In an *Entertainment Weekly* cover story that appeared just before this episode aired, Damon Lindelof warned fans that they would be using a flashback device "in a way we never have before and never will again." He added, "It'll either blow people's minds or chase them away for good." In a way, one could say this episode didn't contain a flashback at all.

How you view this episode depends entirely on how you interpreted Desmond's flashback, and there are two schools of thought on this. Either he physically left the island and time-traveled to the past as a second chance to change the course of his life, or, thinking he was about to die, his life flashed before his eyes, but in such a way as he *believed* he could change the course of events.

In the time travel theory, fans believe that Desmond literally left the island behind, and traveled back to his past with Penelope, before the army, before his disgrace, before meeting Jack in a stadium, before going on his race around the world, and before pushing a button for three years. He still retains some memories of his future that come to him in flashes, and quickly realizes (with the help of a creepy ring lady) that reliving our lives with knowledge of what is coming cannot be done. The course of events has already happened, and they can't be changed. He returns to the island with the ability to see into the future, because it extends from his ability to see the future when he went back in time.

In the other theory, Desmond began to turn the key, and his life flashed before his eyes, but he was an active participant in it, rather than a passive viewer of it. This is a more religious theory, and one supported by accounts of real-life near-death experiences where people's lives flashed before their eyes in minute detail, with one second feeling like several weeks. What Desmond saw was his past, but everything in it made him unhappy, and his longing to go back and change things actually made him believe he was going back to correct his mistakes. But the creepy ring lady tells him that's impossible. The fact that we see him finish turning the key the instant the flashback is done lends credence to this theory. He's immediately knocked unconscious by the electromagnetic force, and wakes up with the ability to see into the future. Either the electromagnetic force somehow gave him this new ability, or perhaps he's had it all along, and it just hasn't been as pronounced as it is now.

Both theories explore the idea of destiny versus free will, which is a common theme in the show (see page 194). Jack's father believed that everything could be chalked up to fate, but Jack saw that as a cop-out: if everything is predetermined, then we don't have to take responsibility for our actions. Jack believes that our lives are own responsibility, and we have the choice to do what we want and must live with the consequences of our actions. In Desmond's flashback, however, the ring lady convinces him that no matter what we do, certain things are destined for us and we don't have free will. In explaining to him that he will eventually push a button for three years, she says, "You don't do it because you choose to, Desmond, you do it because you're *supposed* to."

The tension between free will and destiny informs most of the characters' actions on the island. Locke believes the island is his destiny, yet he also believes he needs to make decisions to help that destiny along, which is a strange combination of beliefs. (Eko, too, believed in destiny, but one that was caused by the

Dominic Monaghan and Henry Ian Cusick on the set of "Flashes Before Your Eyes." The crew had to ship in things like a red British phone booth to make the busking scene in the episode – filmed on Nuuanu Avenue in downtown Honolulu – look like a corner in Covent Garden Market. (RYAN OZAWA)

free will he'd exerted in the past.) Because of the flashbacks playing such a big role in every episode, clearly every character makes their present-day choices with the memories of what they'd done in the past always haunting them.

Unfortunately, the destiny that Desmond can now see belongs to Charlie, and according to Desmond, it'll be short-lived.

Highlight: Charlie singing Oasis' "Wonderwall," a sly admission by the writers that Drive Shaft was heavily influenced by Oasis.

Timeline: This episode is concurrent with "Not in Portland," so it also happens on December 3.

Did You Notice?:

- When Charlie and Hurley are rifling through Sawyer's belongings in his tent, Hurley flips through a copy of Vladimir Nabokov's *Laughter in the Dark*, which is an early book by the author. It's the story of one man's downfall thanks to a sexual obsession, and how he leaves his wife for a younger mistress and eventually destroys his life. More fun beach reading for Mr. Ford.
- There's no "whoosh" sound before the shot of Desmond in the hatch, indicating that this isn't necessarily a flashback.
- When Desmond wakes up in the past, lying on the floor, covered in red paint, the paint can nearby says FUTURE on it.
- When Desmond is sitting in Mr. Widmore's office, you can see a painting on the wall with the word "Namaste" on it, there's a polar bear in the center of the picture with a Buddha near the top, and you can see a little row of houses is painted at the bottom. There was a similar row of houses on the hatch mural in season 2.
- There's another painting that's further behind Desmond as he's sitting in Widmore's office, and it's the same one Claire's boyfriend Thomas was painting in "Raised by Another."
- Desmond tells Widmore that he was in the Royal Shakespeare Company, which was where Henry Ian Cusick actually studied.
- Mr. Widmore says his "foundation" is sponsoring a race around the world, which fueled fan speculation that he was the head of the Hanso Foundation.
- Charlie's middle name is Hieronymus, which means "sacred name" in Greek. It's the name of Saint Jerome, who translated the Bible into Latin, and also the name of famous painter Hieronymus Bosch, who was known

Time Travel

Time travel plays a big role in *Lost*, and while the producers have said the show will never feature an element that cannot be explained by science, they do include time travel as something that is possible. It's possible that Desmond time traveled in "Flashes Before Your Eyes," and we'll see Stephen Hawking's *A Brief History of Time* in the possession of two different people this season (see page 67). The following are some other instances of possible time travel in season 3 (spoiler warning: the last two are for episodes that come later in the season):

- In "A Tale of Two Cities," Jack is listening to "Moonlight Serenade" in his car in the first flashback; could he be listening to the same broadcast that Hurley and Sayid were listening to at the end of "The Long Con"? He's also filling words in on a crossword puzzle that will become relevant on the island, and the newspaper has a bridge game in it from 2006 (probably a prop error, but you never know).
- In "The Glass Ballerina," Ben tells Jack what has happened in the real world, including that Christopher Reeve has died. Reeve starred in *Somewhere in Time*, a movie about time travel.
- In "Further Instructions," in Locke's hallucination Jack is removing his watch, as if removing time from his life. Perhaps Jack doesn't necessarily move on a forward time trajectory.
- In "Every Man for Himself," Jack's about to call Colleen's time of death, but looks around and can't find a clock, as if the Others don't think actual time is important.
- In "Flashes Before Your Eyes," Desmond may have time traveled back to the past, and he believes he has, despite his friend Donovan telling him he hasn't. In the ring store, there are clocks everywhere, pointing to time as the key theme of the episode.
- In "One of Us," Richard mentions to Juliet that when she gets to the island she'll be surprised at "how time flies," as if it moves at a different speed on the island than it does elsewhere.
- In "The Man Behind the Curtain," when Ben sees a vision of his mother and wants to follow her, she says it's not time yet. In that same episode, a young Ben sees Richard in the jungle, looking exactly the same as he does now, suggesting he's immortal or that time moves differently on the island.

for painting demons. It's the Greek variant of the name Geronimo, and could be referring to the phony psychedelic band Geronimo Jackson. Also, the first letters of the name can be rearranged to spell "heroin."

- Charlie looks around to the people standing near him as Desmond begins ranting and says, "This is why we don't do drugs," a moment of dramatic irony if ever there was one.
- When Donovan first comes out of the classroom and is speaking to a student,

he says she needs to run the same test 10 different times and she'll get 10 different outcomes, which contradicts what the ring lady later tells Desmond.

- When Donovan and Desmond are watching the first football game on the television, the wall behind the end zone features ads for Oceanic, the Hanso Foundation, Apollo bars, and something called Kronos (which is Greek for "time").
- In the ring store, there are clocks everywhere, which again points to the theme of time that runs through this — and many other — episodes of *Lost*.

Interesting Facts: Though she never says her name in the episode, the script named Fionnula Flanagan's character Ms. Hawking, clearly a nod to Stephen Hawking (see page 67).

The MacCutcheon 60 whisky that Widmore drank in the scene where he treats Desmond like dirt (one of the more painful scenes we've seen on this show) is not a real brand; the scotch was made up for the show.

Mr. Widmore now stars as Bradford Meade on *Ugly Betty*, where he speaks with an American accent. He's actually a New Zealander. Fionnula Flanagan starred in the Nicole Kidman film *The Others*, playing . . . one of the Others. Hmm . . .

Nitpicks: Claire is wearing an outfit we've never seen on her before that fits her absolutely perfectly. She was pregnant when she boarded the plane, and probably wouldn't have brought a pair of skinny pants with her in her luggage, so where did the new duds come from? And, as mentioned earlier (see page 21), I guess there *is* a beauty salon on the island, seeing as she's got a nice new haircut and all. Also, have the writers never seen a busker on a street corner? They usually don't have crowds like the one Charlie had standing around him, especially if they're only repeating the same two lines of a song (in a mediocre fashion) rather than singing the entire thing. Finally, the pose that Desmond and Penelope take looks very little like the photo he carries around; the red top he's wearing in the photo has a higher collar.

Oops: In "Further Instructions," Charlie's bangs were very short; now they're down past his eyebrows, yet only four days have passed. When Desmond walks by the Royal Scots poster, it has the word "honor" on it, which is incorrect; the British spelling would be "honour." Also, while a Royal Scots poster might appear somewhere inside the British recruiting office, it's highly unlikely it would be the front and center poster outside a British military office in the middle of London. Edinburgh, yes; London, no. Finally, the photographer takes one photo of Desmond and Pen, and only gives them that one copy before Desmond and Pen

Fionnula Flanagan and Henry Ian Cusick rehearse a pivotal scene. (RYAN OZAWA)

split up for good. Yet in the season 2 finale, we see that Pen has a copy of the photo on her bedside table.

4 8 15 16 23 42: The clock in Desmond's apartment reads **1:08** (the sum of the numbers). The courier in the lobby at the Widmore office says he has a parcel for **815**.

It's Just a Flesh Wound: Desmond tackles Charlie and grabs his throat.

Any Questions?:

- After Desmond saves Claire's life, Charlie gets him drunk, then yells at him that he's not a hero just because he risked his life to save everyone on the island, and in fact he's a coward. What is Charlie on about? How does one lead to the other?

- Desmond starts to tell Widmore that he had to look after his three brothers after his father . . . then he's cut off. What was he going to say? Did his father die? Leave the family? Go to prison? Seeing as Desmond is so obsessed with his honor, it could be one of the latter two options.

- What does Ms. Hawking mean when she tells Desmond that if he doesn't do what he's fated to do, "every single one of us is dead"? Who does she mean? Does she believe that if he isn't on the island to turn the failsafe key, the world will explode? Or is she making more of a "go back in time and step on a bug and you change the course of history" sort of comment?

- Hawking tells Desmond that pushing the button will be the only great thing he ever does. Is she telling the truth?
- Who is she? Is she some part of his subconscious? Does she have flashes, too?
- Is Charlie really going to die?

Music/Bands: When Pen is helping Desmond tie his tie, you can hear Sarah McLachlan's "Building a Mystery" (*Surfacing*). Desmond keeps hearing Mama Cass Elliott's "Make Your Own Kind of Music" on the jukebox in the pub, which is the same song that opened season 2 when Des was working out in the Swan station. Charlie performs Oasis' "Wonderwall," from their CD *(What's the Story) Morning Glory?*

 ## A Brief History of Time by Stephen Hawking (1988)

I suffered through *Our Mutual Friend* because Desmond hid the key inside a copy of the book in "Live Together, Die Alone." I forced myself to read Dostoevsky because Locke handed *The Brothers Karamazov* to Henry Gale. But when one of Ben's guards, Aldo, was reading *A Brief History of Time* in "Not in Portland," I threw something at my television in fury.

But after reading it, I'm so glad the writers made me.

I'm not going to lie — *A Brief History of Time: From the Big Bang to Black Holes* is not an easy read. There are paragraphs in here that you can read through five times aloud and still not quite follow. But this is complex, heady material. There's no way Hawking could have dumbed it down for us types who prefer Shakespeare to Newton. Yet he somehow finds a way to take these complicated concepts and explain them to us like a patient teacher would.

I don't think anyone could do justice to this book by summarizing Hawking's book in five pages or fewer, so instead, I'll give a brief overview of what the book contains, pointing out along the way key passages that may or may not ultimately have something to do with *Lost*. If you want to get involved in a serious argument with someone about whether or not Desmond time travels in "Flashes Before Your Eyes," this is the book that should be on your night table.

In chapter one, "The Picture of the Universe," Hawking talks about how we perceive the universe, and recounts the theories of Aristotle (who suggested the Earth was round, and at the center of the universe), Copernicus (the first to argue the sun was at the center), Galileo (who proved it), Kepler (orbits were elliptical and not circular), and Newton. He pinpoints Newton as the true father of modern physics, and thus focuses on his theories of the universe and gravity. Newton postulated that gravity was the most important force in the universe, and that everything was attracted to everything else, but he couldn't explain why the planets and stars didn't just all collapse into one another. At the time, people believed in a static, unchanging, and infinite universe. It wasn't until the twentieth century that Hubble saw through his telescope that distant galaxies were constantly moving away, and he put forth the big-bang model. From that point on, says Hawking, there were certain questions facing physicists: did the universe have a beginning point (and therefore, an end)?; why did the universe begin?; how did it form?; was there a divine creator involved?; what did the universe look like?; what does it look like now? And most importantly, is there one grand unification theory that can explain the entire universe at once?

Next up is chapter two, "Space and Time." Galileo discovered that everything falls at the same rate. Newton explained that this happened because a larger mass will have as much force pulling it up as down, and will therefore not be pulled to Earth faster. British physicist James Clerk Maxwell stated that radio or light waves will travel at a fixed speed. Einstein put forth his theory of relativity, which basically states that "the laws of science should be the same for all freely moving observers, no matter what their speed." In other words, "all observers should measure the same speed of light, no matter how fast they are going." As an object approaches the speed of light, its mass rises because of the weight of the extra energy, and therefore it takes more energy to move faster. Therefore, the energy keeps rising also. The theory of relativity put an end to the theory of absolute time, because each observer would interpret time differently.

To identify a point in space, you need three coordinates. To identify a point in space and time, you need four. Hawking states, "We must accept that time is not completely separate from and independent of space, but is combined with it to form an object called space-time." He then explains past and future light cones, and inside the cone is all possible trajectories and possibilities for the present event. In "Not in Portland," Aldo is holding the book open to two pages of diagrams, and is highlighting passages and taking notes. Those pages appear in this section, where Hawking is showing the future and past cones. The rest of the chapter covers how relativity and gravity are combined, showing how space-time is curved by the mass of the sun.

Chapter three, "The Expanding Universe," talks about exactly that. The universe is expanding away from us. The further a galaxy is away from us, the faster it's continuing to move away. It stands to reason that it must be expanding at a significant rate, or it would slow to a halt and collapse. Hawking likens it to throwing a ball in the air. At first the ball has enough force to move away from us, but at some point it loses that force and gravity takes over, bringing the ball back down. The other option is to be like a rocket ship, and be accelerating fast enough that it does *not* turn around and come back. The universe must be somewhere between the two, expanding at just fast enough not to collapse in on itself, but not so fast that everything doesn't shoot away from everything else too quickly.

Chapter four, "The Uncertainty Principle," gets into explanations of various physics theories. Hawking opens by saying the problems with scientific determinism (that the development of the universe happened because it was following certain laws, and we can therefore predict what will happen next) is that it was resisted by so many people who felt it prevented any way of explaining God's role in the universe. (Interestingly, determinism also goes against the idea of free will; see page 194.) He then explains several groundbreaking theories in quantum mechanics. Max Planck determined that light and waves must be measured in particles called quanta. Werner Heisenberg developed the uncertainty principle, which states that the more accurately you can measure a particle's position, the less accurately you can determine its velocity. The rest of the chapter is about quantum mechanics (how it predicts a number of possible outcomes and the likelihood of each).

The next chapter, "Elementary Particles and the Forces of Nature," is more like a chemistry class than anything else in the book, but provides necessary background in order to understand chapter six. Hawking discusses protons and neutrons, and how it was once thought that these were the smallest things you could find, until it was discovered they were made up of quarks. All things in the universe are made up of particles, and they have a "spin," which explains what each particle looks like from different angles. There are particles and antiparticles, and when brought together they can annihilate each other. Force-carrying particles are emitted by matter particles, and they bump into other matter particles and are absorbed. There are four categories of force-carrying particles: gravitational, electromagnetic, weak nuclear force, and strong nuclear force. Hawking talks about the symmetries C, P, and T. While C states that laws are the same for particles and antiparticles, P says laws are the same for anything and its mirror image, and T states laws are the same in the forward and backward direction of time. However, Hawking argues, the laws of physics would change if one reversed the direction of time.

Chapter six, "Black Holes," is where we get to the good stuff. Stars are formed when a large amount of hydrogen collapses in on itself due to gravity, and the object becomes a ball of heat that we see as a star. The star eventually uses up its fuel, and becomes so massive the internal gravitational pull drags everything, even the light cones, inward, therefore preventing the star from emitting any light. It becomes a black hole. If someone entered a black hole, they'd be ripped in half because the gravitational pull from the interior of the hole would be so strong, so fast, the moment their feet crossed the event horizon (the boundary of the hole) they'd be pulled off by gravity, and the body would continue to be pulled "like spaghetti," as Hawking puts it (*cool*). In theory, he says, an astronaut could enter a black hole, get pulled through a wormhole and come out in a completely different spot, thus performing time travel. But since they'd be spaghetti by that point, the moment any astronaut hit the black hole his time would come to an end, so it wouldn't matter. Black holes may orbit with other stars, and may actually outnumber the stars.

In chapter seven, "Black Holes Ain't So Black," Hawking talks about how his initial theories of black holes have since changed. Another physicist, Jacob Bekenstein, argued that a black hole *could* actually emit something. The second law of thermodynamics states that everything tends to entropy; as time goes on, order will decrease, and chaos and entropy will increase. Bekenstein stated that the event horizon was actually the measure of the entropy of the black hole, and that it could emit radiation. A black hole has never actually been found or seen (which means they are an interesting meld of science and faith) but science would argue that they must exist, and that they must emit gamma rays and X-rays.

Chapter eight, "The Origin and Fate of the Universe," is the longest chapter in the book, and one of the most fascinating. He recounts what happened at the moment of the big bang, and in the following seconds, minutes, hours, and millions of years. He says a big question for physics is how did the universe turn out so perfectly? He says one argument is the "weak anthropic argument," which simply states that the universe is the way it is because it's how we see it, and if we weren't here to see it, it wouldn't be the way it is. He cuts down that argument, and says instead that God must have initially created the universe, and then left it alone after the big bang to form based on the laws He'd given it. (Imagine Jack and Locke hearing *this* argument, which brings together science and faith in such a surprising way!) How else to explain how the universe formed the same way everywhere. Hawking believes that no matter where you go in the entire universe, things would have formed the same way, yet they were forming so fast there's no way light messages could have been sent out to all corners of the universe instructing things to form the same way, so God must have had a hand in it.

To predict how time began, Hawking turns to Richard Feynman's theory of sum over histories, the idea of predicting every possible path in space-time a particle could take. A particle then wouldn't have a single history, but would follow every possible path, and the numbers associated with those paths would represent where the particle is located. Hawking says if you apply Feynman's theory to Einstein's theory that the gravitational field is represented by curved space-time, then following that particle through every possible path available would give us the complete history of the universe. At the time of writing his book, the idea was being put forth that the universe had no boundaries, and was infinite in every direction. But if it has no boundaries and is completely self-contained, with no beginning and no end, Hawking asks, "What place, then, for a creator?"

Chapter nine, "The Arrow of Time," offers the deepest implications for "Flashes Before Your Eyes." Hawking opens the chapter by saying the laws of science do not distinguish between the past and the future, and he asks, "Why do we remember the past, but not the future?" There are three arrows of time: thermodynamic (the direction in which, with time, entropy increases); psychological (the direction in which we remember the past, and not the future); and the cosmological (the direction in which the universe is expanding, not contracting). The reason disorder increases with time is because we measure time in the direction in which disorder increases. If the cosmological arrow turned and the universe began to contract, would other arrows turn? Would people remember the future the same as they do the past? The weak anthropic argument states that the cosmological arrow *must* be facing forward, because that's the only way intelligent beings could exist. However, considering that Desmond tried to go back in time to change his life — to decrease its entropy and put some order back into it — he also changed his psychological arrow, and when the thermodynamic arrow turned forward again, and his life once again became chaotic and disordered, his psychological arrow seems to be flipping backward and forward, occasionally giving him "memories" of the future.

Chapter ten, "The Unification of Physics," talks about the various theories that have been put forward in the hopes of eventually achieving a grand unified theory of physics. Stephen Hawking believes there is a theory, and we will discover it in our lifetimes.

In Hawking's conclusion, he states that the main purpose of science is to discover laws that will allow us to predict events up to the limits of the uncertainty principle. The big question remains, "How or why were the laws and the initial state of the universe chosen?" He says that historically, scientists were preoccupied by questions of what, and philosophers considered the why. Now science has become so advanced philosophers can't keep up (in this way, *Lost* is almost an allegory of history, in that the first season contained a series of characters named after philosophers, like Locke and Rousseau, but by the third season the mysteries were becoming so complicated the characters were named after scientists, like Hawking and Linus). If a grand unified theory exists, he says, then everyone will be able to understand it. "If we find the answer to that," he writes, "it would be the ultimate triumph of human reason — for then we would know the mind of God."

David Hume (1711–1776)

One of the thinkers of the Scottish Enlightenment, David Hume has been called the most important philosopher to write in the English language. He was influenced by the empirical theories of John Locke, and influenced later thinkers such as Immanuel Kant, Jeremy Bentham, and Adam Smith.

Like Locke, Hume believed that all knowledge was derived from experience, and that we can only truly know something by experiencing it through the senses. However, Hume took Locke's theories much further to a radicalized empiricism, and used his arguments to disprove the existence of God, rather than prove it, as Locke had tried to do. According to Hume, all knowledge can be divided into impressions and ideas. Impressions are what we glean from our five senses, and ideas are our reflections on those senses. (An impression is seeing an apple on a table, picking it up and holding it, and biting into it. The idea of the apple is the memory of the look, feel, and taste of the apple after you leave the room.) Therefore, if even our imagination is based on something we've actually seen and felt, the existence of God can't be proven, because we have no proof of Him through our five senses. We also have no way of knowing the connection between the information we receive from our senses and the ideas we get from that information, and therefore we have no way of knowing if our perceptions or ideas can be trusted. We don't know walking into a doorframe will hurt until we do it. Children learn what to do and what not to do by falling and walking into things and hurting themselves, and it teaches them not to do it again. They learn empirically.

Hume's theories on empiricism led to his philosophies on causation. Hume did not believe in cause and effect, but rather in events being "constantly conjoined." In B.F. Skinner's experiment (see page 10) the rat learned through experience that pressing the button would allow a food pellet to fall down. But Hume argued that one action doesn't cause another; it is simply showing that those two actions are correlated, or constantly conjoined. Those two actions will always go hand in hand. Take the problem of induction: we tend to believe that if something happens the same way every time, it will always happen. If the sun comes up every morning, it stands to reason that it will also come up tomorrow. But Hume disagreed, and said there is no basis in reason that one thing leads to another. Just because something has always happened doesn't mean it always will.

Thomas Hobbes said that man is self-interested, and acts purely out of selfishness, but Hume said man acted out of sympathy for others. Hume inspired proponents of utilitarianism — the idea that man will naturally tend toward what is best for all of mankind, and not just himself — through his philosophies that man uses reason to come up with what is best for everyone. He believed that reason doesn't make us do or not do things, but instead we obey our emotional reactions to doing or not doing things. Our reason might tell us that walking off a cliff is okay, but if our emotions dictate that we don't want to end up dead on a pile of rocks at the bottom, we don't do it. As he wrote in his *Political Discourses*, "Reason is and ought to be the slave of the passions and can never pretend to any other office than to serve and obey them." Emotions and sensory perceptions should always come before reason, according to Hume.

Hume came under fire from the religious community for what were deemed his atheistic preachings. Hume did not believe in the existence of miracles, because they went against everything else he believed. They were not natural in character, they were not something we commonly perceived through our senses, and he believed it would make more sense to look at all of the variables and see how a miracle could be rationalized. Was Christ resurrected, or was he not actually dead when they lowered his body from the cross? Hume writes in *An Enquiry Concerning Human Understanding*, "When anyone tells me, that he saw a dead man restored to life, I immediately consider with myself, whether it be more probable, that this person should either deceive or be deceived, or that the fact, which he relates, should really have happened. I weigh the one miracle against the other; and according to the superiority, which I discover, I pronounce my decision, and always reject the greater miracle. If the falsehood of his testimony would be more miraculous, than the event which he relates; then, and not till then, can he pretend to command my belief or opinion." In other words, what is more probable: that a man rose from the dead, or that the person reporting the events is lying?

Is there such a thing as fate and destiny? Proponents of free will state that man is free to determine the direction of his own life. Determinism states that everything has already been decided, and that even if we believe we have free will, we are simply doing what we were meant to do. The two concepts are considered polar opposites, but Hume illuminated that they actually go together and require one another. If no event were determined at all, then everyone would just be doing random things, and there would be no free will at all. Free will coupled with determinism gives rise to the development of character: what a person does determines who he is, and therefore makes each person responsible for his/her actions. If no decision had any real meaning and all were just random and chaotic, then no one could be held responsible for his/her actions.

Hume was a friend of Jean-Jacques Rousseau, until Rousseau (who was famously paranoid) became convinced Hume was planning a conspiracy against him. Rousseau was fleeing a religious controversy in France and went to Switzerland, where he was similarly forced out. Hume offered him a place in his home in England, and Rousseau accepted. Hume tried to integrate Rousseau into society, but the other intellectuals didn't like Rousseau, and Horace Walpole wrote a parody of a letter from the King of Prussia to Rousseau offering to let him come there and be miserable. The letter was printed in the paper, and Rousseau denounced all of them, including Hume, whom he thought was in on it. Hume, out of revenge, published the letters that had passed between them over the topic, and publicly humiliated Rousseau.

Just as his namesake said we cannot know that one thing causes another, but that cause and effect are simply conjoined, Desmond David Hume on *Lost* pushed the button every 108 minutes for three years not because he knew what would happen when he did it, but just because he knew when an alarm went off the action of pushing the button had to follow. He probably questioned his reason for doing so every time he pushed it, but as we saw at the beginning of "Man of Science, Man of Faith," he seemed to be pushing the button out of habit. Hume stated in *An Enquiry Concerning Human Understanding* that "men are not impelled by any reasoning or process of the understanding, but rather from Custom or Habit. . . . Custom, then, is the great guide of human life."

The more important connection between these Humes, as we saw in "Live Together, Die Alone," is that the character on *Lost* is ruled by his emotions and passions, as the philosopher said we are. Just as Hume stated that man will act out of an emotional response to a situation, and will act according to what he believes will be the best thing for the group, rather than himself, Desmond was willing to make the ultimate sacrifice when he turned the key at the end of the episode.

In season 3 (where, like David Hume, Desmond proves he can out-consume Schopenhauer and Hegel) Desmond continues to be ruled by those passions, though they take a different form. He is given messages from the future, and he believes it's his duty to protect Charlie from his imminent death. Just as David Hume believed fate and free will go together and require one another, Desmond believes Charlie is fated to die, but that he could make choices to alter that fate. We will see later in the season how the two obsessions in his life — his need to protect Charlie and his desire to be reunited with Pen — will clash, forcing Desmond to make a crucial decision.

3.9   Stranger in a Strange Land

Original air date: February 21, 2007
Written by: Elizabeth Sarnoff, Christina M. Kim
Directed by: Paris Barclay
Guest cast: Bai Ling (Achara), Diana Scarwid (Isabel), Kimberley Joseph (Cindy), James Huang (Chet), Siwathep Sunapo (Thai Man), Shannon Chanhthanam (Thai Boy)

Flashback: Jack

As Juliet undergoes a trial for killing Danny, we flash back to see where Jack got his tattoos.

Aside from offering the least-liked flashback of season 3 (I blame Bai Ling), "Stranger in a Strange Land" is about not fitting in. The title of the episode is borrowed from the Robert A. Heinlein novel of the same name, a 1961 sci-fi story about Michael Valentine Smith, the son of two astronauts who is raised by Martians on Mars. When they finally bring him "home" to Earth, he is immediately imprisoned and seen as an oddity. He doesn't belong here, just as he wasn't a native Martian and didn't belong there.

Similarly, Jack's life has always been about his inability to fit in. He was never good enough for his father, no matter how hard he tried. He didn't belong in his own marriage, and flees to Thailand to escape the depression he was going through at losing Sarah and the disparagement he received from his parents after the way he had treated his father. In Thailand he's an outsider, yet he's happier there because he can disappear. While he stands out as a foreigner, he's accepted by the locals and therefore finds his place. But when his true nature comes through — his inability to trust people — he forces Achara to mark him with a tattoo expressing his true nature. When the locals see who he really is, they vote him off their island . . . after kicking the snot out of him, of course. Another interpretation could be that by forcing Achara to mark him, Jack has infiltrated their culture and taken something that was deeply spiritual to them.

On the island, Jack is similarly trapped. He's not a Lostie because his fellow castaways have always seen him as someone who is supposed to lead them but not be a part of the group. And he's not an Other, because those people keep him in a cage and refuse to reveal secrets to him. In the depths of Jack's alienation, one can assume he's beginning to see the similarities between the Others and the Losties, one that Tom very willingly points out. When Jack suggests they're killers, Tom uses the old "people who live in glass houses shouldn't throw stones" adage (see page 147). But there's a flaw in Tom's argument: the castaways *react* to what the Others inflict upon them. They don't instigate the killings or kidnappings. They're simply defending themselves.

As Jack is trying to figure out whether or not to help Ben and Juliet, Kate and Sawyer are having similar doubts about belonging. They seemed to be together a couple of episodes ago, but now, postcoitus, Sawyer realizes that Kate isn't with him. She isn't with anyone. Just like Jack, she will spend her life floating between people and situations, and she leaves everyone else feeling her loss. She will remain trapped between Jack and Sawyer, unable to choose either of them, while slowly losing both.

Jack, on the other hand, has discovered a kindred spirit in Juliet. Like him, by the end of the episode, she has become a marked person, an ostracized part of the Others. They make a pact to work together to get off the island, and realize that maybe they can be outsiders — together.

Highlight: Tom folding Jack's paper plate and sandwich in half and cramming it through the bars.

Timeline: The first part of this episode is on December 3, up to Karl talking about the stars. When Jack wakes up the next morning, it's December 4.

Did You Notice?:

The crew of *Lost* spent long hours converting Fort Street Mall in downtown Honolulu into a dazzling Bangkok nighttime street scene for "Stranger in a Strange Land." (RYAN OZAWA)

- When Kate and Sawyer are on the boat, Karl says, "God loves you as he loved Jacob," which is one of the messages that was flashing at him from the screen in "Not in Portland."
- The Thai boy who talks to Jack is wearing a shirt with various Eastern symbols on it, including the Om and ones similar to the Dharma symbol.
- Achara has to help Jack with his kite. The bird on it symbolizes the freedom that Jack will never have, which is why he's unable to make the kite fly on his own.
- The little girl and boy that are with Cindy are the two kids — Zack and Emma — that Ana Lucia had vowed to protect, and she'd promised them they'd be home in L.A. to see their parents soon.

The Indigo Restaurant on Nuuanu Avenue in Honolulu, which had previously been used in "Confidence Man" where Sawyer pulls a con, stands in as both the restaurant where Jack meets Achara's brother, and Achara's tattoo parlor. (RYAN OZAWA)

- When Alex talks to Jack and expresses hostility toward Ben, he immediately guesses Ben's her father.
- Ben tells Jack that he has a terrible bedside manner, which both Christian and Sarah had told him when Jack was a surgeon at the hospital.

Interesting Facts: Thailand is predominantly Buddhist. But according to Sri Krishna Pranami of the Hindu faith, "Dharma means Achara or the regulation of daily life. Achara is the supreme Dharma. It is the basis of Tapas or austerity. It leads to wealth, beauty, longevity and continuity of lineage." Buddhism is driven by a sense of spiritual lineage — something the Others seem to be obsessed with, especially as it appears they have fertility issues.

Isabel is the Hebrew form of Elizabeth, adding yet another to the long line of Elizabeths on this show (see page 29).

In the Book of Genesis, Cain kills his brother Abel, and God drives him away from his lands as a punishment, telling him no crop will grow for him and he will be forced to wander the earth. Cain complains that cursed by God as he is, he will be killed, so God gives him a mark that will keep people away from Cain. He says if anyone kills Cain, seven lives will be taken in revenge. Cain is banished to an area east of Eden (Genesis 4:1–16).

What does Juliet's mark represent? The mark is an upside-down cross in the middle, and on either side of the cross is a curved line that bisects the horizontal. If you go to Symbols.com, and type in 11:10, you'll see the closest symbol to it. It's often used as the symbol for the planet Uranus, and also the alchemical sign for ammonium salt. Some ufologists claim it's a symbol for the planet Ummo, which was mostly a big hoax instigated in the mid-1960s. Jose Luis Jordan Peña claimed to have seen a UFO and communicated with aliens, and soon afterward, a UFO expert began receiving documents backing up the man's claim, including photos and other testimonials. Letters, phone calls, and photos from the alien race, called the Ummites, went out to various researchers and scientists, every

Bai Ling, a staple of every "Worst Dressed" magazine column and the patron saint of gofugyourself.com. (ALBERT L. ORTEGA)

document stamped with a mark similar to Juliet's, though the outside lines were not curved but straight. Other people began claiming to have seen the Ummites. But when cults started popping up, including one called Edelweiss that was branding children with the Ummite symbol, Peña finally came forward to admit the entire thing had been a hoax and he had sent all of the letters and made the calls. It was an experiment to see how something could take on a life of its own, but he didn't realize it would go so wildly out of control. However, there are people to this day who still contend the Ummites are among us. Maybe Ben is one of them.

Nitpicks: Why didn't Jack ask any questions when Cindy was standing right in front of him? Instead he just started bellowing and screaming at her, when for the rest of the episode he spoke calmly to every other person who approached him, including Tom, Isabel, Juliet, and Alex. Maybe he could have gotten some answers, but instead he told them to just go away. Also, at the very end, Juliet is standing at the front of the boat, leaning back against it. You'd think with a fresh wound on her back, the last thing she'd be doing is leaning against it.

4 8 15 16 23 42: Throughout the flashback, Jack wears an infinity symbol around his neck that is shaped like an **8**. The mark on Juliet's back has **8** points.

It's Just a Flesh Wound: Sawyer punches Karl in the arm to make him "cowboy up." Karl punches him back. Juliet has a symbol burned into her back.

Lost in Translation: In case you didn't understand what Achara was telling Jack (Bai Ling has never been a very good actress, much less enunciator), she said, "You are a leader, a great man, but this . . . this makes you lonely, and frightened, and angry." Also, the writers were counting on the viewers not being able to speak Chinese (or perhaps they knew we'd figure this out?) but Isabel's translation of Jack's tattoo — "He walks amongst us, but he is not one of us" — is not accurate. The literal translation of his tattoo is "Eagles high, cleaving sky," or "the eagles fly up on the sky."

Any Questions?:

- How long has Karl been on the island? Where are his parents?
- Jack pushes the button in the cage twice, but never pushes it a third time, avoiding the electrocution that would have happened had he done so. Why does he not push it a third time? Does he lack the faith or hope that something might change on a third push? Does he anticipate something bad will happen on the third push?
- When Jack begins telling Achara about his father, she stops him and says some things are personal. Is this why he doesn't tell anyone on the island about his daddy issues?
- Isabel tells Jack that his tattoo is ironic. Why is it ironic? Her translation sounded like a pretty spot-on description of Jack.
- When Jack is being brought in to Isabel's office for interrogation, Alex is being led out. Was she being questioned about Juliet and what happened on the beach? What did she tell them? Or is she in cahoots with them and

it was all for show? Is Alex working with the Others or against them?

- What did Cindy mean when she said they were here to watch? Why did she keep looking over her shoulder every time he asked her something? Was she aware of the cameras? Was she there to watch the trial?
- If Ethan was the Others' surgeon, why was he the guy that Ben chose to send away to the beach, especially when Ben had only just found out a couple of days earlier that he had a spinal tumor?
- Why does Tom look so disappointed when he finds out that Juliet's sentence has been commuted?
- Achara says that to mark Jack is against her people. Why? Who are her people? Why does his tattoo cause Achara's brother and his friends to go completely ballistic? How did the Thai boy on the beach see the tattoo through Jack's shirt? What about Jack has changed as a result of this tattoo?
- We see later on the beach that the tattoo on Jack's arm is only the line of characters that currently exists under the large 5. When did he get the second one, and why, considering the pain the first one caused him? What about the giant red flower on the underside of his arm?
- Why did Achara write the characters in Chinese, and not in Thai? Is she also a stranger in a strange land?
- When Jack tells Juliet they'll work together, she suddenly looks upset. Why? Has she been tricking him all along, but now feels badly that she's done so?
- Did Kate sleep with Sawyer out of sympathy? Does her heart lie with Jack?

Music/Bands: On the boat, Sawyer sings "Show Me the Way to Go Home," a traditional song that has been covered by numerous musicians.

The Prisoner

Premiering in fall 1967, *The Prisoner* is the brainchild of Patrick McGoohan, who created and starred in the show, as well as wrote several episodes, produced, and even directed. *The Prisoner* is the story of an unnamed man — presumably a spy — who has resigned from a high-level government position, and is subsequently kidnapped and brought to "The Village," a mysterious and surreal little town where he's renamed "Number Six" and asked the same question over and over: "Why did you resign?" His refusal to answer the question causes his inquisitor to try various tricks on him to drag the truth from him. His opponent is Number Two, a person who changes from episode to episode, with the exception of a couple of episodes. It's usually a man, but on two occasions is a woman. Number Two is sometimes confident and haughty, other times nervous and fidgety. Number Two's only job is to get the answer to one question, but it's an answer that never seems to come.

At first, Number Six just wants to escape. He tries running to the water or leaving town by one of the taxis, but a strange white ball suddenly appears, making a roaring sound upon its first appearance and chasing him back to the village. On one occasion, Number Six refers to the ball as "Rover," so it's how fans refer to it. It's made of a parachute material like a weather balloon, which makes you wonder why he doesn't just cut it with a knife (in a parody of *The Prisoner*, Homer is chased by Rover and he turns and pops it with a fork) but it seems to have a strange psychological effect on anyone it catches up to, pressing on their faces and seemingly smothering them.

Number Six is belligerent whenever brought before Number Two in the beginning, demanding to know who Number One is. It's not clear why Number Two keeps changing. Perhaps he/she has failed in the mission and they're replaced as a punishment. Perhaps it's part of the disorientation process so that Number Six can never become too comfortable with one person.

Number Six is unnerved by this strange society that is seemingly trapped on an island with an inhuman monster guarding the perimeter, where people walk around in colorful striped capes twirling umbrellas, where the door to your house opens when you come near it, where your every move is being watched, where everyone is a number, and almost everyone seems to be in cahoots with Number Two. Is Number Six the only real prisoner here, or is he one of many?

The series has a definite Orwellian feel to it. The town salute is, "Be seeing you!" said while the speaker makes a circle with their thumb and index finger, keeping the other three fingers up, holding the circle over their eye, and then flicking their wrist forward like a salute. They all acknowledge they are being watched. Number Six is offended at being made a number and a prisoner — in the opening credits he insists, "I am not a number, I am a free man!" — and one of his famous lines near the beginning of the series is, "I will not be pushed, filed, stamped, indexed, briefed, debriefed, or numbered." As time goes on and Number Six *almost* escapes, he gives up that course, and decides to see it as a game. He becomes a perfect nemesis to the various Number Twos, often driving them crazy, beating them at their own game, pushing them to abandon their posts, and smugly walking back to his apartment to await the next bout of trickery from the new Number Two. It's a lot of fun to watch as Number Six progresses throughout the series — the escape attempts are exciting, and the mental chess games he plays with the Number Twos are just as much fun.

While there's a bit of a burp near the end of the series, with fantasy episodes based away from the village, the final two-part finale ("Fall Out") brings us back to the island, to Number Two, and to the answers. With a surrealism unmatched in

Patrick McGoohan starred in the strange and wonderful cult television series, *The Prisoner*, which has a lot in common with *Lost*. (COURTESY EVERETT COLLECTION)

even the weirdest episodes, the finale blasts The Beatles "All You Need Is Love" during a big shoot-out scene and features the Four Lads' version of "Dry Bones" throughout the episode, as if to suggest some sort of spirituality.

Who is Number One? Why did Six resign? Will he ever get back home? Where is he? All of these questions and more are answered in the finale . . . or not. The finale's psychedelic morass of craziness left a lot of things open to interpretation, to the point where Roger Langley, the author of the DVD liner notes, writes, "'Fall Out' caused many complaints from viewers who did not feel that the series' questions had been answered satisfactorily, causing an exhausted Patrick McGoohan to go into hiding." McGoohan had written and directed the finale (and apparently had been given two days to write it and wrap up everything, explaining why the episode is as insane as it is).

Today there is an annual *Prisoner* convention, held at Portmeirion, the man-made town in Wales where the exterior shots of The Village were taken. Fan clubs exist, and the impact of the series on popular culture has been huge. Ronald Moore, creator of the reimagined *Battlestar Galactica*, has acknowledged that the Cylon Number Six was named after the prisoner's title. In *Buffy the Vampire Slayer*, evil character Ethan Rayne says, "Be seeing you" before running away; and in one episode, Spike was being held in an underground lab with large white balls around, much like the one that keeps everyone in check in The Village (show creator Joss Whedon has admitted to being a huge fan of the show, and once said Number Six was the best television character of all time). On *Babylon 5*, several characters would do the "be seeing you" salute with the fingers to the eye. The show has influenced dozens of musicians, television shows, and films. But possibly the biggest impact has been on *Lost*.

Just as Number Six has been stranded on an island with malevolent forces at work, so, too, are the castaways trapped on an island, and it appears that the plane crash wasn't a random event — someone has put the Losties there. Escape plans have been thwarted, and the Others are somehow watching them all the time. In *The Prisoner*, every character wears a badge with his/her number on it, and when their number is "retired" a different person can take on the number. The numerals 23 and 42 appear often, and the character of Number Eight is often someone working closely with Number Two to try to trick Six. The section of Six's file where Number Two keeps his personality logs is section 42. Four is a common number, usually with a negative connotation: often, Number Two counts down from four instead of three, and something bad happens on one. There are occasional mentions of 16 and 15, but they are rare compared to the other numbers.

Rover is very much like the jungle smoke monster, inhuman and appearing out of nowhere with a bellowing roar, chasing those who step out of line. In many later episodes of *The Prisoner*, Six sees the ball coming and simply slows his walk, stepping to the side as the ball moves by him slowly, as if unsure what to do now that its prey isn't running scared. Similarly, when Eko stares back at the smoke monster, Smokey retreats back into the jungle, but when anyone tries to run away, they are subjected to Smokey's wrath. The interesting difference is that we don't know what Smokey is or why it is appearing, whereas we actually see Rover getting called when Number Two pushes a button and Rover suddenly pops up from under the water. Taking these similarities into account, there's a suggestion that maybe the smoke monster is under someone's control as well, and perhaps it's being called for specific reasons.

Chess is a predominant theme throughout the series, as it will become on *Lost* in "Enter 77" and subsequent episodes.

In the finale of *The Prisoner*, a judge appears before a tribunal and screams repeatedly at a character, "Confess! Confess! Confess!" much like we heard Yemi yell at Eko in "The Cost of Living."

Number Six often thinks he's outsmarted Number Two, just as the characters on *Lost* think they can make decisions to affect their futures, but Ben acts like an evil Number Two, holding the reins and being the one who's really in control. And just as Number Two answers to a mysterious Number One, Ben also refers to a man who is greater than himself, one often referred to as "Jacob." Comments about time are a common theme on both shows. Number Two often lets Number Six get attached to a woman (who is assisting Two), and threatens to hurt her if Number Six steps out of line, just like Sawyer is told Kate will be hurt if he transgresses.

There is a scene in *The Prisoner* episode "Change of Mind" where Number Six is in the mental ward of the Village hospital, and he looks through a window to see a man undergoing "aversion therapy," strapped to a chair and forced to watch a screen that's flashing messages and visuals, much like Karl was subjected to in "Not in Portland." In another episode of *The Prisoner*, Number Six is trained by receiving a shock and learning to conform, just as Sawyer is subjected to the experiment in his cage.

In the end, *Lost* and *The Prisoner* most resemble one another on a fundamental level. In both cases, there is a person (or persons) who is stuck in an unfamiliar place and just wants to go home, who is obviously there for a reason, but doesn't know what that reason is. The reason has something to do with something they've done in their past (one could see the credits of *The Prisoner* as being like the flashbacks that appear in every episode of *Lost*). There is someone bigger and more menacing who is pulling the strings. The characters think they might be in control, but they're not. As the prisoners slowly begin to see the machinations of their gatekeepers, they're able to play some games in return, disarming the people who are keeping them prisoner. And through it all, a roaring faceless monster awaits them in the shadows, reminding them that they're being kept here against their will, with no means of escape.

3.10   Tricia Tanaka Is Dead

Original air date: February 28, 2007
Written by: Edward Kitsis, Adam Horowitz

Directed by: Eric Laneuville

Guest cast: Cheech Marin (Mr. Reyes), Lillian Hurst (Mrs. Reyes), Suzanne Krull (Psychic), Sung Hi Lee (Tricia Tanaka), Billy Ray Gallion (Randy Nations), Caden Waidyatilleka (Young Hurley)

Flashback: Hurley

When Hurley finds a VW van on the island, he remembers the rocky relationship he had with his father.

In season 1's "The Numbers," we discovered that Hurley is worth a whopping $114 million, because he played the mysterious island numbers in a lottery and won, but those numbers have cursed him. He remains immensely lucky (the world could crumble around him, but he'd still be standing) but everyone around him suddenly experiences bad luck. Hurley's backstory has always been about the argument of fate versus free will. Do we have the power to change our futures through our decisions and actions, or has our future already been chosen for us? So far, Hurley seems to believe things are fated, but in this episode he remembers a father who taught him the opposite. He finally realizes that maybe he *isn't* cursed, and sets out to see if he can make his own luck.

This is the first time we've seen the absentee dad, played by Cheech Marin, and just like with so many of the other characters, we can add this one to the almost-full "Daddy Issue" column (see page 153). He ran out on his family, only to return 17 years later when he discovered his son was worth millions. On the island, Hurley finds an old vehicle and believes it's a sign, since the only good thing that ever happened between him and his father was the car they always worked on together.

While the backstory is a little weak in this episode, it's the humor that saves it. "Tricia Tanaka Is Dead" is full of highlights — how boring and morose Hurley is during his television interview; the meteor . . . "or asteroid . . . I don't know the difference" that hits the restaurant; Jin inadvertently volunteering to help Hurley; "Dude . . . Roger was on a beer run"; Jin and Hurley accidentally popping off poor Roger's head; the reunion between Sawyer and Hurley and Jin — "Well, look at that. Somebody's hooked on phonics"; how the Reyes' exude nouveau riche in their tacky décor and Mrs. Reyes' golden personal Jesus; Sawyer's nicknames; Hurley mistakenly calling the dead guy Roger Workman; Sawyer teaching Jin the three things you say to a woman . . . the comedy alone is worth watching this episode.

Meanwhile, as Sawyer and Kate return and Sawyer heads out into the jungle, Kate turns right around and heads back to find Jack. Just as Hurley has convinced himself the van will start despite everyone saying it won't, Kate is determined to save Jack despite him telling her not to try. Sayid and Locke are very interested in what she tells them about the "zoo" they were kept in, but even they think she can't find her way to the other side of the island. But she has something the Others don't — Rousseau.

Ultimately, Hurley recruits Charlie, that other island boy who thinks his fate has already been written, thanks to Desmond's flashes. The two of them decide they have nothing to lose, and jump into a junky old vehicle with no engine and hurtle down a dangerously steep meadow full of boulders. What happens will prove to Hurley that maybe his old man wasn't always wrong, and maybe he really isn't cursed. Will he continue to think that way?

Hurley (Jorge Garcia) decides to stop letting the "curse" of the numbers get to him, and decides to see if he can break it and make his own luck.
(YORAM KAHANA/SHOOTING STAR)

Highlight: Sawyer: "What's your problem, Jumbotron?" Hurley: "Shut up, red . . . neck . . . man." Sawyer: "Touché."

Timeline: Kate and Sawyer return on December 5, and Kate, Locke, and Sayid find Rousseau early the morning of December 6.

Did You Notice?:

- Hurley says, "Death finds me, Dude." Hurley was put in a mental institution because he stepped on a balcony, broke it, and two people fell to their deaths. After he won the lottery, Grandpa Tito died, then Tricia Tanaka and her cameramen, and the guy who jumped from the building where he was seeing his accountant. He was involved in a plane crash where 253 people died on impact, and 27 people have died since then. While on the island, four of the Others have been killed. One can sympathize with him that he actually believes death finds him.

- Locke looks genuinely happy to see Sawyer and shakes his hand, but the last real encounter he had with him was when Sawyer humiliated him.
- This episode marks the return of Walt's evil dog, Vincent. Everywhere Vincent goes, death and destruction follow. In this case, the death happened about 20 years earlier, according to Hurley, but still . . .
- Hurley tells his parents he's going to get rid of the houses and the livestock. The *what?!*
- Looks like Mr. Reyes went to the same school of con artistry as, well, pretty much everyone else on the island. Except he graduated at the bottom of his class.
- Sawyer sits in front of his tent at the end of the episode as if he's returned home.

Interesting Facts: When Hurley is letting the "butlers" go, he calls them Mr. Tron and Lady Tron. Ladytron is an electronic band from Liverpool, England. They took their name from the Roxy Music song "Ladytron," from the band's debut album.

Nitpicks: Hurley's flashback seems to happen right before he leaves for Australia, and he's in the crash on the way back. Yet we see Randy firmly ensconced as Locke's boss at the box company in "Walkabout." He doesn't come off as someone who'd *just* gotten the job. Does Hurley's flashback last a lot longer than it seems, or is there a consistency error here?

Nikki and Paulo — Why?: In this episode, Paulo continues his obsession with bathrooms when he complains that they're out of oat bars, and then tells Nikki to stay behind because they need to go find bananas. He seems to be having some serious "regularity" issues. When Hurley shows up to the group, excited that he's found a van, both Nikki and Paulo act with derision, like they are *so* above a vehicle in the jungle.

Oops: When Vincent is first coming out of the jungle, the hand is in his mouth, but in the very next shot, the arm is turned and the hand is away from his mouth.

4 8 15 16 23 42: The vw van has an **8**-track. The license plate on Mr. Reyes' Camaro at the beginning is **429** PCE. If you assign numbers to the letters, they add up to 24 (a reverse **42**). The first three numbers add up to **15**.

Any Questions?:
- Why did Hurley hire Randy? *Was* it a revenge fantasy? Why is Randy so happy to be there? We know Randy's next job was at the box company, so did Hurley feel some weird loyalty to him and install him at the other company he owned?
- How did Roger die?
- Why was there a bunch of junk in the van?
- The psychic was hired by Hurley's dad, but Hurley cut the Tarot deck. How did the Death card end up where she needed it to be?

Music/Bands: The song playing at the beginning and end of the episode is "Shambala" by Three Dog Night (*Cyan*). Shambhala, in the Tibetan Buddhist tradition, is believed to be a mystical city beyond the Himalayas, and only people with the right karma will ever find it. When Hurley is eating dinner with his parents, you can hear Mozart's violin Sonata in A, "Tema con Variazioni."

3.11   Enter 77

Original air date: March 7, 2007
Written by: Damon Lindelof, Carlton Cuse
Directed by: Stephen Williams
Guest cast: Anne Bedian (Amira), April Grace (Bea Klugh), Shaun Toub (Sami), Eyad Elbitar (Arabic Man #1), Taiari Marshal (Waiter)

Flashback: Sayid
While heading north to find the Others, Sayid and co. come upon a shack in a clearing, inhabited by a man who claims to be the last living member of the Dharma Initiative.

"Enter 77" is a fantastic episode, possibly the best of the season thus far (and trust me, they just get better and better from this point on). Sayid has been all but absent this season, so it's great to have an entire episode focus on him. As with the other Sayid episodes ("Solitary," "The Greater Good," "One of Them"), the focus is on Sayid's past as a torturer, and how he's haunted by what he did. In "Enter 77," we discover his past caught up to him long before he came to the island.

Despite the violence of Sayid's flashback, it's a bittersweet story of mercy, love, and redemption. Sami's love for his wife drives him into a rage at the very thought of what Sayid did to terrorize her, but Amira has learned something through her anguish: forgiveness. She gives Sayid the pardon and mercy that he refused her when faced with the same option. Amira is played beautifully by Anne Bedian, and in the scene where she sits on a chair holding the cat, telling him the story of how she found the feline, you can almost hear the sound of Sayid's heart breaking in two. Her husband doesn't need to come in and finish the job of destroying Sayid: she just did.

Now, in the present, Sayid uses his skills as both torturer and tortured when facing Mikhail. He knows the man is lying, but he's also able to keep up a front and lie right back, the same way he did to Amira. As Locke sits in the other room, playing chess against a supercomputer, Sayid plays a mental chess game with Mikhail, where both combatants know the score, but are playing the game because the situation calls for it. Ultimately, Sayid offers Mikhail the mercy that he'd never shown his previous victims, but, one wonders, to what end?

Meanwhile, on the beach, Hurley and Sawyer have a less intellectual game of back and forth, when Hurley challenges Sawyer to a game of table tennis, with high stakes. Hurley surprises him, and once again, the con man is conned.

While Sayid seems to be trying to find redemption on the island, Locke seems to have gone completely crazy in this episode. This is the first of several episodes where Locke's behavior is baffling at best. He cannot resist the lure of another computer, another button to push. After saying he'd searched every nook and cranny of the house (when we know he hasn't looked anywhere) and hadn't found any hatches, he missed the obvious one under the carpet of the living room. When told to guard Mikhail, he wanders off like a child with attention deficit disorder, and once again gets wrapped up in his game until Mikhail turns the tables. In "Further Instructions," Locke came to the realization that he's not a farmer, he's a hunter, but his behavior has altered since then. He got a message from Eko's stick, and he thinks the island is speaking to him once again. Perhaps, through the computer, he's looking for "further instructions," and can't be bothered with helping out Sayid and Kate. At this point in the season he's not working alongside anyone else, but is on his own.

The YMCA on Richards Street in downtown Honolulu, which has previously been used as Sayid's mosque in "The Greater Good" and Hurley's mental institution in "Dave," stands in as both the patio of Sayid's restaurant, and the exterior of Sami's restaurant in "Enter 77." (RYAN OZAWA)

Highlight: Hurley hustling Sawyer at table tennis.

Timeline: Lostpedia lists the events of this episode as happening on December 9, 2004, three days after the previous episode; there's clearly a gap, but we don't know for sure that three days have passed.

Did You Notice?:

- There has been a lot of confusion on the show (and among the fans) about whether the hatch exploded or imploded. On the one hand, Desmond said that turning the key would pull the magnetic force inward and implode the hatch. Yet everything that was in the hatch blew out of it, which suggests an explosion. Hurley and Sawyer disagreeing on what actually happened was a nod to the fact the writers have been inconsistent on this.

- The cover stories on the issue of *Guns & Ammo* are, "Choosing the Right Caliber for Defense," "The New Breed of Deer Guns and Optics," and "Stories from the Bush." Perfect bathroom reading.

- When Kate immediately tries to come to Sayid's defense after he's been shot, Locke pushes her aside, leaving Sayid to fend for himself.

- The "ping-pong ball" that Sawyer brings over is, in fact, a golf training ball.

- Mikhail says he's at the Flame station, which was marked on the blast door map (seen in "Lockdown") as being just northwest of the Swan station.

- Mikhail refers to the Others as "the Hostiles," which is how Kelvin Inman always referred to them.

- During Sayid and Kate's fight with Mikhail, Locke is in the very next room, yet he only comes in at the very end of the fight. It's as if he wanted Mikhail to overpower Sayid and Kate.
- The viewers know that Sayid is lying to Sami the moment he says he'd never torture another woman, because we know from "Solitary" that he tortured Nadia.
- While Amira's cat and Mikhail's cat looked the same, they're not. Amira's cat has a black smudge on his nose that the other one doesn't.

Interesting Facts: Mikhail Bakunin (1814–1876) is the name of one of the founding fathers of anarchism. He was a Russian rebel who despised injustice and called for a general uprising of the people that would lead to freedom. He was aligned with Marx in his economic theories, but separated from Marx and his belief that socialism could be built up by taking over the state. Bakunin, on the other hand, called for the destruction of socialism and the state. He believed a revolution should direct violence toward the institutions, not toward other human beings.

Nadia Comaneci was the first gymnast to receive a perfect score at the Olympics. In 1976, at the age of 14, Comaneci performed on the uneven bars, and scored a perfect 10. Nadia won the gold medal in the event, and went on to win two more golds, a silver, and a bronze. During the ABC Wide World of Sports coverage of her in 1976, they played the theme song from *The Young and the Restless* over montages of Nadia's events, and the song was renamed, "Nadia's Theme." Her birthday is November 12, so if Mikhail is telling the truth, that's his birthday, too.

Nitpicks: Sayid never would have taken a sip of the iced tea before waiting for Mikhail to do it first.

Nikki and Paulo — Why?: In yet another example of literal bathroom humor, Paulo apparently reads *Guns and Ammo* while doing his business in the forest. (Notice how the roll of toilet paper still has the wrapping on it, as if he wasn't actually able to go.) His pale imitation of "macho" withers in the presence of Sawyer, and despite Sawyer's rudeness, we can't help but roll our eyes and hope Sawyer decks him when Paulo calls him "Heelbeely." Meanwhile, Nikki is over at the ping-pong table whining at Sawyer about playing nice, and his comment — "Who the hell are you?" — echoes what a lot of fans were saying at home.

4 8 15 16 23 42: Mikhail says that 4 men came to his yard and told him not to cross the imaginary line. There are C-4 explosives everywhere in the basement. The Dharma binders are marked DI 90M1654-21644, and the numbers all add up to **42**. Marvin Candle says on the computer message to enter 24 (a reverse **42**) for a pallet drop; 32 (a reverse **23**) for mainland communications, 38 (**23** + **15**) for a satellite connection; 56 (**16** + **16** + **16** + **8**) for sonar access; 77 (**42** + **23** + **8** + **4**) if there's an incursion by the Hostiles.

It's Just a Flesh Wound: Sayid is shot in the left arm. Mikhail and Sayid beat each other up. Kate kicks Mikhail in the head. Klugh hits Kate and slams her head into the pavement, and Kate beats her in return. Mikhail shoots Klugh and headbutts Locke. Sayid hits Mikhail with the butt of his gun.

Lost in Translation: When Sami says to Sayid that they are both Iraqi, he isn't actually speaking Iraqi, but he is using an Arabic dialect.

As Locke is wandering through Mikhail's house, he finds a manuscript lying upon the table, written in Cyrillic, and with marginal notations in a red pen. The translation (provided by Lostpedia) is as follows:

Sayid (Naveen Andrews) recalls a life-changing encounter in his past in "Enter 77." (JACK DARRIN/SHOOTING STAR)

. . . were lost in his land, and they should
. . . force and, if necessary, through complete social
. . . in some measure pushed <u>Andrey</u> [the notation in red here says, "My name is also Andrey"] away. Nadji was not
. . . Afghan resistance, however he was an excellent
. . . He was a second cousin of an influential
. . . who controlled one of the northwestern
<u>. . . ical specialist</u> helping

. . . Mujahideen used against . . .

. . . of courage Nadji compensated with his wits . . .

. . . of a fundamentalist. Just like all the radicals of that time, Nadji . . .

. . . at his madrasah believed that they are holding back the West and . . .
were paving the way for Allah, so that he could erase the infidels from the
face of the Earth, at the time that Andrey thought that the fall of
Afghanistan will become an impulse for a new social revolution [the notation in red says, "I have forgotten so much about Afghanistan"]

. . . "The Pakistanis arrived today," Nadji reported with a strong accent
in grandiloquent Russian.

. . . We knew that the ISI would be involved. And you . . .

. . . report this?" Andrey knew that he . . .

. . . "I thought that you . . .

Could the document be about Sayid? Nadji is very similar to Najeev, the
name Sayid is using when working as a chef. It's also similar to Nadia. The notation, "My name is also Andrey" is a curious one, although it could simply be a
wink to the fact that the actor who plays Mikhail is named Andrew.

Later, during the showdown outside, Mikhail and Klugh begin speaking in
Russian. The rough translation is:

Klugh: Mikhail! You know what to do.
Mikhail: We still have another way.
Klugh: We cannot risk. You know what to do.
Mikhail: We still have another way.
Klugh: We cannot risk. You know the conditions.
Mikhail: We have another way.
Klugh: They know us. We will not let them [unintelligible]. You know what
to do. It is an order.

Any Questions?:

- It seems very suspicious that Rousseau just suddenly wanders back into the
jungle when they arrive at Mikhail's place. On the one hand, she's a solitary
creature who prefers to keep to herself and to stay away from others, but on
the other, she returns when they have the upper hand, and seems very intent
on killing him. When she told Sayid that 16 years ago she was part of a sci-

Sawyer's Nicknames

Kate: Freckles, Shortcake, Sweetheart, Kiddo, Magellan

Danny: Boss, Chinatown, Broken Nose Man, Blockhead

Alex: Sheena, Underdog, Sister, Lollipop, Sally Slingshot

Karl: Chachi, Cheech, Bobby

Ben: Big Kahuna, Sucker, George, Captain Bunnykiller, Bug-Eyed Bastard

Jack: The Doc

Charlie: Oliver Twist, The Munchkin, Jiminy Cricket

Hurley: Snuffy, Blockhead, Ese, International House of Pancakes, Jumbotron, Avalanche, Grimace, Hero

Jin: Jin-bo

Sun and Jin: Crouching Tiger and Hidden Dragon

Roger: Skeletor

Paulo: Zorro, Pablo

Nikki: Nina

Nikki and Paulo: Jabronis

Locke: Tarzan, Bald Bastard, John-Boy

Charlie, Hurley, Aaron: Three Men and a Baby (he counted Hugo twice)

entific expedition, could she have been part of the Dharma Initiative?

- When Locke and Kate ambush Mikhail, he begins shouting, "We had a truce! You said I could stay here!" Was it all an act, or has he broken away from the Others somehow?
- Kate finds some fresh meat in Mikhail's kitchen. Where did that come from? Did he recently kill a cow?
- What sort of manuscript is Mikhail typing?
- Did Sayid take one of the Dharma binders?
- Why was Klugh hiding in the basement? Why did she tell Mikhail to shoot her? Why does Mikhail smile when Rousseau suggests there's no reason to keep him alive? Is there something they know that we don't? Are they immortal?

Ashes to Ashes: Miss Bea Klugh (not necessarily her real name) was an island resident and one of the mysterious Others. She was Michael's chief interrogator during his capture at their camp, and she was studying Walt's behavior. She enjoyed book clubs and kidnapping people.

3.12   Par Avion

Original air date: March 14, 2007
Written by: Christina M. Kim, Jordan Rosenberg
Directed by: Paul Edwards
Guest cast: John Terry (Christian Shephard), Gabrielle Fitzpatrick (Lindsey), Julian Barnes (Dr. Woodruff), Rhett Gils (Officer Barnes), Anne Elizabeth Logan (Head Nurse), Danan Pere (ER Doctor)

Flashback: Claire

Claire believes she's come up with a way to get everyone off the island; meanwhile, Sayid, Locke, and Kate discover a large fence on their way to the Others' camp.

Claire's two previous flashbacks dealt with her pregnancy and impending motherhood. In "Raised by Another," we see how far she went to give her baby up for adoption, and how she ended up on the island. "Par Avion" is also about motherhood, but the focus is on Claire's relationship with her own mother. And how Claire was a totally rockin' Goth chick.

The episode definitely has its revelations. We discover that despite Claire's laid-back, sweet demeanor, she harbors a dark secret: she believes she caused the car accident that put her mother into a coma. After last season's "Two for the Road," many fans speculated that Claire and Jack were actually half-siblings, sharing the same father, and that was confirmed in this episode. Of course, Claire never asked Christian his name, and it's doubtful Jack carries a photo of dear old Dad in his pocket, so they may never find out.

This is an episode about hope and false hope. When Claire sees a flock of birds migrating, she sees a possible way off the island. Charlie worries that Claire's placed all her hopes in a paltry attempt at rescue, and that maybe the birds aren't even tagged. He worries that if other people listen, they'll all start to have false hope.

Goth chick Claire works in a tattoo and piercing place in "Par Avion." (MARIO PEREZ/© ABC/COURTESY EVERETT COLLECTION)

"There is hope, and there is guilt, and believe me, I know the difference," says wise Christian in Claire's flashback, and he knows that her mother will never wake up, and doesn't want Claire to spend the rest of her life thinking she might. What is interesting about this statement coming from Christian, of all people, is a conversation we saw him have in one of Jack's flashbacks in "Man of Science, Man of Faith." After Jack delivers a too-honest prognosis to Sarah — her spine is crushed and she'll never walk again — Christian follows Jack into the hallway and tells him, "Even if there's a ninety-nine percent possibility that they're utterly, hopelessly screwed, folks are much more inclined to hear that one percent chance that things are going to be okay." When Jack counters that doing so would be giving nothing more than false hope, Christian says yes, but it's still hope. Apparently something's changed in him, as if he realizes that in this situation, the only person being hurt is the one who *could* move on with her life.

Meanwhile, the person who should be wracked with guilt is Locke, but he seems to be getting by just fine. As Locke continues to act alone and move away from the group, he lies to Sayid, throws a man to his death, and then shrugs the whole thing off with a big, "Well . . . *no one* consulted with me!" whine session. It's a wonder Sayid didn't grab Locke and throw him in after Mikhail. If his aim is to push everyone away so he can be on his own, he's doing a damn good job.

Even though Desmond runs around trying to save Charlie yet again, and Claire pushes Charlie out of her tent for lying to her yet again, all turns out well in the end. Claire and Charlie attach a note to one of the tagged birds, and watch as it flies off. Claire refers to her mother in the past tense, as if indicating that she's finally let her go. Claire is the island mother, but in many ways she's also still a child. Charlie will never be allowed to fully be Aaron's father because Claire keeps pushing him away. Just as her mother refused to allow Christian into Claire's life, Claire is reluctant to let any father into Aaron's. Perhaps this flashback will show her where her petulance has gotten her in the past, and now that she knows what Desmond believes is in store for Charlie, she'll stop pushing him away. Before it's too late.

Highlight: When Rousseau suggests they shoot Mikhail like a dog, Locke replies, "No, I like dogs."

Timeline: December 10

Did You Notice?:

- Sayid argues with Locke, who tells him he didn't know there were explosives in the basement. And Sayid believes him, which could be the first time we've ever seen someone put one over on Sayid.

- Rousseau tells the group that whatever Mikhail says will be a lie, which is exactly what she said about "Henry Gale" in the season 2 episode, "One of Them."

- Mikhail looks to each one of them and says they're not on Jacob's list because they are flawed (Kate), angry (Locke), and weak and frightened (Sayid). We can only assume each of those characteristics is meant to describe the person he's looking at, but interestingly, in "Stranger in a Strange Land," Achara tells Jack that he is angry and frightened.

- It's interesting that Claire worked in a tattoo parlor, since in his last flashback, her half-brother showed what happened after he got a tattoo.

- Christian tells Claire that he used to come to visit her and he'd sing to her. In the season 1 episode, "Raised by Another," she says her father used to sing "Catch a Falling Star" to her.

- Since Claire's mother would have been in a coma during the events of "Two for the Road," the woman in that episode that Christian goes to see, banging on her door in the middle of the night, must have been her Aunt Lindsey.

Nitpicks: Aunt Lindsey blames Claire for causing the accident, but somehow doesn't seem to blame the fact that Mommy wasn't wearing a seatbelt? Also, there's a scene where Sun is spooning food into Aaron's mouth. It's not clear if she's giving him crushed melon, or just spooning milk into his mouth from the melon shell, but either way, an eight-week-old child would not be on solid foods, and would not be eating with a spoon.

Another thread in the motherhood theme of this episode involved Rousseau and Alex, and I don't buy Rousseau's response to Kate. She's bracing herself for upset, so she can't bring herself to ask about Alex, but what about the basic questions: Is Alex healthy? Was she being treated okay? Was she happy?

Jin, Sun, and Claire almost catch the birds in the trap when Desmond shoots his gun. Later we discover it's because he needed to keep her from trapping the birds, because he had a flash of Charlie dying trying to grab one. But if Claire had caught a bird in the trap, then Charlie wouldn't have had to venture out onto the slippery rocks, so Desmond's reasoning makes no sense. Later, when Desmond actually catches the bird, there's no way it would have sat still like that while he was approaching it.

We hear Charlie's voiceover reading the letter, which is about how they feel like they've been forgotten and left behind, but they won't give up hope, and there is new life on the island, and blah blah blah . . . if anyone does find the note, they'll assume it had been written hundreds of years ago by Shakespeare, not someone actually *looking to be rescued*. How could she have possibly fit all of that on that tiny piece of paper? Sadly, no one will find the note, because Charlie and Claire forgot one important thing: water and paper don't mix. They didn't put it into any tiny vial that would actually protect it, so the moment that bird lands on the water for a rest, the note will be history.

Oops: In the season 1 episode, "Raised by Another," Claire takes the pregnancy test and tells the baby's daddy, Thomas, that she's pregnant. He asks if she's going to keep it, and she says, "My mom would disown me." He replies, "She pretty much has already." But now we know her mom's been in a coma for months, possibly years at that point. The writers could argue that they were referring to her comatose state, but then it would turn their words into a joke, and there's no way Claire would have joked about her mother being in a coma. Also, when Claire goes to see the psychic, her friend tells him that Claire hasn't told her mother about the pregnancy yet, and when he looks concerned, Claire suggests maybe she shouldn't tell her. At the end of the episode, Dominic Monaghan holds the bird to let it fly away, and you can see the note still tucked into his hand, not attached to the bird. The producers have confirmed this was a production error, and we can assume Charlie attached it to the bird.

4 8 15 16 23 42: Mikhail was recruited into the army when he was 24 (a reverse **42**). Over the hospital loudspeaker, you hear an announcement for Dr. Alanson to pick up line **4**. Another announcement tells a therapist to call 10**58**. Claire's mom's hospital room is 2**12** (21 + 2 = **23**).

It's Just a Flesh Wound: Mikhail appears to suffer a cerebral hemorrhage when Locke pushes him through the sonar fence.

Any Questions?:

- What did Desmond tell Charlie at the beginning of the episode? Did he give him the detail about the rocks, or did he just tell him to dissuade Claire from catching a bird?
- Why did Locke lie about the C-4?
- Mikhail is clearly talking about Jacob when he says the man who brought them all here is a "magnificent man." Will we ever see Jacob?
- Mikhail begins to say, "The John Locke I know was para—" but is cut off by Rousseau. Does he mean the Locke he knew through his files? Or did he actually know Locke off the island? Is there a personal reason Locke threw Mikhail into the sonar fence to kill him? Is he hiding his former paralysis from everyone else?
- Why does Mikhail say "thank you" when Locke throws him through the fence to die? Why does John smile at him when he says it, like they're in cahoots?
- Why is Jack playing football with the Others?!

Ashes to Ashes: Mikhail Bakunin was part of the Russian military working as a medic, and did a tour in Afghanistan. He is one of the mysterious Others, though often claimed to be the last living member of the Dharma Initiative. He worked in communications, and was a sneaky bastard.

3.13   The Man from Tallahassee

Original air date: March 21, 2007
Written by: Drew Goddard, Jeff Pinkner
Directed by: Jack Bender
Guest cast: Kevin Tighe (Anthony Cooper), Brian Goodman (Ryan Price), Cleo King (Government Worker), Patrick J. Adams (Peter Talbot), Barbara Baehler (Mrs. Talbot), Marlene Forte (Detective Mason), Don Nahaku (Detective Reed), Stephen Bishop (Kincaid)

Flashback: Locke

As Kate and Sayid attempt to rescue Jack, Locke confronts Ben and tells him he wants to find the submarine.

It's time for . . . Name that Locke Screw-up! That's right, folks, just pull your chairs on up, and let's review. This is the sixth Locke episode we've had in the series. "Walkabout" revealed that Locke had been in a wheelchair, worked at a box company, and seemed to be everyone's underdog. "Deus Ex Machina" showed us how his mother had given him up to make a few extra bucks, and his father had conned him out of a kidney. In "Orientation," he went to anger management classes, met Helen, and she talked him out of stalking his father's house late at night. Cooper finally died (hooray!) in "Lockdown," only to show us that he was actually alive and conning some people into thinking he was dead (boo) and once again he convinced Locke to help him out, which caused Locke to lose Helen. In "Further Instructions" Locke seems to have finally gotten past his father and his own anger, and he has joined another group of people who accept him for who he is, only to accidentally introduce a fed into the mix who threatens to destroy everything they'd built up. Oops.

On the island, Locke has endured a rollercoaster of emotions and events. In season 1 he believed he'd been healed and blessed by the island, and was an instant disciple to the island and its bidding. He discovered the hatch and spent most of the season trying to open it. In season 2, Jack took over the hatch, and Locke began to resent the fact that he was being treated like Jack's underling. Locke pushed the button faithfully for most of the season, until the doubts that Jack had put in his head started to speak louder than his faith. Sawyer convinced Locke that Jack was after the guns, and when Locke moved them, Sawyer took all of them. When Henry Gale suddenly appeared on the scene, Locke believed for a moment he had someone on his side, until Henry tricked him. He snapped, decided he wasn't going to be their buttmonkey any longer, took over the hatch, ousted Eko, and refused to push the button . . . only to discover he'd been right the first time, and in *not* pressing the button, he risked blowing up the island and killing everyone on it.

Locke's behavior has changed drastically in the third season. In seasons 1 and 2, the story line had followed Locke so closely that we always knew what was going on in his head and why he was acting the way he was. In season 3, it's no longer clear what he's thinking about because we're only seeing him from the point of view of the other characters. The last thing we saw happen from Locke's point of view was discovering that he's destined to be a hunter. He believes he has to stop reacting to things around him, and become an active participant, making them happen for himself, and not taking into consideration anyone else. He's following a premonition to get to the other side of the island, and along the way he's acted against Sayid and Kate. He's blown up important information, lied to both of them, killed a man, and now he's acting alone, intent on blowing up the only possible means of rescue that these people may have.

So when he arrives in Ben's room, we know this is the first time they've seen each other since Benry tricked him in "Two for the Road." But what he doesn't seem to have figured out is that Ben is no less a con man than Locke's father had been. Ben knew Locke would come and he needed him to blow up the sub so that he could squirm out of a promise to allow Jack and Juliet to leave the island.

In the backstory, we *finally* discover how Locke ended up in the wheelchair, after so many teasers in the other episodes. It comes as no surprise that Cooper is the one who does it, but it's *how* he does it that's so devastating. Even knowing that this is the episode where the accident will be revealed, the moment of Locke being thrown out of a window comes as a shock, and only moments after Cooper had said, "I'm a con man, not a murderer." It's like a liar telling you he'd never tell a lie. The performance Terry O'Quinn gives throughout this episode — and especially at the end, when he looks down and sees his future in two useless legs — shows again what an extraordinary actor O'Quinn is.

The history of Locke is that he will always be a pawn, and never a player. (No wonder he took such an interest in the chess game at Mikhail's place.) Cooper used him, "the island" used him, and now Ben is using Locke for his own gain. Even with Alex warning Locke that Ben always makes people think they're making the decisions, he doesn't wake up and realize he's being played.

Or is he? There's definitely something in Ben that's changed. As Locke says, he's not healing as quickly as he should be on the island. Bullet wounds heal in three or four days. But it's been several days, and Ben is still in a wheelchair, and the wound on his back is not healing. Ben takes offense to Locke lecturing him about not appreciating the island, and asks Locke why he thinks he knows this island better. "Because you're in a wheelchair, and I'm not," Locke replies bluntly. Locke has regained his communion with the island, just as Ben has lost his. Ben recognizes in Locke the person he should have been, and he needs to keep Locke onside if he wants to find a way to heal himself. And if that means bringing the one person to the island that will keep Locke occupied, then Ben will do it.

Highlight: Ben's response when Locke asks him how they get electricity: "We have two giant hamsters running on a massive wheel in our secret underground lair."
Timeline: The A-Team arrives at the camp the night of December 10, but the rest of the episode happens in the early morning of December 11.
Did You Notice?:
- In every Locke flashback, we always know it's happened after the previous one because of his slowly receding hairline.
- When Peter arrives at Locke's apartment, there are hieroglyphics and illustrations on Locke's TV tray, and one of them is the number 40, which is an important Biblical number.
- Pay attention to the television show that Locke is watching (it'll make sense in the next episode).
- Whose side is Tom on? He seems to have aligned himself with Jack, warning him about the cameras in the room as if he doesn't want him to get caught.
- Ben tells Locke that if he joins them, he'll show him things he's always wanted to see, as if he were recruiting him into a cult. Considering the police officer in "Further Instructions" told Locke that his psych profile said he was easily swayed, it appears Ben's been reading the same file.
- When Locke wheels Ben into his living room, you can see a copy of *A Brief History of Time* sitting on a side table.
- The scene of Locke looking down into the sub is almost exactly the same as when he was looking down into the hatch.

- Just before Anthony throws Locke out the window, he pours a drink of MacCutcheon whisky, the same whisky that Desmond's never-would-be-father-in-law poured. Like Widmore with Desmond, Anthony clearly had no intention of letting Locke drink it.
- The nurse tells Locke, "I don't want to hear about what you can't do," repeating back Locke's mantra.
- Ben tells Locke that Locke had appeared to him like a dream come true, just like he said earlier that having a spinal surgeon fall from the sky made him believe in God.
- At the end of the episode, the hallway that Ben and Locke go down to see Cooper looks exactly like the hallway outside Rachel's apartment in "Not in Portland."

Interesting Facts: Locke calls Ben a "Pharisee." The Pharisees were a Jewish religious party that existed from 515 AD – 70 BC, and they believed in the oral tradition of the Torah over the written version.

In "Not in Portland," Juliet meets with Dr. Alpert. In this episode, Ben refers to the same man as Richard. Richard Alpert, a.k.a. Baba Ram Dass, was the cohort of Timothy Leary, and he studied the effects of mind-altering drugs on human beings. He conducted psychological experiments and is a follower of dharma and eastern philosophy.

Nitpicks: Why does Locke trust that Anthony really will break it off with Peter's mom? Cooper hasn't exactly been a rock of trustworthiness so far.

Oops: There are some errors on the paperwork that the government worker has on her desk while dealing with Locke. First, it says his birthday is May 30, 1956, but in "Further Instructions," his license said his birthday was November 15, 1946. The date in this episode is probably more correct, since it's more believable that he's just shy of 50, not 60 (and that his mother was 16 when she had him, and not six). Also, the date on the paperwork is February 4, 2002, but he was put in a wheelchair in 2000, four years before the plane crash, and in this scene, he's still walking. Later, when Locke goes to Anthony's apartment, the apartment number is 3801, which would mean he's on the 38th floor, not the 8th. The view from the apartment looks much higher than eight floors up. Also, when Ben is in his living room, the clock says 3:24. When Alex comes in with the backpack, the clock reads 12:35. When she hands him the bag the clock is at 4:12. As he leaves her, the clock goes back to 12:35.

4 8 15 16 23 42: Also on the paperwork, it says that Locke's address is **168**

O Canada

You can always tell when someone is lying or is evil — they use a Canadian reference.

- Kate tells Ray she's from Canada in "Tabula Rasa."
- Sawyer tells Jess he has an investor from Toronto in "Confidence Man."
- Ethan tells Hurley he's from Ontario in "Solitary."
- Nathan tells Ana Lucia he's from Canada in "The Other 48 Days" (he was actually telling the truth, but we were meant to believe he was an Other based on the Canuck reference).
- Peter tells Locke that "Adam Seward" claims to be from Ontario.
- Mikhail tells Bonnie and Greta that he thought they were on assignment in Canada in "Through the Looking Glass."

San Juan St., zip code 92780 (the numbers add up to 26, 2 + 6 = **8**). There are **4** candles atop the piano that Jack is playing. Locke mentions again that he'd spent **4** years in the wheelchair. When Locke begins eating chicken in Ben's kitchen, the clock reads 3:24 (a reverse **42**). Locke falls **8** storeys before breaking his back.

It's Just a Flesh Wound: Locke has been beaten when he's handcuffed to the pipe, probably by Ryan, possibly by Jack. Cooper's also been beaten.

Any Questions?:

- Where did Karl go?
- Rousseau disappears into the jungle again. Was she ousted from the group after some disagreement? Is Ben, in fact, Alex's real biological father and not an adoptive one, and Rousseau lied about the circumstances of her birth? Did they want to do tests on Rousseau because she somehow had come to term on the island without dying?
- Is Anthony Cooper really the guy's name? Is he really Locke's father?
- Peter says he obtained Anthony/Adam's medical records. How did he get those? How did he find out his name was Anthony Cooper in order to get the medical records?
- Kate looks at Jack in astonishment when she arrives at his "house" in Otherville. Is it because he's just hanging around and not trying to escape, or because she didn't know he could play piano?

- Jack tells Kate the kids are all safe. Does he know more than he did the day he was confronted by Cindy in the cage?
- Did Locke actually blow up the submarine? First of all, when he's walking up the dock, he's soaking wet. If he'd boarded the sub, planted the explosive device, and got off, he'd be dry. There's no reason for him to have gone into the water to plant it on the side of the submarine, since he'd do far more damage by blowing it up from the inside. Could he have somehow piloted the submarine somewhere else, swum back, attached the explosives to the end of the dock, and blown it up instead?
- When he's handcuffed to the pipe, one side of his face is bruised. Who hit him?

3.14   Exposé

Original air date: March 28, 2007
Written by: Edward Kitsis, Adam Horowitz
Directed by: Stephen Williams
Guest cast: Maggie Grace (Shannon), Ian Somerhalder (Boone), Billy Dee Williams (Mister LaShade), William Mapother (Ethan), Daniel Roebuck (Arzt), Jacob Witkin (Zuckerman)

Flashback: Nikki and Paulo

Suspicions abound (and fans cheer) when Nikki and Paulo are found dead.

Razzle frickin' dazzle!

Characters fans love to hate: they run rampant in television shows, and sometimes the writers ignore the angry outcries of fans (as in the case of Joxer on *Xena: Warrior Princess*) or they phase them out quietly (think Riley on *Buffy the Vampire Slayer*). But in this episode, the writers take the fans' pleas seriously, and give us back a gift that completely makes up for having to suffer these fools for the past few months.

Some of you may have watched this episode and thought, "Who the hell are these people? Were they introduced in this episode just to kill them off?" Despite the diehard fans hating Nikki and Paulo with every fiber of their being from the moment they first appeared in "Further Instructions" to the announcement that this would be a Nikki/Paulo–centric episode (and I am not alone in this one), there were many casual viewers who never noticed them, and to them they were about as distinguishable as the trees on the island.

We know there were 48 survivors, yet fewer than 20 of them actually have names, and the rest are just background characters, or "socks," as the producers call them (short for "sock puppets"). From about midway through season 1, fans began wondering aloud why the writers weren't taking advantage of all the socks in the background, and why they weren't introducing them to just play smaller roles like Scott and Steve, or Rose. By the beginning of season 2, the writers were already talking about bringing two characters forward and giving them a backstory. By season 3, those characters had become Nikki and Paulo.

There are two elements I adore about this photo. One makes me laugh out loud, the other makes me lose my train of . . . what was I talking about again? (MARIO PEREZ/©ABC/ COURTESY EVERETT COLLECTION)

And then it backfired. Fans immediately retaliated, hating these characters and wondering why time was being wasted on them when Rose and Bernard had completely disappeared. Fan conspiracy theories began popping up — were Nikki and Paulo Others who had infiltrated the camp? Did the electromagnetic surge at the end of season 2 actually make Rose and Bernard about 20 years younger . . . and Latin American? Fans thought Nikki was brusque and unlikable; Paulo was dull and went to the bathroom too often.

So, in a rare moment of television executive *mea culpa*, the producers of the show decided to nix their plans of several flashbacks focusing on Nikki's television show, *Exposé*, and get rid of them immediately. This episode is one extended apology to the fans.

And what an apology it is! I had been imagining all sorts of gruesome deaths for these two, but I never came up with something as cruel and vicious as the writes did. (Bless them!) But before ridding us of them forever, they used this episode as a sort of clip show, reminding us of key moments of the series, but inserting Nikki and Paulo into old footage and scenes. Just as Tom Stoppard's *Rosencrantz and Guildenstern Are Dead* retold Shakespeare's *Hamlet* through the eyes of Hamlet's two bumbling friends who have not much more than a couple of lines, now we see the entire span of the show through the eyes of these two morons. Past characters who have been killed off were brought back, the most refreshing being Arzt (that other background character brought forward only to give him a funny death). Shannon and Boone also return.

The episode contains several in-jokes as well. Hurley, the avid television viewer, knows exactly who Nikki is. Sawyer, representing the casual viewer, is constantly saying, "Who the hell's Nikki?" Nikki tells Zuckerman that she's just a guest star on the show, and we all know what happens to guest stars. Zuckerman suggesting they can still bring her back next season even if she's killed off on the show. Hurley excitedly grabs the script, saying *Exposé* is the greatest show on television, "even better than *Baywatch*" (ha!), and discovers that a long-time character on the show was actually the evil mastermind behind everything, a nod to fans who believe that Locke or Jack or one of the main characters actually orchestrated the crash and is behind everything.

A humorous subtext of the episode was that everyone theorizes about what's going on, and are often way off, which makes us wonder how many of their other theories are wrong. Charlie notices grit under Nikki's fingernails. Hurley thinks Paulo did it. Several people think Sawyer did it. Jin is convinced the monster did it. Sawyer thinks Nikki and Paulo were in cahoots with the Others.

In the end, Nikki and Paulo die not only because we hated them, but because of greed. We discover that they weren't actually dead the entire time, but have been bitten by spiders that cause a paralytic state, which means during the entire episode of people talking around them and digging their graves, they've been completely conscious and aware that they're about to be buried alive (of course, one could assume they were unconscious, but I'd prefer to think of them as being completely aware of what was going on — it's much more horrific that way). In the final moment, just as they throw the dirt on them, Nikki's eyes pop open. But it's too late. It seems even in death, they are as overlooked and unnoticed as they were in life.

Highlight: The final 30 seconds. I was cheering. Yes, I am evil.

Timeline: This episode runs concurrently with the previous, so it's December 11.

Did You Notice?:

- There was no "Previously on *Lost*" segment at the beginning, as if the writers knew many people wouldn't remember them being on *Lost* previously.
- In the previous episode, in the scene where Locke is watching television and Peter comes to his apartment, Locke is watching an episode of *Exposé*.
- Billy Dee Williams is playing the Cobra. On *Star Wars*, he played Lando Calrissian whose ship was the *Cobra*.
- His character's name, Mister LaShade, is an anagram for See Dharma List.
- The director of the episode of *Exposé* is listed as Stephen Williams on the clapboard, who also directed this episode (and many others) of *Lost*.
- The diamonds are hidden in a wooden Russian doll, which is ironic, since if any two characters had absolutely *no* layers, it's these two.
- At the airport, Paulo's carrying a shoulder bag that has *Exposé Season Four* written on it.
- Boone is running around looking for pens, which is a reference to the pilot episode, in which he began collecting pens after the crash so Jack could perform emergency tracheotomies.
- Arzt says he's going to be the next Darwin. Darwin argued that animals evolved through survival of the fittest, where the weaker members of a species would be killed off. Arzt would die about three weeks after his discussion with Nikki.
- As Hurley and Charlie are digging the grave, Vincent pulls the blanket off Nikki and Paulo, as if to alert everyone they're not actually dead.
- Sawyer refers to Sayid, Kate, and Locke as the A-Team, which is a term fans had been using for them for a long time.
- The smoke monster is nearby, but doesn't actually do any damage.

Interesting Facts: Sawyer is reading Agatha Christie's *Evil Under the Sun*. Generally considered one of Christie's finest Poirot murder mysteries, this one has one of the best twist endings of the bunch, and I can't bear to ruin it if you haven't read it. It's the story of Arlena Marshall, a beautiful woman married to a man named Kenneth, who comes to a seaside retreat. Patrick Redfern, Arlena's lover, is also there, much to the chagrin of Patrick's wife. When he leaves to apparently have a tryst with her, another woman asks to come along in the boat. When the boat comes to shore, Patrick finds Arlena lying there, dead. The ensuing mystery

"Exposé" Timeline

Day	What happens to Nikki and Paulo	Episode	Inconsistency
80 days ago/ Day 1	They read the obit in the airport; see Shannon and Boone fighting; survive the crash	"Pilot"; "Exodus": Shannon is angry that they didn't get their first-class tickets, which saved their lives in the end	None
75 days ago/ Day 6	N&P are looking for their suitcase; Ethan tells them if they need anything he can help them find it; Arzt yells that Boone took the water; Jack gives his speech	"White Rabbit": Boone took the water because he believed someone needed to take responsibility; Jack finds the caves and tells people they're not going to be rescued, it's time to start learning to live on the island	None
57 days ago/ Day 23	Nikki talks to Arzt about his bugs, gets him to draw a map, and she and Paulo find the plane and the Pearl station door	See next box (Boone and Locke won't find the plane for another 18 days)	See below
48 days ago/ Day 32	Nikki and Paulo overhear Kate arguing with Shannon and Arzt; they go to the waterfall and Paulo finds the case, but doesn't tell Nikki	"Whatever the Case May Be": Jack and Kate get the case with her toy plane in it, and Jack puts the key around his neck; just as Paulo hid the case from Nikki, Kate hides the truth from Jack	The events of "Whatever the Case May Be" actually happened on Day 23, not Day 32

involves false alibis, attempted voodoo magic, strange items washing up on shore, and when the killer is revealed, we discover that things are not what they seem, and people are not who they appear to be. As good as the twist at the end is, though, it's nothing compared to the one at the end of this episode.

Day	What happens to Nikki and Paulo	Episode	Inconsistency
32 days ago/ Day 48	Paulo sneaks into the Pearl station and hides the diamonds in the back of the toilet; he overhears Juliet and Ben talking about how they're going to get Jack	"Abandoned": This is the day Shannon was shot (the episode "The Other 48 Days" confirms that). (Henry Gale will be captured on Day 56, and Eko and Locke will find the Pearl station on Day 63)	Since Ben's already in costume as Henry Gale, it seems strange that it'll be another week before they'll find him
9 days ago/ Day 71	Back at the Pearl station, Paulo sneaks the diamonds out while Nikki, Desmond, Locke, and Sayid see Mikhail on the television	"The Cost of Living": Same events happen, and Eko dies	None

Several promotional photos were released in advance of this episode, and in one series, Nikki is screaming and looking like she's having a nervous breakdown after the hatch explosion, and Paulo has his arms around her comforting her. Then he takes her down the beach and sits with his arms around her while she cries. Perhaps the writers thought this moment was a little too tender, and would make fans feel guilty for wanting them dead.

Many of the scenes of the crash were reshot, but others were actual footage from the pilot episode, with Nikki green-screened into it. For example, when she stops and looks up at the wing of the plane teetering dangerously, she's been superimposed onto the original footage.

Nitpicks: Shannon is even more hostile and annoying than she was in season 1, which is inconsistent. And why would Ben tell Juliet his plan is to find out what Jack's emotionally invested in and exploit it? Talk about putting all his cards on the table, especially when that's exactly what he's doing to Juliet.

Oops: The newspaper with Zuckerman's obit that Paulo is reading in the airport is dated September 24, 2004, two days *after* the crash. Also, after Nikki gets the map from Arzt, Paulo complains that they should have gone to Ethan. But they're on Day 24, and Ethan had kidnapped Charlie and Claire and disappeared over a week earlier. And back in "Flashes Before Your Eyes," when Desmond was

The Fountainhead by Ayn Rand (1943)

Sawyer is reading Ayn Rand's *The Fountainhead* on the beach. The book is very dense and complicated, but Rand's basic theme is the promotion of individualism. Howard Roark is the main character, a man who refuses to play by the rules, and who is kicked out of architecture school for not adhering to the lessons of the old masters. Throughout the book he maintains his individualism, while scoffing at his rival, Peter Keating, who is content to follow the status quo. Roark becomes involved with Dominique who similarly hates society and convention (though his initial contact with her is through rape), whose father owns a quarry where Roark has been forced to work. After Roark is set up by a vengeful journalist and is sued for work he'd done on a building, losing the case, Dominique leaves him for Keating. The marriage doesn't last long because Peter "sells" Dominique to another man, Wynand, a newspaper publisher, for money and a contract. Wynand is friends with Roark, and doesn't know about Dominique's past relationship with him. Keating, meanwhile, requires Roark's help on a public housing project, but when Keating changes Roark's designs, Roark dynamites the place. Wynand defends Roark in his paper, but is pressured by investors to retract his defense, and Dominique leaves him for compromising his principles. At his trial, Roark gives a lengthy speech about individualism, and the jury finds him not guilty. He marries Dominique, and a few months later Wynand asks him to build a skyscraper in New York to be called the Wynand Building, one that would symbolize the supremacy of man and his unbending devotion to his principles.

The Fountainhead is an allegory where the characters are more archetypes than fleshed-out people. The book would appeal to Sawyer, a man who keeps to himself and lives his own way. The book eschews sentimentality and emotion, and instead upholds reason as the most important human attribute. Just as Dominique switches loyalties from one man to another, depending on their integrity and honor at the time, so too must Sawyer think Kate does the same thing, going to Sawyer when he seems like the sympathetic one, and turning to Jack when he's done something worthy.

watching the soccer game on the television, one of the backboards flashes an ad for *Exposé*. However, if the show was entering its fourth season when the plane crashed in 2004, it would have begun, presumably, in 2001, and not the mid- to late-90s, which is approximately when Desmond is in the scene.

4 8 15 16 23 42: Most of the flashback day counts are Hurley's numbers: 84 (**8**, **4**), **8**0, 75 and 57 (each of the latter two add up to 12, which is **8** + **4**), 48 (**4**, **8**), 32 (reverse **23**), 12 hours, **8** hours. At the end of the *Exposé* scene, the guy snaps the clapboard shut and it reads 01 **16** 07 00 (1 + 1 + 6 + 7 = **15**). *Exposé* is filming season **4**. The diamonds are worth $**8** million. Inside the back of the toilet at the Pearl station, you can see a 22 written (2 + 2 = **4**). When Paulo finds the walkie and turns it on, it reads 21**8** 1**88**.

It's Just a Flesh Wound: Sun punches Sawyer in the face. Nikki throws a Medusa spider at Paulo, paralyzing him. Another spider bites her.

Any Questions?:

- Jin says something to Hurley at one point and Hurley says, "Yeah, I know." Is he starting to understand Korean?
- Locke tells Paulo that things don't stay buried on this island. What did he mean? He explains that the beach is eroding but his comment sounded more significant.
- Why are Juliet and Ben so convinced that Jack won't do the surgery willingly?
- Will Sun and Sawyer have serious tension between them now?
- Was Paulo telling the truth when he said he didn't want Nikki to leave him, or was he conning her?

Ashes to Ashes: Nikki and Paulo, we hardly knew ye . . . thank God.

Music/Bands: Nikki's *Exposé* character comes down the runway and strips to Wreckx-N-Effect's "Rump Shaker" (*Hard or Smooth*).

Rodrigo Santoro (Paulo)

He may be half of the most reviled couple on *Lost*, but in his home country of Brazil, Rodrigo Santoro is a megastar. Born August 22, 1975, Santoro was a journalism major before he switched his focus to theater. He began appearing on Brazilian television in his teens before moving to film, but his big break came when he starred in *Carandiru*, an Argentinian film directed by Hector Babenco (director of *Kiss of the Spider Woman*, *At Play in the Fields of the Lord*, and *Ironweed*). The movie was the true story of horrific conditions in Argentina's Carandiru prison, and Santoro played a transsexual named Lady Di, who marries another man while inside the prison. The film didn't make him a star in North America, but it caught the eye of other producers and directors, and soon he was appearing in such films as *Charlie's Angels: Full Throttle* and *Love, Actually*. He was named one of *People* magazine's "50 Most Beautiful People" in 2004.

Santoro was called in to meet with the producers on *Lost*. He said he hadn't seen the show, but "I knew about *Lost* in Brazil," he says. "It was big, not just in the States but all around the world." He was given the first two seasons on DVD to watch, and he watched the entire thing. "I watched everything in a row, and I really liked it. Thought it was a

Yep, he's a cutie all right, but it wasn't enough to make fans like his character. (MARY LEAHY/AGENCY PHOTOS)

great, great show and just great writing and just a great opportunity." The writers said they'd write him a part, even though they still weren't sure what part it would be. Santoro trusted them, and said as long as he wasn't cast as a stereotypical Latin lover type, he would take the role.

While appearing on *Lost*, Rodrigo got his true big break by starring in the blockbuster hit *300* as Xerxes, for which he had to undergo a painful transformation. Not only did the slim actor have to shed an additional 35–40 pounds, but every hair on his body was removed through waxing and shaving — including his eyebrows. "I have a lot of respect for women after that," he laughs. The movie was a massive hit, and propelled him into the public eye.

Because of *Lost*, despite Nikki and Paulo remaining in the background for the most part until their explosive episode, "Exposé," Rodrigo has become recognizable to the public. "Everywhere I go, people know me and then they ask me about what will happen on the next episodes. I tell them that they really don't want to know because it would spoil it," he says.

Despite being a heartthrob in movies, Santoro didn't get the same reception from *Lost* audiences. "I don't know how long I will be there, but you can't control things," he said, when he probably already had an inkling that his character would be killed. "You can just build a character. I don't prepare too much because who knows what will happen with this show." And in the case of Paulo, that was a good decision.

Kiele Sanchez (Nikki Fernandez)

She nagged at Hurley, visited the Pearl station, nagged at Paulo, yelled at Sawyer . . . and then she was dead. Nikki was never going to be a fan favorite, but that hasn't slowed down Kiele Sanchez. Half Puerto-Rican, half-French, Sanchez was born on October 13, 1977. She showed a love of acting at the age of 13, but ended up in the public eye in a major way when she tried out for MTV's national VJ search competition, *Wanna Be a VJ.* Sanchez made it into the top five before being eliminated, but she caught the eye of a talent agent. She starred in the short-lived shows *That Was Then* and *Married to the Kellys* before getting attention on the WB program *Related,* starring as Anne Sorelli. As is common in television these days, that show was canceled after less than a season.

Nikki Fernandez: the epitome of When Good Television Ideas Go Terribly Wrong. (STHANLEE MIRADOR/SHOOTING STAR)

After getting what should have been her big break on *Lost,* Sanchez discovered quickly that fans hated her character. There was an outcry from viewers against Nikki and Paulo, and the writers soon realized there was only one way out — they had to be killed off. In their final episode, "Exposé," the script called for the couple to be mistaken for dead before being buried alive. It was a horrific situation for Sanchez. "I am horribly claustrophobic — I can't even have a blanket over my face — so I didn't have to do a lot of acting. I was genuinely terrified," she says.

Damon Lindelof claimed responsibility for the mishap. "People hated them before they even opened their mouths to say anything significant because it felt like they were crashing the party," he admitted. "The easiest thing would have been to just write them out and forget they ever happened, like the cougar on [season 2 of] *24.* But that's not *Lost.* We should at least own up to it." And own up to it they did.

It hasn't slowed down Sanchez, however, who has already moved on to some other pilots. But while her time on *Lost* was short, no one can say it wasn't memorable. After that final episode, no one will be saying any longer, "Who the hell's Nikki?"

3.15 Left Behind

Original air date: April 4, 2007
Written by: Damon Lindelof, Elizabeth Sarnoff
Directed by: Karen Gaviola
Guest cast: Kim Dickens (Cassidy), Beth Broderick (Diane), Fredric Lane (Marshal), Shawn Lathrop (Federal Agent), Andrew Meader (Johnny), Bill Ogilvie (Man)

Flashback: Kate

After the Others abandon camp and leave Kate behind, she wakes up in the jungle handcuffed to Juliet.

"Left Behind" is a fantastic episode, full of suspense, questions, and revelations. The Stepford Locke knows Kate's secret, Kate discovers that Jack knows about her and Sawyer, the Others abandon camp, Old Smokey is back, and Sawyer tries to make nice.

The episode is about abandonment (and it's *not* a Locke episode?) where Kate is abandoned by the Others, her mother, Locke, and, most painfully, Jack.

Most of the characters on this show have been abandoned at some point, and they want to know *why*. Jack couldn't let Sarah go without knowing why she'd left him, and who she was with, and why she was with him. Sawyer, if he ever finds the real Sawyer, intends to show him the letter he'd written to him, as if hoping the man will reveal to him why he did what he did. Locke continued to stalk his father after Cooper stole his kidney, and when he finally comes face to face with him again, asks him why he did it. All of the Lostaways want to know why the Others are treating them the way they are. And now Kate needs to confront her mother, just to know why she'd turn her in when Kate thought she'd done the right thing by her.

In the middle of the second season, we discovered that "what Kate did" was burn down her mother Diane's house, with her mother's husband (who turned out to be Kate's father) inside. In flashbacks previous to that one, we saw her mother avoiding her and abandoning her, so the revelation that Kate was actually doing something to help her mother — whose marriage was full of physical and emotional abuse — came as a surprise. In this episode, however, we see the effects of Kate's actions from her mother's point of view for the first time. She points out that what Kate did was kill the man that she loved, and that her life had changed for the worse, not the better. Kate's

The gas station where Kate meets Cassidy is located on Old Fort Weaver Road in Ewa (West Oahu).
(WENDY BACHILLER, AKA KANAHINA)

heart was in the right place, but she'd misread the situation, thought she knew what her mother wanted, and was wrong.

Now, she's done it again. Thinking she was off to rescue Jack, she trekked across the island with Locke and Sayid to the Others' camp, only to discover that Jack was doing just fine without her, and had been given a ticket off the island. By leading Locke to the camp, she enabled Locke to blow up Jack's only chance off the island. She's been guilt-ridden ever since, but has never really realized the impact of her actions. Kate has spent her entire life running, but she can't run away this time. Juliet's taken care of that by handcuffing herself to Kate and carrying her far away from the camp, forcing her to listen to the cold hard truth about what Kate's *really* done to Jack.

This is also yet another episode about the con games. Kate encounters Cassidy — now linking Kate to Sawyer with only one degree of separation before the crash — as Cassidy's running one of Sawyer's old con games. The two of them run a smaller con on the feds who are watching Diane's house. But more important are the cons that are happening on the island. We can never trust the Others, so it's not clear if they've really left (or where they're going) and if they've really taken Locke or if he's fallen for something. Juliet cons Kate throughout the episode into believing that it was the other Others who put them together, against Juliet's will. And on the beach, Hurley cons Sawyer into believing that the Lostaways are all planning on voting him off the island, or out of the group at least, showing that

Hurley's actually not the sort of stupid guy we've been led to believe he is. In fact, Hurley is pretty perceptive to realize that while Sawyer's a con man, he's also the easiest guy *to* con (plus Hurley's probably watched too many episodes of *Survivor*).

While the Sawyer con is funny and causes Sawyer to realize that sometimes being nice is kind of nice, Juliet's con further blurs the picture of Juliet's sincerity: it was effortless for her to pull the wool over Kate's eyes, even though she comes across to us in her flashbacks as someone who is trustworthy. Can they really trust Juliet, or is Jack making a huge mistake at the end of the episode?

Highlight: Sawyer trying to clean and gut a fish.

Timeline: The first part of the episode happens on December 12, and Juliet and Kate arrive back in Otherville on December 13.

Did You Notice?:

- At the beginning of the flashback, Kate is wearing a hat that says, "Cowboy Up" on it, which is what Sawyer had said to Karl in "Stranger in a Strange Land."

- Cassidy is pulling Sawyer's jewelry con from "The Long Con," and even does it at a gas station, where he showed her. She seems to have forgotten the most important element that he taught her, however: that the key is to have an accomplice pretend to buy the jewelry as if to vouch for its authenticity.

- Hurley refers to "Steve" as one of the guys on the island, but it's actually Scott, showing that Scott's long con is still going on (see *FL*, page 97).

- This episode had a lot of homages to earlier episodes: there's a backgammon game in the billiards room where Kate is, which is a game that was very near Locke's heart, as seen in earlier seasons (see *FL*, page 15); Sawyer is re-reading *Watership Down*, a book he was always reading in season 1 (see *FL*, page 55); Kate handcuffed to Juliet was reminiscent of her being handcuffed to the marshal; Jack dislocated his shoulder in "The Moth" and Charlie had to reset it for him; Hurley handing Desmond some food when Desmond looks so desolate reminds us of the scene near the beginning of season 1 when Hurley hands out little airplane food trays to everyone looking so upset.

- In the first season, it was Sawyer's voice that would always calm down Aaron (as Charlie discovered) and make him stop crying, but now Sawyer's voice scares him.

- Diane tells Kate the first thing she'll do if she ever sees her again is yell for help, and the next time Kate sees her — when she visits her in the hospital

Kate unknowingly gets a little closer to Sawyer during one of her flashbacks in "Left Behind."
(JEAN CUMMINGS/MOONGLOW PHOTOS)

in the season 1 episode "Born to Run" — that's exactly what Diane does.

- When Kate tells Juliet that she doesn't know anything about Jack, Juliet rattles off that she knows where he was born, what his parents did, that he was married, who he was married to, why he got a divorce, how his father died, his height, weight, birthday, and blood type. Kate seems humbled, yet everything Juliet knows about Jack she got from a file. Everything Kate knows she knows because Jack told her.

- When Old Smokey comes toward the sonic fence, watch how the front of the monster has split off into three large sections, as if it's a three-headed monster. In this moment, it resembles the Greek mythological creature, Cerberus. Cerberus was the three-headed dog who guarded the entrance to Hades. He allowed the spirits of the dead to enter the underworld, but ensured none of them would leave. Perhaps the smoke monster serves a similar purpose, if the fans who believe the island is some sort of purgatory are to be believed.

Pre-Island Relationships

We've seen several characters in deep, intimate relationships before they were involved in the plane crash on the island. The following is a list of who everyone was involved with romantically before they stepped onto the plane. (Spoiler warning: Desmond's contains a spoiler for "Catch-22.") In most cases, their romantic relationships were about as disastrous as their filial ones.

Jack: Jack was married to Sarah, a woman who appeared to be paralyzed but whom Jack "fixed." He kissed a woman whose father was one of Jack's patients, but immediately regretted it, and when he went home to confess to Sarah, she confessed that she'd been having an affair and was leaving him. Jack was also briefly involved with a woman in Thailand, but that ended badly.

Kate: Kate had a childhood sweetheart named Tom, who married someone else after she left town. He died when he was in a car with Kate and she was trying to escape police. She got married to a police officer named Kevin while she was on the run, but he knew her only as Monica, and when she realized she shouldn't compromise his job, she left him.

Sawyer: He was involved with a woman named Cassidy, but was conning her out of her life savings the entire time. She claims to have gotten pregnant by him, and had a daughter, Clementine.

Locke: John was in love with a woman named Helen whom he'd met through an anger management class. They moved in together, and he was going to propose to her until she found out that he'd been keeping a big secret from her, and she left him.

Sayid: When he was employed by the Republican Guard to torture dissidents, he encountered Nadia, a woman he'd known when they were both kids. He fell in love with her, despite having to follow through on his orders, and helped her escape. He's spent the rest of his life since then trying to locate her.

Sun: Besides Jin, she was involved with a hotel owner's son named Jae Lee, who died tragically, right before she and Jin left Korea.

Desmond: He was engaged to a woman named Ruth, but left her days before the wedding when he felt he had a calling to become a monk. When he was dismissed from the monastery, he fell in love with Penelope Widmore. After two years he asked her father's permission to marry her, and her father said no. Desmond left her, but is still deeply in love with her.

Claire: Claire was involved with a guy named Thomas, who impregnated her, got scared, and then told her she'd gotten pregnant on purpose. He left her alone to raise the baby.

Hurley: He was in love with a girl named Starla who worked at a record store. He asked her out, and she accepted, but after he became rich, his best friend ran off with her.

Michael: He was in a common-law relationship with a woman named Susan who refused to marry him, but was in love with him. Together they had Walt, but when Walt was two, Susan began an affair with another lawyer at her law firm, and left Michael for him. She took Walt with her, refusing to allow Michael to see him.

- Juliet stood and stared right at the monster without blinking, just as Eko did (though she had a fancy sonar fence protecting her, where Eko didn't).
- When Kate approaches Jack at the end of the episode, he wakes up with the same start as Juliet had in the jungle. Could the two of them be in cahoots somehow?

Interesting Facts: The infamous *Left Behind* series of books, written by Tim LaHaye and Jerry B. Jenkins, tell the story of the Rapture, when millions of devout Christians suddenly disappear as they are drawn up into Heaven and rewarded for being faithful to God, while God's wrath comes down on the rest of the world. So far, there are 16 books in the series, and as of mid-2004, MSNBC was reporting that the books had sold more than 62 million copies. They obviously have a massive audience, but their publication has also been rife with controversy, as several groups have claimed they focus on God's anger and not God's love, and that the books are tinged with racism and intolerance for other religions.

Nitpicks: Diane tells Kate that she can't help loving the man she did, which seriously calls into question Diane's maternal instincts. It's not just her daughter who is the selfish one: Wayne had been abusing Kate, too, and there's a suggestion of sexual molestation. While it's never been confirmed if he molested Kate, the way he spoke to her in "What Kate Did" when he was drunk, commenting on how her chest looked in her top, suggests that he's been making these comments to her for some time. Diane's never stopped to think what effect having this alcoholic, abusive, sexual deviant in the house has had on her daughter, and because of that, she has no right to throw it back in Kate's face. Even if Kate stayed mum on the subject and never told her mother how he was treating her, does Diane really think it was okay to have him beating her up with her daughter in the house? Also, Cassidy says that the feds interrogated her for half an hour, and in all that time, they never noticed how bad her wig was, and it never slipped off to one side, giving her up? Finally, why does Hurley say everyone on the beach is eating boar because of Sawyer? Desmond was the one who shot it.

Oops: When Kate is talking to Cassidy, the glass she is holding is empty, yet she then picks it up and drinks the suddenly full glass in one shot. When Cassidy throws the chili at the end of the flashback, it only lands on Diane's apron, but when Diane stands up the mess is suddenly everywhere. Later, after Juliet and Kate fall in the mud and get to Otherville, their cleanliness keeps changing. One second Kate's face is clean, the next it's dirty again. Juliet is clean at the perimeter, but dirty later when she's talking to Jack.

Kate's Aliases

In "Left Behind," Cassidy notices that Kate's named herself after a saint, which is how she comes up with all of her names.

Annie ("Tabula Rasa")

Saint Anne was the mother of the Virgin Mary. She had been infertile for most of her marriage, and prayed to God to allow her to have a child. She gave birth to Mary late in her life, and gave her to the church for a life of devotion. In Canada (which is where Kate claims she is from when she goes by this name), she is the patron saint of the province of Quebec, and is known as Saint Anne de Beaupré.

Maggie ("Whatever the Case May Be")

There are several Saint Margarets, but two stand out as patron saints. Saint Margaret of Cortona lived a scandalous life in the thirteenth century by taking many lovers. She became a penitent, and nursed the ill and received messages from God, which she passed on as speeches about the dangers of vice. She is the patron saint of several groups, among which are the falsely accused, the mentally ill, and reformed prostitutes. Saint Margaret of Antioch (third century) is surrounded by myth and legend, but as the story goes, she was tortured and imprisoned for being a Christian. In prison, the devil appeared to her in the form of a dragon, and swallowed her, but disgorged her when the cross she was tightly holding irritated his throat. When authorities tried to execute her by fire and drowning, and she survived both, several onlookers converted to Christianity. She was eventually beheaded, and is the patron saint of childbirth.

Joan ("Born to Run")

One of the most popular saints is Joan of Arc, who is the fifteenth-century patron saint of soldiers and France. As a girl she heard voices in her head of saints (one of them Saint Margaret of Antioch), and by the age of 17 knew the voices were telling her to help reclaim France from the English. She went to the king, and eventually was given a small army. Her ensuing military successes gave the king his victory, but when she was captured and given to the English, he would not help her. She refused to renounce her claims that she heard voices, and was burned at the stake as a heretic.

Monica ("I Do")

Saint Monica is the patron saint of wives and women who have suffered abuse. She lived in the fourth century, and was married to a violent man, whose equally obstinate mother lived with them. Monica had three children, and through her persistence and prayer, convinced her husband and mother-in-law (and her children) to convert to Christianity.

Lucy ("Left Behind")

Saint Lucy is the patron saint of blindness. Living in the fourth century, she devoted her life to Christ, but her mother tried to arrange a marriage to a non-Christian man. Lucy realized the only way she'd change her mother's mind would be to prove the power of Christ. She prayed for Christ to cure her mother's longtime illness, and when her mother was cured, she dropped the marriage plans. Her betrothed reported to the Roman authorities that Lucy was a Christian, and she was tortured and killed. Some legends say her eyes were gouged out but were healed by God, hence her being the patron saint of the blind.

4 8 15 16 23 42: Cassidy says all the necklaces are 18-carat gold. Sawyer says he can't use nicknames for 3 days, 10 hours, and **15** minutes. The monster makes **4** flashes at Juliet and Kate. Juliet has dislocated her shoulder **4** times. When Juliet runs to the sonic fence, she types in the code **1623**. Kate's license plate at the end of the episode is 4ON DVB. If you assign a number to each letter based on its placement in the alphabet, O is the **15**th letter, D is the **4**th, and all together they add up to 60 (**15** x **4**).

It's Just a Flesh Wound: Kate tries to clock Juliet with a pool cue, but Juliet flips Kate onto her back. Kate punches Juliet in the face several times. Juliet flips Kate onto her back again. Kate dislocates Juliet's shoulder.

Any Questions?:

- Where did Juliet get the superstrength judo skills from? Is her lightning-quick reaction to Kate attacking her at the beginning proof that she really could have carried Kate all the way into the jungle?
- Why is Locke's hand bandaged?
- Where did the Others go? Why did they leave Juliet behind?
- Why did the monster make those bright flashes at Kate and Juliet? Was it taking pictures?
- How did Juliet dislocate her shoulder the other three times?
- Why didn't Old Smokey go up and over the fence? We saw Kate and the others go over the fence; does it suggest there's something mechanical about the monster that short circuits when it hits the fence?
- Jack's house has been completely trashed. Did the Others ransack it before leaving, or did Jack put up a big fight when they tried to gas him?
- Is Cassidy sincere or a con artist? In "The Long Con" she seemed to be playing Sawyer while he thought he was playing her. In "Every Man for Himself," she showed him the picture of her daughter, and it's still not clear the child's his. In this episode, one minute she comes off as an amateur in her gas station con, the next minute she seems to be reading Kate like a book when they're talking in a bar, immediately teaching Kate how to lie properly about a fake name. Is she really pregnant by Sawyer, or is she a brilliant con artist who gets the trust of her victims by pretending to be naïve?

Music/Bands: When Kate's flashback opens, we hear Patsy Cline's "Walkin' After Midnight," which was also featured in "What Kate Did," and is playing on the radio in "Two for the Road" when Christian and Ana Lucia go to Claire's aunt's house.

3.16　One of Us

Original air date: April 11, 2007
Written by: Carlton Cuse, Drew Goddard
Directed by: Jack Bender
Guest cast: Brett Cullen (Goodwin), William Mapother (Ethan), Robin Weigert (Rachel), Joah Buley (Other Dude), Tyrone Howard (Airport Guard)

Flashback: Juliet

When Jack, Kate, and Sayid return to the beach with Juliet in tow, the others don't trust Juliet, until an emergency situation with Claire forces them to make a decision.

Suspicion is one of the hallmarks of life on the *Lost* island. After Nikki and Paulo died, people looked at Sawyer as if he had done it. When Boone died, no one could look Locke in the eye. When the raft caught on fire, suspicions were everywhere, until they finally settled on Jin, the one castaway who couldn't verbally deny the charges. But now Juliet has shown up, and unlike everyone else on that beach, she didn't survive a fiery plane crash. She has no significant trauma that she's lived through with everyone else that would help her bond with them. In fact, not only is she not one of them, but she's one of the enemy, part of that race of Others who kidnaps, kills, imprisons, and tortures. No wonder eyebrows are raised and backs are turned.

This episode contrasts with season 2's similarly titled "One of Them." In that episode, Rousseau finds a man in a net who says his name is Henry Gale. Sayid doesn't believe him, and takes him back to the hatch to torture him into telling the truth. Gale never wavered throughout his time in that underground prison, and Sayid never stopped believing that Henry was lying. Sayid saw something of himself in Henry Gale, and he knew all the tricks of the trade — how to spot a liar, how to catch them in that lie — and as we saw in the flashback in "Enter 77," he learned how to use those lies himself. Turns out . . . he was right. Henry Gale was Benjamin Linus, leader of the Others, and not a poor man who'd fallen from the sky on a balloon ride gone wrong.

Now Sayid is suspicious again, but he's not quite as convinced as he was with Ben because Juliet is different. She's never denied who she is or said Sayid was wrong. At the beginning of this episode she looks him right in the eye — the same way she does with everyone — and tells him that if she told him everything, he would kill her. Her admission completely throws him off his game. Where's

Behind those lovely smiles, these two are definitely plotting something. Do you trust them?
(ALBERT L. ORTEGA)

the lying? The denials? The begging for mercy? Juliet gives him none of those things, and he's not sure what to do next. And unlike Henry Gale, Juliet has Jack in her corner.

From a dramatic standpoint, she has *us* in her corner as well. For, to the viewers at home, Juliet is indeed one of us. We've seen her journey, her abusive husband, the wonderful thing she did for her sister. We've seen that she just wants to go home, that she's been emotionally tortured on the island, that her attempts to apply her groundbreaking research to the problems on the island have all been for nothing, draining her of all motivation. She's been on an emotional rollercoaster, and ultimately, has been promised a passage home, only to have her means of escape destroyed by Locke. With "Henry Gale," the audience was never given a backstory. We only had his word to go on, and we wavered from week to week, knowing something was fishy about the guy, but never able to put our fingers on it. He *seemed* sincere, but he was also odd. Juliet has become familiar to us through her flashback, while Ben, a year later, remains alien and Other to us.

When the group arrives on the beach, however, they're met with a bunch of people who have not seen Juliet's backstory. She's as much an enigma to them as Ben is to us. All they know of her is what Kate and Sawyer have told them — she did help them escape, but she also helped keep them in cages, forcing them to break rocks. She'd held a gun on them, allied herself with the enemy, and stood by while these things happened. Now Jack is backing her up and telling everyone to leave her alone, and it's causing some suspicion among the ranks about Jack as well. Who's to say Jack hasn't been assimilated in some way? But then a crisis happens that will allow Juliet to prove herself, and it changes how everyone perceives her. They still don't completely trust her, but they'll let her stay in the camp. And now they're suspicious of Jack, too.

And by the end of the episode, we realize they should be. The final flashback has got to be one of the most gasp-worthy twists since we realized Nikki and Paulo were still alive and Locke used to be in a wheelchair, making this episode the highlight of season 3 so far.

Highlight: Ben approaching Mikhail's house and complaining that he never keeps his walkie on. "Mikhail! It's Ben! I'm here with Juliet. We're approaching the house, don't shoot us."

Timeline: The first part of this episode is on December 14, and they return to camp on December 15 (it seems strange Lostpedia has it taking four days to get to the north side of the island, but only one to get back). Juliet retrieves the medicine on December 16.

Did You Notice?:

- The title of this episode actually comes directly from "Stranger in a Strange Land," when Ben told Jack that Juliet was "one of us."
- *Now* we know why Karl was being psychologically tortured in Room 23 — if he was in love with Alex, there's a chance he'd get her pregnant, and Ben knew that would lead to Alex's death. Clearly he was forcing Karl to get away from his daughter to keep her safe.
- Inside Mittelos, on the wall it says Herarat Aviation. The is an anagram for Earhart. Amelia Earhart was a famous pilot in the 1930s who disappeared over the Pacific Ocean in 1937 during a flight (sounds like another plane we know). Fans have speculated that maybe she landed on this island, or that she started Dharma, or that one of the bodies the Lostaways discovered in

the caves in season 1 was supposed to be Earhart.

- When Juliet wakes up on the sub and walks to the opening, she passes two men sitting at a table. The one in the foreground has a black-and-yellow shirt, and it has one of the I Ching symbols on the back of it that make up the Dharma symbols (see *FL*, page 195). The one on his shirt is, not surprisingly, the symbol for Water.
- When Ben and Juliet are talking in the flashback on the rocks, he talks about Jacob as if Jacob is God, and when he says, "unless of course you don't have faith in him," Juliet is silenced immediately.
- No one asks where Locke was until hours after they've returned, when Desmond finally asks Jack.
- The mark on the tree is really similar to the one that was burned into Juliet's back.
- In the previous episode, Hurley had told Sawyer that Claire was very influential, and if he can get her vote, then he'll be able to stay. Now Juliet proves that is true.
- No wonder Ben balked at Locke's choice of Dostoevsky in season 2: when Juliet comes to Ben's house to show him the X-ray, the books around him appear to be mostly mass-market pap. Some of the titles are Kitty Kelley's *The Royals*, Tim LaHaye and Jerry B. Jenkins' *Assassins* (the sixth book in the *Left Behind* series), James Patterson's *Pop Goes the Weasel*, Barbara Michaels' *Stitches in Time*, and the feminist classic *Women Who Run with the Wolves*.
- Now we know that in "Enter 77," despite what Mikhail said, the satellites *did* work, he knew about the plane and everyone on it, and he was involved with the Others. Sayid sees through his ruse and guesses that after the Others lost communications, Mikhail was sent out to the house, but now we know he'd actually been there the whole time.
- The man filming Juliet's sister in the park is Richard, the man with the dark eyebrows who recruits Juliet in the first place. Clearly he has Ben's complete trust, since he moves back and forth between the island and the mainland and always comes back.

Interesting Facts: The name of the woman who dies on the operating table is Sabine. The Sabines were a tribe of people in ancient Italy whose women were kidnapped by the Romans in order to help populate their then-new town. When the fathers came to Rome to reclaim the women, the Sabine women threw themselves and their children between the two armies.

The park where Rachel is playing with Julian is called Acadia Park. Acadia was a settlement of French colonists in the Maritimes in the seventeenth century. When France seceded its Canadian territories to England, the Acadians refused to pledge allegiance to the Crown. Many of them fled to parts of the United States, and several stayed put. There are still many Acadian people living in the Maritime provinces today (especially Nova Scotia and Newfoundland), and their culture is very vibrant. Henry Wadsworth Longfellow wrote a famous poem about the Acadian plight in 1847, called "Evangeline."

Nitpicks: Juliet is the last one to arrive at the camp. While that works dramatically, there's no way Sayid would have let her walk behind all of them, because he doesn't trust her. In the flashback, Ethan tells Juliet she shouldn't have drunk the tranquilizer juice quite so quickly. As a doctor, shouldn't he have told her to slow down *before* she downed the entire thing? When she wakes up on the sub, she walks a little too steadily for someone who's just been heavily sedated for so long. Also, the evening Jack and company return from the other side of the island, everyone in the camp has questions. Claire begins spitting up blood, Juliet says she needs to get the medical supplies near the cave, and Jack lets her go. The caves were only about an hour's walk from the beach, so, running, Juliet should have gotten there much quicker. But when she arrives it's daylight. Why did it take her so long? Does nighttime last only two hours on the island? And Sawyer calls Charlie, Hurley, and Aaron "three men and a baby." According to the timeline, his week isn't up, so why did they let him get away with the nickname?

When Juliet confronts Sawyer, she says he shot a man the night before he got on the plane. That seems to be off. Sawyer met with Christian in a bar, and Christian told him to do what he had to do. He returned to the site of the shrimp shack and killed Frank Duckett. Then he was caught by the police and thrown in jail for three days before being deported. Meanwhile Christian went missing for a few days, drank himself to death, Jack was called, he took some time making his decision, got on a plane to Sydney, had to wait for his father's body to be located, dealt with the body itself, and *then* got on the plane.

Finally, in "Every Man for Himself," Jack looks at Ben's X-rays, which Ben says are a week old. But in this episode we saw that the X-rays were actually over two months old, since he had them taken a few days before the plane crash. Of course, Ben could have had more X-rays done in the meantime so they're not the same ones, but if that were true, Jack would have been given all of the X-rays in that episode so he could chart the tumor's growth.

Oops: When Juliet is about to climb up the ladder, her hair is neatly pinned back on the top. By the time she gets to the top of the sub, her hair is completely disheveled and doesn't look pinned back at all. When Ben tells Juliet that her sister's cancer is back, he hands her a medical report on her sister that she opens up, reads, and is horrified by. Unfortunately, the camera zooms in on the report and we see it's for a *male* patient who weighs 187 pounds (look in the top right corner), and suffers from heart problems. Juliet is a doctor, so she would know if the report was false, so the mistake can only be chalked up as yet another error on behalf of the prop department. Also, during the flashback of the crash, the first part is from the season premiere, but in the new part they filmed for this episode, Ben's hair is gelled and spiked, where it's dry at the beginning of the scene.

4 8 15 16 23 42: Juliet discovers a tumor on Ben's L4 vertebra. Ben says Claire will be symptomatic in 48 hours (**4**, **8**). Watch when Juliet is tying the tarp onto her hut at the very end: she makes an **8** with the rope before pulling it tight.

It's Just a Flesh Wound: Claire spits up blood after an implant in her is triggered.

Any Questions?:

- Richard says Juliet "created life where life wasn't supposed to be." Does he believe women on the island aren't *meant* to have children? That would point to the island epidemic being a spiritual problem, and not a medical one.
- Is it possible that the island is actually very close to the U.S. mainland, and Juliet was actually drugged so she wouldn't know the sub had traveled no more than, say, 50 miles?
- How does Ben (or Jacob) cure cancer? Why is there no cancer on the island? More importantly, how was he able to cure someone's cancer who *wasn't* on the island? If that's possible, it raises questions about the season 2 episode, "S.O.S.," where Rose revealed to Bernard that she didn't want to leave because if she did, her cancer would return. Maybe it's not the island.
- Sawyer suggests Sayid should just torture Juliet, and Sayid says he no longer does that. Since when? He vowed never to do it again after he tortured Sawyer, and then he tortured Henry Gale brutally. Does he mean only since his memory of Amira when he was at Mikhail's house?
- Juliet clearly doesn't trust that Ben saved her sister, so it's understandable that she confronts him in his kitchen. But why is she assuming his tumor is cancerous? Even a benign tumor would cause pain on his spine, so of

course he's concerned by the fact he has a tumor. Yet she's immediately assuming it's malignant. Why?

- Juliet asks Sayid if the other castaways know what he did in Basra. In 1991, the city revolted against Saddam Hussein and Hussein's army responded with much bloodshed in return. In 1999, there was a second revolt, and Hussein's army once again responded with mass executions. Was Sayid involved in one of these?

- What is making these women die? Why can't they take them off the island? If Ben is so worried about Alex's wellbeing, why not take her off the island? Will something happen to anyone who leaves? Will they suddenly get cancer or something? Does the island heal all, but infect you if you try to leave?

- What part of Juliet's story was true? If they really were just taking Claire to keep her alive, why did Alex think she had to save her? What was Ethan intending to do to Claire? Was he really acting alone or was the kidnapping all part of the plan?

- Has Ben promised Juliet again that she's going home? How? She knows the sub is gone; does he have a backup sub? Why is she spying for him?

- Tom mentioned in "Not in Portland" that Ben and Juliet have history. Was he referring to the stormy relationship they had after Juliet found out Ben had a tumor?

Music/Bands: When Juliet is talking to Goodwin in bed, we can hear "Addio del passato" from Giuseppe Verdi's *La Traviata*. The lyrics of the aria are appropriate for Juliet's mindset at that time, with lines such as, "Farewell past, happy dreams of days gone by;/ The roses in my cheeks already are faded" and:

> The joys, the sorrows will be soon over,
> The tomb confines all mortals!
> Neither tears nor flowers will my grave have,
> No cross with a name that covers my bones!
> Oh, comfort, sustain a tired soul,
> And may God pardon and make her his own!
> Ah, all is finished.

Elizabeth Mitchell (Juliet Burke)

Coming into a show with an established cast is never an easy feat. (See Nikki and Paulo.) Suddenly coming into that show as the bad guy is even harder. And the bad *girl*? Virtually impossible. But as the elusive Juliet, one of the mysterious Others, Elizabeth Mitchell has somehow pulled it off.

Born in Los Angeles on March 27, 1970, Mitchell moved to Dallas with her lawyer parents as a child and grew up in Texas. She attended London's British American Drama Academy, though she says people tended not to take her acting ambitions seriously. "I had terrible acne, frizzy hair, and I was scrawny and paunchy at the same time . . . I definitely didn't take Hollywood by storm." An early role was on the soap opera *Loving*, but because fans didn't like her character, she was fired only a few months after starting. She moved around into various forgettable roles until landing the role opposite Angelina Jolie in

Elizabeth Mitchell has so far been a hit as Juliet on season 3 of *Lost*.

(YORAM KAHANA/SHOOTING STAR)

HBO's critically acclaimed movie, *Gia*, where she played Jolie's bisexual lover. More character roles began coming in, including films like *Nurse Betty* and *Frequency*, and Mitchell got a semi-regular role on *ER* as Kim Legaspi, Dr. Kerry Weaver's girlfriend. Since then she guest starred in shows like *Spin City*, *Law & Order*, *CSI*, and *House*, before being cast as Mrs. Claus in *The Santa Clause 2*, which made her instantly recognizable to children everywhere.

But it was her role as Juliet on *Lost* that moved her from that "where do I know her from?" status to that of a regular star on a hot TV show. Mitchell was thrilled to get the part. "My husband and I both were [fans of the show before I joined the cast]," she says. "The first episode made our jaws drop. It was really an astonishing episode."

The producers of the show were equally excited to have her in the cast. Her audition was to play opposite Jack as he was hanging in his cell by various chains connected to the ceiling, and she came in and tackled the character in a way no one else had done. Damon Lindelof said, "The scene is basically, 'Get off the f—ing table because it's futile!' but somehow she made it seem like a mommy talking to a small child who's banging his head against the wall. There was something so disquieting about it."

Juliet, like many of the characters on *Lost*, is heavily nuanced, and how Mitchell portrays her is just as important as how she is written. There's something about the honesty in Mitchell's face that makes us *want* to trust her. Part of the ambiguity in the character could be that Mitchell herself doesn't know if Juliet is good or bad. "She definitely has something on her mind and is trying to get something accomplished. She's the way most of us would be if we were pursuing a specific objective." But even if Juliet turns out to be a "bad guy," Mitchell believes that Juliet is acting out of a belief that what she is doing is right. "Even if you're bad, you always think you're good. I think she's operating towards an objective she feels to be the right thing. She's doing everything she thinks is right. That can lead to fairly ambiguous behavior depending on who she's trying to convince of what at what time."

Audiences and critics alike have responded to Juliet in a positive way. *TV Guide* columnist Michael Ausiello put *Lost* at number 9 in his list of top 10 things on television in 2006, and raved, "The casting of Elizabeth Mitchell alone was enough to clinch its spot in my top 10."

While maintaining a house in Washington State, Mitchell and her husband, improv acting teacher Chris Soldevilla, live in Hawaii with their son, C.J., who wasn't quite a year old when Juliet got the part on the show. Their schedules allow for them to both take care of their son without having to put him in daycare, and when Soldevilla is away, Mitchell is able to take him on her weeks off.

With Juliet becoming so popular, however, those weeks off might become less frequent. While the writers' reticence at answering any questions began eating away at the patience of fans early in the season, Juliet was a mystery everyone loved trying to figure out. But don't look for Juliet to reveal herself too soon. "She's so good at reading other people that she knows how to block you from reading her," says Mitchell. "I like the tremendous amount of freedom in there."

Carrie by Stephen King (1974)

Stephen King's *Carrie*, one of his most popular books, is a terrifying examination of telekinesis. The book is the story of Carrie White, an outcast in high school, raised by a single Christian fundamentalist mother. The book is structured as a chronological story of Carrie's humiliation in school, the discovery of her telekinetic power, and a play-by-play of the horrific revenge she exacts on those who have wronged her (and everyone else, for that matter), but interspersed throughout the book are snippets of newspaper articles, court transcripts, and books written in the aftermath of the destruction she wreaks, so we know where the book is going before we get there.

When Carrie menstruates for the first time after a gym class, the other girls throw tampons and sanitary pads at her, yelling, "Plug it up!" The gym teacher at first chastises Carrie for not dealing with the problem, but soon discovers Carrie thinks she is dying because even at 16, she knows nothing about menstruation. In disgust, the teacher bars the perpetrators from the upcoming prom, but in the end, the only girl who remains barred is Chris, who had been the ringleader.

Carrie's mother would scare even other Christian fundamentalists. She preaches at Carrie about her "dirtypillow" breasts, and tells her that because she got her period, she's officially evil and unclean.

Carrie soon realizes she has the power of telekinesis, and likens it to a muscle flex in her brain. She practices lifting and moving things with her mind. Sue Snell, one of the girls who had been involved in the tampon attack, feels deep remorse for what she did to Carrie, and convinces her boyfriend, Tommy, to take Carrie to the prom. Carrie makes her own dress — in harlot red, her mother says. Carrie floats her mother out of the room, and her mother silently vows to kill Carrie when she gets home, because she believes the Devil has returned.

At the prom, things seem to be going well until Chris, the one girl expelled from the prom, organizes with her boyfriend Billy for Carrie to be crowned prom queen and at the crowning they pour a bucket of pig's blood over her head. Carrie walks out of the school gym, humiliated, locks all of the doors of the school with her mind, and turns on the sprinkler system, thinking she would ruin everyone's clothes and hair. However, she looks through a window in time to see the lead singer of the live band electrocuted when he grabs a mike, and girls' dresses catching on fire. Something inside Carrie snaps, and she realizes she's just created a possible massacre. Rather than open the doors and let out the other students, she goes whole hog, walking through town in a maniacal rampage, exploding gas stations, blowing up buildings, overturning cars, and bringing down power cables on people, leaving dozens dead in her wake.

At home, her mother is waiting to kill her, and manages to stab Carrie in the shoulder with a knife. Carrie stops her mother's heart and kills her, and manages to crawl out to a roadhouse where she kills Billy and Chris before dying herself. Sue Snell publishes a book after the event to tell her side of the story, the courts try to determine who caused this destruction and how, telekinesis experts proclaim it a sign of things to come pleading with the authorities not to sweep the Carrie White case under the carpet, and many of the town's remaining residents sell their properties and move away.

In "A Tale of Two Cities," Juliet says *Carrie* is her favorite book, and she says so with some defiance. In "Not in Portland," we see a copy of the book on Rachel's bedside table. In "One of Us," Ben says he finds it incredibly depressing. Why is this Juliet's favorite book? Could it be the revenge fantasy element? Does she somehow identify with a girl who's been pushed too hard by a vicious mother? Perhaps Ben would find it depressing because of the way he was treated as a child (see "The Man Behind the Curtain").

There's a condemnation of childbirth and female menstruation in the book by the mother, and she believes women are punished for being women. One character in the book believes she might be pregnant, and when she's with Carrie in Carrie's final moments before dying, she sees menstrual blood running thickly down her legs, perhaps miscarrying the baby. Juliet could see a link between the fate of the women in this book and the fate of the women on the island, doomed to suffer simply because they wanted to bear children. Mrs. White constantly reminds Carrie that childbirth and the pain it brings was Eve's punishment for being a sinful woman, and perhaps there's an entity on the island who feels the same way. Every prominent woman in the camp has been either kidnapped, hurt, or killed, so someone or something certainly has it in for the women.

We will see a terrifying moment of telekinesis later in the season. What is interesting is that throughout *Carrie*, experts weigh in on what happened to Carrie and state that telekinesis is purely the domain of women, particularly pubescent women. But on *Lost* we will see a male exhibiting powers of telekinesis, turning these theories on their head. Walt seemed to have telekinetic powers (if the visions of Walt throughout season 2 were actually Walt projecting himself somehow), and maybe the Others were so fascinated by him because they'd read *Carrie* and were intrigued to find a male who could do the things Carrie could do. Finally, the book follows a very distinct structure that the show follows (flashbacks, present-day accounts, several mysteries), some of which will become more prominent by season 4.

3.17　Catch-22

Original air date: April 18, 2007
Written by: Jeff Pinkner, Brian K. Vaughan
Directed by: Stephen Williams
Guest cast: Sonya Walger (Penelope), Andrew Connolly (Brother Campbell), Joanna Bool (Ruth), Jack Maxwell (Derek), Andrew Trask (Brother Martin)

Flashback: Desmond

Desmond receives a flash that Penelope is coming to the island to rescue him and he leads Hurley, Jin, and Charlie into the jungle to help find her.

"Catch-22" is a term that refers to circular logic that goes nowhere, and the frustration that results (see page 139). Desmond faces a moral conundrum in that he needs Charlie to go on the journey with him because Charlie appeared in his flash, but he also knows Charlie will die. If he saves Charlie's life, the outcome of his flash might change (in this case, Penelope won't come to save him), but if he doesn't save his life, he'll live with the guilt of not having done so. It's not *quite* as cut-and-dry as a genuine Catch-22, but close enough.

In Desmond's flashback, we discover that not only was he a monk before he met Penelope (!) but he was engaged to be married before becoming a man of the cloth. He left Ruth at the altar because he believed he had a higher calling and had to meet it. Ruth sees right through his cowardice, however, and says to him, "Next time you want to break up with someone, Des, don't join a monastery. Just tell the girl you're too bloody scared." Her words echo the ones we heard earlier in "Flashes Before Your Eyes," when Desmond told Penelope that they couldn't be together because of outside factors. Like Ruth, Pen sees the truth, and tells him to "have the decency to admit that you're doing this because you're a coward." Brother Campbell also sees to the heart of Desmond's problem, telling him, "You've spent too much time running away to realize what you may be running toward." Brother

Desmond (Henry Ian Cusick) is forced to make a desperate decision in "Catch-22."

Campbell's words suggest Desmond has a destiny of some kind, which is what Ms. Hawking had told him in "Flashes Before Your Eyes."

On the island, Desmond is forced to stop running. He's tried before — he ran from the hatch when he thought it was going to explode, and he got onto a boat and tried to escape the island — but his attempts are always thwarted. By the end of the season, the boat had turned around and forced him back to the island to face up to his destiny. He returned to the hatch he'd tried to escape, and in the end he had to cause the explosion, and the only way to do it was to be in the middle of it. But now Desmond is moving one step forward. Rather than being made to stay put, unable to leave, he's actually running *toward* something for the first time in his life — and he hopes that something is Penelope.

Meanwhile, on the beach, Kate finds out what it feels like to be one of the two outside points of a love triangle, rather than the middle person the other two are fighting over. She's happy to have Jack back, but he's distant and unfamiliar to her, and instead is cozying up to Juliet. In becoming hung up on Jack's strange actions, however, she unwittingly becomes distant to Sawyer, only using him to take out her frustrations (in a manner he's only too happy to oblige). It doesn't take Sawyer long to figure things out, but when he does, he doesn't seem particularly hurt by her mixed emotions. Instead, he just asks her to be honest with him. His own Catch-22 is that he loves Kate, but she still has feelings for Jack. But her feelings for Jack drive her to Sawyer's bed to work out her emotions. For the time being, it's a Catch-22 he'll live with.

As Desmond runs toward the woman he loves and finds her hanging from a tree, the timeline cuts between the present and the past, creating a sense of urgency and sadness, and putting us in Desmond's head. Desmond believed he wanted a religious life, but he wasn't cut out for it. Realizing that fact put him on the path of true love, but he couldn't face that, either. Now he knows what he's done wrong, and is finally ready to make the commitment it's taken him his entire life to make. But when he comes face to face with his destiny, he discovers it just might be too late.

Highlight: Sawyer asking Kate if he needs to make her a mix tape to show her how he feels (and then actually manages to find a tape).

Timeline: Desmond and co. set off on December 16, and they get to the pilot on December 17.

Did You Notice?:

- Hurley believes that The Flash could best Superman in a foot race. The comic that Hurley carried onto the plane was a Spanish version of *The Flash and Green Lantern*.
- Desmond tells Jack he needs a first aid kit because he'd twisted his ankle. The first time he met Jack, Jack had just twisted his ankle running in the stadium.
- After Sawyer bests Jack at ping-pong, Jack insists on best two out of three games, showing once again that he can't let things go.
- The book containing the photo of Penelope and Desmond is *Ardil-22*, which is the Portuguese edition of Joseph Heller's *Catch-22*.
- Ruth tells Des it's a good thing a shepherd didn't help him up when he'd fallen (it was a monk . . . so he decided to become a monk). But interestingly, in "Man of Science, Man of Faith," we saw that it was Desmond who helped a Shephard when he'd fallen.
- When Desmond comes into Brother Campbell's office at the end of the episode, there's a photo on the desk of Campbell with Ms. Hawking, the creepy ring lady from "Flashes Before Your Eyes."
- When Desmond is carrying the cases of wine out to Pen's car, they're marked 1989, so they're not the vintage he was bottling earlier.

Interesting Facts: This is the first episode co-credited to writer Brian K. Vaughan, who is a comic book writer best known for *Y: The Last Man*, *Ex Machina*, *Pride of Baghdad*, and *Runaways*. The latter comic is about a group of teenagers from L.A. who run away and become superheroes to counteract what their villainous parents have done. One of his biggest fans is *Buffy the*

Vampire Slayer creator Joss Whedon, who stepped in to write several issues of the series.

When Desmond is bottling the wine, the label says the vintage is 1995. If the plane crashed in 2004, and Desmond had been on the island since 2001, and we know he was with Penelope for two years (starting in 1995) before they broke up, then it means four years passed between breaking up with her and coming to the island. It's likely that the time is less, however; wine bottling legislation states worldwide that the date on the wine label should indicate the year in which most of the grapes were harvested. The grapes could have been aged, so it's not necessarily 1995 in which Desmond is bottling the wine. Ruth mentions that the closest thing to a religious experience she'd ever seen Desmond have is when Celtic won the Scottish Cup, and she could be referring to 1989 or 1995. It's more likely she means 1995, and he's been at the monastery for one or two years.

Moriah is commonly recognized among biblical scholars as the mountain where God told Abram to sacrifice Isaac. God wanted to see if Abram really loved Him, so He told him to go to the mountain and kill Isaac to prove it, but God stopped him just before Abram completed the task. Other scholars suggest Moriah refers to the land of the Amorites, which were a group of Semitic people.

After Jin's ghost story, Hurley asks him if he's heard the one about the chupacabra. A chupacabra is a creature that has become urban legend in the Americas, predominantly Puerto Rico, Mexico, and the southern United States. According to legend, it sucks the blood of animals, mainly goats (the name translates to "goat sucker"). It is usually described as lizard-like, with scales down its back and yellow eyes, and is purportedly extraterrestrial in nature. Sightings of the chupacabra began in 1990, and there are several photos and videos found online of alleged chupacabras, though most experts maintain the creature is mythical.

Sawyer gives Kate her "mix tape," which turns out to be Phil Collins' greatest hits. It seems to be a throwaway joke, but a look at the track listing on the tape shows that the titles of the songs could easily apply to Kate, her relationship with Sawyer, or even to other people on the island: "Another Day in Paradise", "True Colors," "Easy Lover," "You Can't Hurry Love," "Two Hearts," "I Wish It Would Rain Down," "Against All Odds," "Something Happened on the Way to Heaven," "Separate Lives," "Both Sides of the Story," "One More Night," "Sussudio" (maybe not that one), "Dance Into the Light," "A Groovy Kind of Love," "In the Air Tonight," "Take Me Home."

Nitpicks: The wine label says there are 500 bottles of wine, yet later Brother Campbell says there are 108 cases. Since there are a dozen bottles in a case, either someone's math is way off, or they're making more than just Cabernet Sauvignon at Moriah Vineyards. Also, a vineyard in Scotland? Making something other than an ice wine? Not likely.

Finally, the biggest nitpick of the episode is the very Catch-22 of the title. Desmond believes that everything must happen according to the flash that he saw; in other words, Charlie must die before he can make it to the pilot. But if you freeze-frame the flash at the beginning of the episode, when Desmond is cutting down the pilot, you can clearly see Charlie and Jin holding the parachute that catches her, which means Charlie *had* to be alive in order to help Desmond find the pilot. Was his flash giving him conflicting information? Why didn't he know he needed to *save* Charlie's life in order to be reunited with Pen, rather than let Charlie die?

Oops: When Hurley stammers to Jack that he's hanging out with Desmond because they're friends, the first aid kit is over Desmond's shoulder. As they walk away, it's in his hand with the strap wrapped around it, and he unwinds it and puts it on his shoulder.

4 8 15 16 23 42: Desmond insists that **4** guys have to go to find Penelope. Sawyer jokes that if they don't play ping-pong every **108** minutes, the island will explode. Jack says that he hasn't played ping-pong since he was 12 (**8** + **4**). Desmond has saved Charlie's life **4** times. The monks bottled **108** cases of wine.

Lost in Translation: When Jin is telling the story, this is what he says: "And the girl turned to the man who saved her and said, 'Thank God. I was afraid you were the Hook Man.' And the man looked at the girl with a smile and said, 'Don't worry, little girl. My hook is . . . *still in your father's head!*'" Which makes Hurley's comment — that he loved the part about the bird — even funnier.

Any Questions?:

- Why did the helicopter go down over the island? What caused it to malfunction?
- Why didn't anyone in the main beach camp see or hear the helicopter?
- Why does Brother Campbell have a picture of him with Hawking on his desk? Has he been down the same path as Desmond? Is he similarly just someone helping Desmond along to his destiny?
- Who is the woman in the plane? Why did she have a photo of Desmond with her? Did Penelope send her? Does she have anything to do with the

men we saw at the end of season 2 in the blizzard? They were speaking Portuguese, and this pilot has a Portuguese book with her.

Music/Bands: When the guys are walking along the beach looking for the wire, Hurley, Jin, and Charlie are whistling "The Colonel Bogey March," made famous in *The Bridge on the River Kwai*. When Desmond is drunk, he's singing the Celtic Football Club song.

Catch-22 by Joseph Heller (1961)

Catch-22 is in many ways like an adult, twentieth-century version of Lewis Carroll's *Through the Looking-Glass* (see page 204). Set in 1944, near the end of the Second World War, it's about the absurdity and insanity of war, seen through the eyes of someone everyone else thinks is insane, but he may be the only sane one in the madhouse.

Yossarian is a bombardier whom everyone else sees as a hero, but he's a self-professed coward. He doesn't want to fight in the war, he doesn't want to fly the planes, and when he proclaims that he hates going into combat because everyone is trying to kill him, the other officers look at him like he's mad, when he's actually right. Yossarian is dogged by the idiotic Colonel Cathcart, who waits for the men to achieve the allotted number of missions before they can go home (at the beginning of the book the number is 40) and then raises the requisite number of missions. Yossarian, who'd achieved the 40 missions, begins to put himself into the hospital to try to avoid flying more. He asks Doc Daneeka to declare him insane and unfit for battle. Daneeka replies that he can do that, but Yossarian must request it. When Yossarian requests it, Daneeka says he's just hit on Catch-22, which states that any man who requests a leave based on insanity must actually be sane — because only a sane man would want to leave a war — and therefore Daneeka cannot grant his wish.

The term "Catch-22" becomes synonymous with a circular argument that gets a person nowhere. Throughout the novel, the dialogue is laugh-out-loud hilarious, especially when two characters become involved in a heated verbal battle — by the end of the discussion they often seem to be arguing the opposite of what they were at the beginning. In one example of the insane logic of the book, we get a description of Major Major's father, who is an alfalfa farmer who works very hard at not actually growing any alfalfa. The government pays him for the bushels he doesn't grow, and with his money he buys more land to give him more space to not grow alfalfa. "He invested in land wisely and soon was not growing more alfalfa than any other man in the country."

The book is written in a nonlinear fashion, divided instead by character, telling each one's story while still maintaining the novel's main themes — the absurd bureaucracy of war and the futility of language. Several stories are retold, seen through the lens of one of the other characters: Hungry Joe is a former *Life* magazine photographer who is obsessed with having sex with women, but not as obsessed as he is with photographing them, and he can never seem to do both at the same time. Major Major Major Major (born Major Major Major before being promoted to Major) is a lonely man, made lonelier whenever he gets a promotion, and he ultimately decrees that people are only allowed to see him in his office when he is not there. Nately is a nineteen-year-old with rich parents who falls in love with a prostitute, known only as "Nately's whore" throughout the book. When she finally falls in love with him, he dies on his next mission, and she somehow blames Yossarian and spends the rest of the book hiding in bushes, trying to kill him.

Milo Minderbinder is the mess hall officer who begins an import/export business through military channels, couching it as a "syndicate" that will benefit everyone; at first it's amusing, as he seems to be paying more for things than he ultimately sells them for, but soon we find out that he's the political head of most of the states he buys from, and therefore owns the materials already. When he accepts a contract from the Germans to earn money for every squadron of his own men that he can shoot down, and bombs his own camp, his story takes on a ridiculous and horrifying turn. Orr is Yossarian's annoying roommate, who seems to get shot down on every mission he goes on but always escapes unscathed. One day, Yossarian gets word that Orr has rowed to Sweden, and he realizes he was being shot down on purpose as practice runs all those times. McWatt is Yossarian's pilot who likes to "buzz" the camp by flying low, until he accidentally kills a young soldier. Chief White Halfoat is an alcoholic who threatens his roommate, Flume, saying that one night he'll cut his throat in his sleep. Flume goes to live in the forest, waiting for Halfoat to die of pneumonia. Lieutenant Scheisskopf (German for "shithead") is an incompetent who is obsessed with organizing parades every Sunday for the men to march in, but is reassigned to work with General Peckem. Peckem plots throughout the book to take over General Dreedle's position (Dreedle is the head of Yossarian's squadron), but when he finally does, Scheisskopf is promoted to Peckem's superior and Peckem is unable to do anything.

The only other character in the book who seems to be sane is Chaplain A.T. Chapman. He is a timid man, often pushed around by all of the dim-witted corporals and generals, but unlike everyone else except Yossarian, he looks around him and sees nothing but death and destruction. Over the span of the book, he begins to lose his faith, questioning basic tenets of Christianity (if Adam and Eve were the first man and woman, and they only had two sons, how were their sons able to procreate?), and wondering if he has any true purpose. He is the only one who lobbies on Yossarian's behalf to get Cathcart to stop raising the requisite mission number, but no one will listen to him.

An ongoing theme is our inability to use language to actually communicate. In fact, the less said the better, in this novel. When Yossarian is in the hospital he is given a job of censoring letters, and he begins signing them all as Washington Irving. He censors them all at his whim, sometimes crossing out all verbs, other times removing nouns, and in one case deleting everything in the letter but "Dear Mary" and writing "I long for you tragically, A.T. Chapman, Chaplain, U.S. Army" at the bottom. Eventually the bureaucracy starts to notice that the strangest letters going out have been signed off by Washington Irving, and they begin an investigation into who is doing it, eventually pinpointing the poor chaplain.

By the end of the novel, Yossarian discovers that Catch-22 is just a made-up clause, when he meets an Italian woman who tells him that some prostitutes were thrown out onto the street, and the soldiers who did it cited Catch-22. "Catch-22 says they have the right to do anything we can't stop them from doing," she tells Yossarian. Yossarian asks why she didn't insist on actually reading Catch-22:

> "They don't have to show us Catch-22," the old woman answered. "The law says they don't have to."
> "What law says they don't have to?"
> "Catch-22."

While the book is still one of the funniest novels in the English language, all of the comedy in the book is tinged with the knowledge that what is really going on around Yossarian is horrific. After Yossarian leaves the woman he walks through the streets of Rome and sees nothing but degradation wherever he goes. In one alley, a man beating a dog while others look on. In another, a man beating a small boy while others look on. Four drunken soldiers gathered around an Italian woman, ready to rape her, while she begs them to "Pleeshe don't." A wounded soldier being beaten by the police. A woman standing on a street corner and crying into a dirty dishtowel. "The night was filled with horrors, and he thought he knew how Christ must have felt as he walked through the world, like a psychiatrist through a ward full of nuts, like a victim through a prison full of thieves."

Throughout the book, Yossarian keeps thinking of a particular gunner named Snowden. The scene is played out again and again, with Yossarian in battle, the plane taking a hit, and Yossarian hurrying back to where two tail gunners are, with Snowden lying on his back with a wounded leg and the other man in a dead faint next to him. Yossarian keeps remembering that he tended the "wrong wound," but describes the leg wound as being very serious. Only at the very end of the book do we get the complete, grisly scene. Snowden had been conscious the entire time, looking directly into Yossarian's eyes and saying quietly, "I'm cold, I'm cold," while Yossarian, unsure of what else to say, simply said, "There there," as he worked to close up the leg wound. Snowden keeps repeating his words, as Yossarian repeats his, until the tourniquet is tied. Only then does Snowden finally motion with his head toward his armpit, and Yossarian unzips the top of Snowden's uniform and all of Snowden's insides come spilling out. Yossarian screams, staring at the mess in front of him, while Snowden continues to quietly insist, "I'm cold, I'm cold." Realizing once again that words won't help, Yossarian simply cradles Snowden and repeats, "There there" while his gunner dies. Yossarian realizes the human body is nothing but garbage, that Snowden will be disposed of somehow, thrown away to rot, and that his own fate will be no different. The army sees him as human trash that can be tossed from one mission to the next. It's this incident that sparks his actions throughout the novel (since this scene actually precedes most of the novel's plot).

At the end of the novel, Yossarian is given his own Catch-22, when he wages his own personal protest at having to fly more than 70 missions, and Colonels Korn and Cathcart come to him and offer him a way out — they will let him go home if he agrees to be a hero and will trumpet the greatness of the squadron and the colonels to everyone. Yossarian realizes that to do so would compromise everything, and justify all of the death and madness he'd witnessed for so long. But to continue flying missions would also undercut anything he believes in. The novel ends with him running away to Sweden, narrowly escaping Nately's whore, who is waiting in the bushes with a knife.

On *Lost*, *Catch-22* is in the pilot's possession when she crashes to the island. Desmond's photo is inside the book, suggesting his connection to it. The novel represents much of the lunacy that Desmond has been living through for the past three years. When he first arrived, he was told he had to push a button every 108 minutes to save the world, but wasn't told what would happen if he didn't. He was lied to, just as Yossarian is lied to throughout the novel, and like Yossarian's endless missions, Desmond ended up being stuck in the Swan station for three years, rather than the few months he'd originally anticipated.

At the end of season 2, Desmond faces the ultimate Catch-22, when he has in his hands a key that could save everyone on the island, but if he turns it, he will die. Unlike Yossarian, who admits to being a coward and thinks of himself first (even though ultimately, he doesn't), Desmond decides he will turn that key anyway, and he does.

And just like Catch-22 is based on a lie, it turns out Des doesn't die when he turns the key. Instead he's put into a daily conundrum, where he can see the future but is helpless to do anything about it. He sees a flash of Charlie's death, and tries to save him, but is cursed to have to keep on saving Charlie. At this point he knows that fate will not rest until Charlie is dead, but he can't live with the guilt of *not* saving him, so he keeps doing it. Like Yossarian, Desmond just wants to go home. Throughout *Catch-22*, Yossarian is the biggest troublemaker, yet he seems to escape the clutches of the bureaucracy, just as Desmond doesn't seem to be on the radar of the Others at all. The novel ends with Yossarian running, but we don't know if he makes it away successfully or not. Will Desmond see an escape route and take it, leaving the others behind?

3.18   D.O.C.

Original air date: April 25, 2007
Written by: Edward Kitsis, Adam Horowitz
Directed by: Frederick E.O. Toye
Guest cast: Byron Chung (Paik), Alexis Rhee (Older Woman), John Shin (Mr. Kwon), Esmond Chung (Paik's Associate), Jean Chung (Paik's Secretary)

The canal where Sun meets with the mysterious woman at the end of "D.O.C." was filmed near Chinatown in downtown Honolulu, along College Walk at N. Kukui St., near the Ho Tong Temple. (RYAN OZAWA)

Flashback: Sun

When Juliet discovers that Sun is pregnant, she gives her an ultrasound to determine if she conceived the baby on the island — which will tell Sun who the father is.

"D.O.C." is an episode about shame. In most of the Jin and Sun flashbacks we've seen so far, shame has played a vital role in their background story. Jin was ashamed of where he'd come from, so he kept his father's existence hidden from Sun, opting to say that his father was dead instead of admitting he was a lowly fisherman. Jin accepted a job in a hotel, only to walk away from it when the manager made him feel the shame of where he'd come from. Sun has been ashamed about her affair with Jae Lee, and while she doesn't seem worried that Jin might find out, she's more upset about the guilt she feels and the fact that the baby may be Jae Lee's. In this episode, we discover that not only did Sun know about Jin's supposedly shameful past, but she helped him cover it up the same way she pretended her father wasn't the monster he really was. And, in doing so, unwittingly helped send Jin down a path of servitude.

So, is Sun really the Machiavellian master manipulator of the relationship, when all along we thought Jin was pulling the strings? Because she kept the truth from him, can she be blamed for what ultimately happened to him? On the one hand, if she had allowed Jin's mother to walk away without the money, she might have exposed Jin for what he was, and we can only imagine how Paik would have treated Jin after that. Jin's father, who knows him better than anyone, knew that Jin would become self-destructive, closing himself off from Sun and everyone around him, unable to deal with the dishonor of having a prostitute for a mother. Mr. Kwon begged Sun to keep it to herself. She complied, paying off the black-mailer, and in doing so, took the money from her father, putting Jin in Paik's debt. On the one hand, she has forced her husband to become a servant to her father. But what if she'd told him the truth — would Jin be in an even worse state than he is now? In "The Glass Ballerina," Sun tells Colleen that the Others don't know her, and then she shoots her. In this episode, she tells Jin's mother, "You know how powerful my family is. My husband believes that you are dead. Do not force me to make that a reality." We are slowly discovering that this seemingly quiet, subservient woman is actually a powerhouse. But now that we know she knew what her husband was doing all along — and was instrumental in forcing him into that position — it removes much of the sympathy we had for her going to Jae Lee and considering running away from Jin. She helped turn him into a monster, and then tried to leave when she didn't like what he'd become.

The most surprising moment of the episode, however, occurs with Desmond and company as they're trying to revive the pilot, who seems to be speaking in every language but English. When Mikhail suddenly emerges from the jungle, we can't help but be shocked. Did he rise from the dead? Was he somehow not dead at all (because we all know blood shooting from the ears with extreme force heals pretty quickly)? What is going on? Like Sayid, Desmond cannot bring himself to kill Mikhail, despite Charlie goading Des the same way Rousseau did Sayid. Mikhail tells them the same story he'd told Sayid about being a medic, and he manages to save the pilot's life. But when she finally speaks English again, her revelation to Hurley about the supposed fate of Flight 815 is a surprising and baffling one.

Juliet has definitely earned Sun's trust (and our sympathy, until she leaves that message on the recorder at the end). It's clear the castaways are beginning to turn away from Jack, believing he may be one of *them*. Sun's suspicions are raised when Jack begins asking her about her baby, especially when he asks if she's had any bleeding. Understandably, she worries that she may suffer the same fate as Claire.

Others vs. Losties

Back in "Stranger in a Strange Land," Tom suggested to Jack that he was living in a glass house and throwing stones when he accuses the Others of being bad people. Again, in "D.O.C.," Desmond points out to Charlie that the Losties have done far worse to the Others than vice versa. Let's compare the transgressions of the two groups (I'll only include instances up to "D.O.C." to avoid spoilers):

Others:
- Allegedly kidnapped Rousseau's daughter Alex
- Kidnapped 12 people from the Tailie camp (Karl claims it was to give them a better life)
- Killed Nathan, the man in the pit that Ana Lucia had mistaken for an Other
- Kidnapped Cindy
- Kidnapped Claire and Charlie, and left Charlie hanging from a tree, near dead
- Killed Steve
- Injected Claire with what Juliet says were drugs to keep her alive, but they also implanted her with a device that would cause her to become very sick in "One of Us"
- Kidnapped Walt and forced him to undergo tests
- Kidnapped Michael and convinced him to lure Jack, Kate, and Sawyer to them
- Shot Hurley, Jack, Kate, and Sawyer with tranquilizer darts
- Kidnapped Jack, Kate, and Sawyer and let only Hurley go
- Injected Jack and Kate with something, threatened Kate, electrocuted Sawyer several times, conned Sawyer, kept them all in cages
- Shot at Sawyer and Kate as they tried to leave
- Mikhail shot Sayid in the arm
- Ryan beat up Sayid as he was handcuffed to a swing set
- Gassed Sayid, Jack, and Kate
- In Other-on-Other action, Juliet killed Danny; Ben put Karl through psychological torture; Mikhail killed Bea Klugh

Losties:
- Eko killed two Others when they tried to kidnap the Tailies
- Ana Lucia killed Goodwin (in retaliation for the kidnappings)
- Charlie killed Ethan (also in retaliation for kidnapping)
- Beat the snot out of "Henry Gale" and kept him locked up
- Killed Colleen (when she was threatening Sun)
- Locke threw Mikhail into the sonar fence (but he's better now)
- Kate hit Juliet and dislocated her shoulder

It would seem that Tom was wrong; the list of transgressions by the Others far exceeds that of the Losties. However, the body count is higher with the survivors; they've killed five Others, but have only lost two of their own. Does that make them "good people"?

While Jin is away with Charlie, Desmond, and Hurley, he has no idea the emotional rollercoaster his wife is on. (YORAM KAHANA/SHOOTING STAR)

In the season 1 episode, "Raised by Another," Jack asks Claire several questions about her pregnancy, including whether she was seeing an ob/gyn in Sydney and why she let her fly so close to the end of her pregnancy; how the ultrasound was; how she'd been feeling overall; whether she's eating enough, and how many weeks along she was. Time has made everyone suspicious, but Jack is just asking questions that would be standard coming from any ob/gyn or midwife.

Although Sun knows that all of the pregnant women on the island die, she still seems determined to have the baby, even if it will kill her, but it's unclear whether or not she'll tell Jin what could happen to her. Considering her other lies were also to protect him, but led to his suffering, one can only imagine what will happen to him if she dies and he finds out later that she knew all along she would.

Highlight: Hurley pretending to call his mother on the satellite phone.
Timeline: The first part of this episode is December 17, and when Juliet and Sun leave the Staff station, it's the morning of December 18.
Did You Notice?:
- The opening scene was a callback to the season 2 scene where Sun was kid-

napped from her garden.

- The pilot speaks Chinese, Spanish, Italian, Portuguese, and finally English.

- Mikhail tells Desmond that if he "fixes" the pilot, they must let him go. Interestingly, Jack said he "fixed" Sarah when he made her walk again.

- When Mikhail and Desmond put the tube into the pilot's chest, Hurley doesn't pass out the way he did when Jack was working on the marshal, even though blood was shooting from the tube in the pilot's lung. After 90 days of death and destruction, he's no longer queasy around blood.

- When Juliet comes to Sun in the night and claps a hand over Sun's mouth, it's an echo of Ethan doing the same thing to Claire in "Raised by Another."

So many things have happened during the short marriage of Jin and Sun that the happy times seem like more of a dream than reality. (YORAM KAHANA/SHOOTING STAR)

- If Sun conceived off the island, she will live, but the baby is Jae Lee's. If she conceived on the island, she will die, but the baby is Jin's. Now *that* is a Catch-22.

- In one corner of the ultrasound room, you can see the crib and wall hangings that had been in Claire's nursery when they were keeping her.

- We've seen several moments of Juliet on her own, being honest, and her "I hate you" to Ben after she'd shut off the tape recorder was one of them. Coupled with what we've seen in "Not in Portland" and "One of Us," and the scene at the very beginning of the season of her crying alone in her house, the writers are definitely painting a sympathetic portrait of Juliet, even if we know she is deceiving everyone on the beach.

Nitpicks: Hurley's never been known for his intelligence, but in this episode he was especially stupid — first he shoots off a flare gun, then tells Mikhail about the sat phone. Also, Mikhail says that the pilot will be better in a day and a half, yet at the beginning of the season, Kate was put into handcuffs for a few hours, and a week later the marks from the chafing were still on her wrists. Apparently bullet wounds heal, but blisters don't?

There were a few inconsistencies with the way Juliet handled the ultrasound that seriously calls into question her abilities. First, she asked Sun when she and Jin *last* had sex, because that would determine conception. The baby could have been conceived eight weeks ago, but by Juliet's logic, if they'd since had sex the day before, then she must have conceived one day ago. What a stupid question. Secondly, an ultrasound technician has to measure the baby on screen to see if it's healthy, and they use those measurements to determine the age of the baby. Juliet just passed the wand over Sun's stomach, and boom, somehow knew the age of the baby right to the day without doing any measurements.

Oops: Juliet says Sun is 53 days pregnant. She took the pregnancy test on Day 60. It's now Day 90. That means her last period was 23 days before the pregnancy test, but the earliest a test would work is at 28 days. . . . And remember, at the time she said her period was late, which it wouldn't have been. Also, according to the World Health Organization, the average sperm count is 20 million. Juliet says the average sperm count is between 60 and 80 million and on the island it's five times that much. Not only is she way off (once again showing that as a fertility doctor, she'd make a good plumber), but at that rate, these island men would be impregnating their own underwear.

4 8 15 16 23 42: Charlie says it's an **8**-hour walk back to the beach. Juliet says the baby is **8** weeks old, or 53 days (5 + 3 = **8**). Jin's mother tells Sun to meet her in 3 days at 5 o'clock (3 + 5 = **8**). Paik's safe code is 734.

It's Just a Flesh Wound: Jin beats Mikhail in the jungle, and the pilot has a branch in her rib cage and requires a tube forced into her lung.

Lost in Translation: When the pilot speaks Brazilian Portuguese, Mikhail tells everyone that she said "thank you," but she actually says, "Eu não estou só," which means "I am not alone."

Any Questions?:

- How did Mikhail survive what happened at the sonar fence? He actually says to Desmond that he's already died once this week; is he just being sarcastic and facetious, or is there something more to what he's saying?
- Where did Jin learn his kung fu fighting skills? In season 1 he ran at Michael on the beach and just punched him and rolled around in the water,

but he never used crazy spin kicks. Later, in "…In Translation," Michael beat him up and he didn't fight back. Juliet said that the island increases a man's sperm count; could that be a factor in why he's suddenly such a ninja? (We've also seen Ben and Ethan fight with seeming superpowers.)

- Where did Sun get the file on Mr. Kwon, including his photo?
- Juliet tells Sun she'll be safe if she conceived off the island, which brings us back to an earlier question: Why did the Others kidnap Claire? Clearly she conceived off the island, so her baby — and she — would be safe. If the injections were to keep her safe, they were useless because she was already fine. Was Claire the first mother they'd seen on the island who'd conceived off-island, and therefore she's the one they're basing their new presumption on? What about Rousseau? She'd presumably conceived off the island and gave birth on it, so wouldn't she have been the previous test case to prove women who conceive off the island don't die?
- What did the pilot mean when she said she wasn't alone? Is there someone else on the island? On a boat nearby?
- Mikhail says the pilot will be better in a day, maybe a day and a half, because wounds heal quickly on the island. Why didn't the marshal's wound heal in season 1? Mikhail says the key is keeping it clean, and we know the marshal's wound was infected. But Jack was giving him antibiotics, and coupled with the healing properties of the island, one would think that would be enough to make him heal.
- When Charlie threatens to take Mikhail's other eye, Mikhail says, "Sorry . . . what?" Is he referring to Charlie's possible hearing loss after the hatch explosion?
- Now that Sun knows she conceived on the island, is there a possibility she'll consider an abortion? Is anyone on the island qualified to give her one? Would ABC have the courage to raise the issue?
- How will Juliet get samples of the other women? It's not like getting hair or saliva will tell her if they're pregnant. In "One of Us" did she get Claire's sample somehow?
- What did the pilot mean at the end when she said Flight 815 was found and all passengers were dead? Is it a ruse? Have the writers been lying all along and they really *are* in purgatory?

3.19   The Brig

Original air date: May 2, 2007
Written by: Damon Lindelof, Carlton Cuse
Directed by: Eric Laneuville
Guest cast: Kevin Tighe (Cooper), Kimberley Joseph (Cindy)

Flashback: Locke

Locke approaches Sawyer and tells him that he's kidnapped Ben, explaining that when Sawyer hears what Ben has to say, Sawyer will want to kill him.

"The Brig" is an episode about revenge, and the effects of that revenge on different people. Sawyer finally gets his revenge on the "Sawyer" who's dogged him all his life. Locke also gets his revenge on his father by having Sawyer kill him. For three seasons, we've seen Locke's life repeatedly ruined by his father. He suffers from anger issues because of what his father did to him, he doesn't trust other people, and while both of these would suggest he's a violent man, he's the opposite. He's unable to lash out at people, even when they deserve it, because of his underlying fear that he's the spineless coward his father has made him out to be. Yet we recently saw him throw Mikhail into the sonar fence, suggesting that there's been a change in him.

During those same three seasons, we've seen Sawyer's life completely dominated by the man who conned his parents out of $38,000, and caused both of their deaths. As some fans speculated as long ago as season 2 (see *FL*, page 183), that man was the very same Cooper. Sawyer has suffered indignity, hardship, and given himself over to a life of crime all because of what "Sawyer" did to him. Now Sawyer and Locke come together to finally put an end to the hold that Cooper/Sawyer had on them, but the outcomes for each are very different.

The episode was filled with other revenges. Ben resents Locke because the Others think he is special. He gets his revenge by setting up Locke in front of everyone and making him look like the coward Cooper always told him he was. Over on the beach, Kate finally voices her resentment of Juliet when she tells Jack — in Juliet's presence — that no one trusts him anymore. He used to be the good doctor, the leader, the one everyone went to with personal problems, the guy they all trusted above anyone else. This entire scene ranges from annoying to mysterious. Kate has known about Naomi for all of three seconds before running to Jack (after Sayid made her swear not to do just that). Jack is similarly irritating

Parent Issues

In my previous book (see *FL*, page 73), I outlined all of the parental issues we'd seen of the characters, thinking most had been explored in the first two seasons. Nope. There were still a *lot* of parental skeletons in the closets of these people. So I'll try not to cover territory I outlined in that book, and just carry on with what we learned in season 3 (warning: Charlie's and Ben's entries contain spoilers for the next two episodes).

Locke: His father was the one who paralyzed him, throwing him out of an eight-storey window. In return, Locke manages to kill him — with a little help from a friend.

Kate: When Kate confronted her mother about why she had turned her in, her mother told her that she loved Wayne, and Kate had killed him, so she would never forgive Kate. Of course, she chooses to overlook the fact that Wayne was abusive to both of them.

Juliet: There is no mention of either of Juliet's parents, which is interesting.

Desmond: While we also don't see or hear of his parents, his potential father-in-law is a head case who tells Desmond he's worth less than a mouthful of whisky.

Sun: Sun has known all along what her father does, and admits she chose to keep quiet about it. Mr. Paik puts Jin in his debt to pay off money that Sun has asked from him.

Charlie: Despite what we've seen of Charlie's harsh father in season 2, we see that Charlie has at least one happy memory of his father being a supportive and loving man.

Hurley: His father walked out on the family when Hurley was a child and returned 17 years later when he heard his son was wealthy.

Eko: We have no mention of his parents, so they're either dead or have been arrested, leaving Eko and Yemi to fend for themselves.

Claire: Her mother was put in a coma after being in a car accident while Claire was driving, and is still in the coma when Claire gets on the flight. Claire lives with the guilt that the last thing she said to her mother was that she wished she were dead. Claire discovers that her father is none other than Christian Shephard, but since she never asks his name, she doesn't realize she's Jack's half-sister.

Jin: Jin seems to be the *only* one with a good father (at least we *think* he's his father), but Jin is ashamed of him and tells everyone — including Sun — that he is dead. Jin's mother was a prostitute who dumped Jin on Mr. Kwon and left, only to return — like Hurley's father did — when she found out her son had married money. He doesn't know who she is, but Sun does.

Ben: Ben's mother died giving birth to him, but he's seen a vision of her on the island and has idealized her in his mind. His father was a verbally abusive alcoholic, and Ben ultimately killed him.

when he smugly tells Kate that whatever she has to say, she can say in front of Juliet. His comment is a return to the holier-than-thou Jack Shephard we had to suffer through for parts of seasons 1 and 2, but it's also hurtful because of what he and Kate have been going through personally recently. If there was ever a time that she needed to talk to him about how she feels, it's now, and if that were what she really wanted to do (the news about Naomi being a cover story), he doesn't even grant her the dignity of doing it in private.

These moments of spitefulness pale in comparison to what happens at the *Black Rock*, however. One can't help but wonder if Locke turned to Sawyer not only because he realized that Sawyer was the only other person on earth who hated Cooper the same way he did, but because it was his own subtle revenge on Sawyer. In season 2, Locke had been on an emotional rollercoaster all season, his newly discovered faith from season 1 slowly trickling away as everything he did turned out to be a mistake, everything he believed in turned out to be wrong. In "The Long Con," Sawyer tricks Locke into moving the guns, and Sawyer takes them all, declaring himself sheriff. Locke has barely exchanged two words with Sawyer since, and perhaps this entire thing was orchestrated to deliver to Sawyer the same pain he'd given him.

Josh Holloway delivers a searing performance in this episode, his best of the series. From the moment in the jungle where he pushes Locke to the ground and hisses at him to stop calling him James, to his ultimate act of vengeance on Cooper in the brig, Holloway has Sawyer run the gamut of emotions in a way we've never seen. During his conversation with Cooper, he moves from anger at being locked in to confusion about who Cooper is to exasperation with the guy who believes he's stuck in Hell . . . to his moment of revelation. The second he realizes he's face to face with his lifelong nemesis, Sawyer begins to act out the scene he's played in his head for almost 30 years. But Cooper doesn't play along — he refuses to read the note in full, instead filling in the rest with a condescending "blah blah blah blah." He shows no remorse, and instead insults Sawyer's mother and Sawyer himself. He pushes Sawyer to his limit, and Sawyer suddenly turns into an animal in a blind rage. The instant he's fulfilled his lifelong goal, however, he stands back and suddenly becomes the eight-year-old boy who'd originally written that letter. His pain has not gone away. His parents are still dead. He feels no satisfaction from killing the man. He realizes his life has been for nothing.

Locke, on the other hand, is filled with peace. He has finally lain to rest the man who had turned him into the person he hated. No longer is Locke the cripple whose father tried to kill him; the easy mark who gave his kidney to a con man when all he wanted was his father back; the target who lost the love of his life when he helped that con man retrieve a sum of money. He has triumphed over Cooper, even if he wasn't the one who dealt the final blow. Unlike Sawyer, Locke's revenge has left him satisfied, fulfilled, and on a new journey.

Ben tells Locke to do something drastic to end his father's (Kevin Tighe) reign of terror – will Locke follow through? (MARIO PEREZ/© ABC/ COURTESY EVERETT COLLECTION)

Highlight: That strange moment of Enlightenment thinkers coming together on the *Black Rock*. "Rousseau." "Locke."

Timeline: Richard gives Locke Sawyer's file on December 19, Locke reads it with Cooper trapped in the brig on December 20, and Sawyer kills Cooper on December 21.

Did You Notice?:

- The pilot's name is Naomi (see page 158 for the significance of her name). Her last name is Dorrit, which is probably a reference to Charles Dickens' *Little Dorrit*, a satirical novel about the government of the Victorian age, which takes place mostly in a debtor's prison.

- Despite the distinct possibility that Locke is trying to punish Sawyer in some way, when he turns to him in the jungle and tells him how hard it must have been to have lost his parents the way he did, he looks genuinely sympathetic.

- When Hurley first approaches Sayid to ask if he can keep a secret, Sayid is digging a hole. Why?

- In "One of Us," Sawyer calls Ben a "bug-eyed bastard," and in this episode,

Cooper refers to him as "Bug-Eye." Looks like the apple doesn't fall far from the Sawyer.

- Locke tells Sawyer this is a slaving ship, but doesn't say how it could have ended up in the middle of the island, nor does Sawyer ask.
- Ben hands Locke a knife and tells him to kill Cooper, which means he needs Locke to do it with his bare hands. Locke similarly locks Sawyer in a room without a gun, forcing him to do it the same way.
- When Rousseau comes to take the crate of dynamite, Locke says, "Be careful, it's unstable," and the look between them indicates that maybe he isn't talking about the dynamite.
- The file that Richard hands to Locke is a French police report on Sawyer.
- Cooper says he guesses he "didn't raise no dummies," but he didn't raise Locke.
- If the world assumes everyone on Flight 815 is dead, then no family members or loved ones are out there wondering where the survivors are anymore.
- Ben's retort to Locke — "Don't tell me what I can't do, John" — is a clear echo of Locke's favorite line from season 1.

Interesting Facts: The title of the episode focuses on the ship itself. A brig was a large ship that required an equally large crew, and was often the choice of pirates because they were good warships, but was more commonly used to carry a lot of cargo. (In the case of the *Black Rock*, the cargo was slaves.) The symbolism of Locke taking Cooper to a brig and forcing Sawyer to kill him there points to the fact that both men have been carrying their own cargo, or emotional baggage, for most of their lives because of this man, and now it's finally time to dump that cargo and move on.

Like Kate's aliases, Cooper's aliases — Alan, Anthony, Ted, Tom, Louis, Paul — are all named after saints (the exception is Blessed Alan de la Roche, who was not fully canonized).

Nitpicks: At the beginning of the episode, we see Locke burning pages in a file. Later, it's clear that he was sitting in the *Black Rock* while doing it, only a few feet away from boxes of dynamite. Locke isn't *that* stupid. Also, can a person really bail out of a helicopter without the parachute getting caught in the propeller?

4 8 15 16 23 42: The first Locke flashback is **8** days ago. If Kate's tent is five over from Sawyer's, there are **4** tents between them. Naomi says the plane was found off the coast of Bali in a **4**-mile trench. Cooper swindled Sawyer's parents out of $38,000 (**23** + **15**). Naomi's ship is 80 nautical miles northwest of the island (**42** + **23** + **15**).

It's Just a Flesh Wound: Sawyer's feet are cut up from walking through the jungle barefoot. Sawyer kills Cooper by wrapping a chain around his neck.

Any Questions?:

- Ben keeps saying Locke brought Cooper to the island. What does he mean?
- Ben tells Locke that the Others are moving camp to a new place, then changes that to "an old place, actually." Where does he mean? The beach? Some ancient ruins?
- Why is everyone looking at Locke with such admiration? What exactly are they looking for? A messiah? Cindy tells Locke, "We've been waiting for you." What does she mean?
- Has Cindy been completely assimilated by the Others? Is she a willing member now, or is she guarded? Are the other people in the background more survivors from the tail section who had been kidnapped?
- Ben tells Locke that they will go to the beach and kidnap the pregnant women, and adds that this isn't the first time they've done this. When is the last time? Was Rousseau taken by them? Is he referring to Claire? The Tailies?
- Is Ben telling the truth about being able to walk only after Locke showed up, or has he been able to walk the entire time?
- Ben tells Locke that a person needs to make a gesture of commitment to be part of the Others. Did all of these people have a hazing ritual of some kind before they were accepted into the group? Did Ben?
- Cooper is tied to what appears to be an ancient rock pillar. Where did it come from? Does it have something to do with the four-toed statue we saw at the end of season 2?
- How has the wreckage of Flight 815 been found with all of the bodies on board? Did some organization (possibly Hanso or Widmore) orchestrate the media reports to say it had been found, and then produced false photos and reports?
- Naomi says they were given GPS coordinates in the middle of the ocean. One of the favorite fan theories is that if you take Hurley's numbers and turn them into coordinates — latitude 4.815, longitude 162.342 — and type them into Google Earth, it takes you to a spot in the Pacific Ocean.
- Why is Ben so insistent that Locke kill Cooper? And why does he have to do it with his bare hands, and not a gun? Why do the Others want Locke to do it? Do they all have daddy issues? Why does Ben hit Cooper? Does he have a personal vendetta against him, or does he just hate him because he's a terrible father?

- Sawyer's file contains the information that he killed a man in Sydney, which only Sawyer knows about, and Locke's contains information about his Walkabout tour. Where did the information in these files come from? They aren't exactly police reports.
- Locke says the *Black Rock* is a nineteenth-century slaving ship. Is that true?
- Why was Rousseau getting dynamite? Is she making more bombs in the jungle?
- When was Sawyer in France?
- What really happened to Cooper? Was his accident orchestrated? He mentions a paramedic who smiled at him in the ambulance; could it have been one of the Others?
- How did Locke get the tape recorder out of Ben's tent?
- All of Locke and Sawyer's flashbacks have been about Cooper's impact on their lives. Do we need to see flashbacks of either of them anymore? Will their flashbacks take a new direction?
- Why was Cooper referred to as the Man from Tallahassee? Was he rear-ended in Tallahassee on the I-10?

Ashes to Ashes: Anthony Cooper (a.k.a. Alan Seward, Ted MacClaren, Tom Sawyer, Louis Jackson, Paul somethingorother) believed he died in a car crash driving along I-10 when he was hit from behind, but he was taken to an island where he was beaten by several people and eventually killed by James Ford. He will not be missed.

Biblical Names

One of the most common occurrences on *Lost* are people who have names taken from the bible. Aside from the obvious religious name — Jack's father Christian — several characters are so named for a reason, and might end up fulfilling what their biblical counterparts did.

Jacob: Jacob is the son of Isaac, who is the son of Abram. Isaac is the boy who Abram almost sacrificed on Moriah (see page 138). Jacob is quiet and is his mother's favorite, but his brother Esau, the stronger outdoorsman, is Isaac's favorite. Jacob is a trickster, however, and when his father is blinded by old age,

Jacob dons an animal skin to feel to his father's hand that he is Esau, the hairier brother, and this way receives his father's blessing, which gives him all the rights as the firstborn. Jacob leaves home, and one night has a dream where he sees a stairway of angels ascending to Heaven. God speaks to him and tells him that he will have numerous descendents, and God will protect him.

Benjamin: Jacob has twelve sons, and the youngest one is Benjamin. He is protected by all the other brothers after they'd stupidly sold their brother Joseph — he of the amazing technicolor dreamcoat — into slavery.

Aaron: He is the brother of Moses, and plays a significant role in the exodus through the desert. While God speaks to Moses, Aaron relays many of the messages from Moses to the people. Aaron is revered as a prophet by many religions, even though he is involved in making the Golden Calf when Moses is on the mountain. God is about to smite Aaron, when Moses steps in on his behalf and stops it.

John: "John" is one of the most important names in the bible. John the Baptist is a public minister who preaches about Jesus and eventually baptizes him. He is beheaded by King Herod a few months after the baptism of Christ. John the Evangelist (also John the Apostle) is credited with writing the Gospel of John and is one of Jesus' apostles. John the Divine (or John of Patmos) is credited with writing the Book of Revelation.

Michael: Archangel Michael appears in the Book of Daniel, where Daniel identifies him as Israel's guardian angel. Daniel prophesies that at the end of time, Michael will appear to signal the Day of Judgment has arrived. In the Book of Revelation, Michael is described as leading God's army into battle with a dragon, and Michael and his angels are victorious.

Ruth (Desmond's ex-fiancée): Ruth is the central figure of the Book of Ruth. She is a Moabite who marries an Israelite man. When he dies, she remains loyal to her mother-in-law, and returns to Israel with her and vows her devotion to God. She remarries an Israelite and through him becomes the great-grandmother of King David.

Naomi: Ruth's mother-in-law, who remains by her side and brings her back to Israel, helping to buoy her devotion.

David (Hurley's father): David is the king of Israel, and the author of the Psalms. God chooses David to reign over Israel after King Saul, and Saul brings David to his court to play the lyre for him. David's brothers are in the army, and come upon a giant named Goliath. David walks out onto the battlefield, fearless, and hits Goliath between the eyes with a stone shot from his slingshot, killing him. David becomes best friends with Saul's son, Jonathan, and Saul makes him the commander of his army. When Saul becomes jealous of David, worried he will take his throne, he tries to have him killed, but his attempts are thwarted. Eventually Jonathan and Saul are killed in battle, and David becomes king, reigning for 40 years before his son Solomon succeeds him.

Tom (an Other)/Thomas (Aaron's biological father)/Tommy (Charlie's drug dealer): Thomas is one of Jesus' twelve disciples. When Jesus appears to the disciples after the Resurrection, Thomas is not among them. They tell Thomas what they have seen, and he says he would have to see Jesus with his own eyes, along with the scars and holes from the crucifixion. Jesus appears to him and Thomas believes, but Jesus says men who can believe without seeing are the happier ones. It's from this story that we get the term "Doubting Thomas."

Matthew and Luke (two of the Others): Two of Jesus' apostles, and authors of two of the Gospels.

Danny (an Other): Daniel is a prophet in the Christian religion, and the central figure of the Book of Daniel. Though he never speaks directly to God, he receives visions from Him, and can interpret dreams. He becomes an advisor to the king of Babylon, but as such has to deal with jealousy. His three companions are thrown into a fiery furnace for being associated with him, but the next day the furnace is opened and they are still standing there, untouched. Daniel is thrown into a lion's den, but he, too, is untouched.

Mary (Sawyer's mom): The most significant Mary is the Virgin Mary, mother of Christ, who conceives Jesus immaculately. The other Mary is Mary Magdalene, who is a disciple of Christ and stands at the base of the cross until Jesus dies. She is crying at the door of Jesus' tomb when He arises and comes to her, and she is the first person who sees Him resurrected.

Adam (one of the Others; one of Cooper's pseudonyms): Adam is the first man whom God created to live in the world He has made.

Peter (son of the woman Cooper was conning in "The Man for Tallahassee"): Peter is one of Jesus' twelve apostles. At the Last Supper, Jesus tells Peter that he will deny Christ three times before the cock crows. Peter refuses to believe this, but does exactly that. After Jesus is arrested, a woman from the High Priest comes to Peter and asks if he knows Jesus, and he says no, he doesn't, then says it again, and then repeats it to men who ask him a third time.

Elizabeth (various women): Elizabeth is the mother of John the Baptist, and a descendant of Aaron.

3.20   The Man Behind the Curtain

Original air date: May 9, 2007
Written by: Elizabeth Sarnoff, Drew Goddard
Directed by: Bobby Roth
Guest cast: Jon Gries (Roger Linus), Doug Hutchison (Horace Goodspeed), Sam -
antha Mathis (Olivia Goodspeed), Carrie Preston (Emily Linus), Sterling Beaumon
(Young Ben), Madeline Carroll (Annie), Jenn Boneza (Dharma Welcomer), Gregory
Suenaga (Dharma Rep. #1), Diamante Kielo (Dharma Rep. #2)

Flashback: Ben

*As Ben takes Locke to meet the mysterious Jacob, the Losties all find out about Naomi,
and what Jack's been keeping from them.*

Okay, what . . . was *that?*

As mentioned earlier, the key purpose of flashbacks is to align us with the characters and allow us to feel sympathy for them by seeing some of their memories.
We've been waiting a very long time to see Ben's flashback, but unlike Juliet's, which
pretty much summed up everything we need to know about her, the first look at
Ben's previous life is more like a season 1 flashback. We see only snippets of his life,
we get some sympathy for why he's become the way he's become, and we also
caught a glimpse of just how evil he could be. And, as is the general *modus operandi*
of the *Lost* writers, his flashback left us with *far* more questions than answers.

"The Man Behind the Curtain" — the new best episode thus far — contains
several biblical references. And of course, it focuses on Locke (since Eko is gone).
In season 1, Locke was the original island disciple. He believed that the island had
healed him, and that it had something to tell him. In season 2, Locke's faith was
shaken by Jack's relentless reason, and by Henry Gale. Eko entered the scene as the
island's prophet, the would-be priest who quoted the Bible and told biblical stories
to Locke. When Locke stopped believing in "the button" — a symbol of blind faith
if ever there was one — Eko stepped in to walk Locke's path, and the disillusioned
Locke went further than Jack ever had, just to shake Eko's faith.

By season 3, Locke had prevailed; he'd been right in the first place, and he tried
to resume his mission. But his journey was becoming a solitary one. His faith in
the island had been restored yet again, and he admonished the wheelchair-ridden
Ben for not realizing the island's greatness. Locke no longer needs to defend his
faith to people like Jack, and he refuses to believe in false prophets like Ben.

Jon Gries (Roger), Sterling Beaumon (Young Ben), and Doug Hutchison (Horace) star in the flashback of this stunning episode. (MARIO PEREZ/© ABC/ COURTESY EVERETT COLLECTION)

Ben's jealousy of Locke is front and center in this episode. In "The Brig," it was unclear why Ben wanted Locke to kill his father in front of everyone. Now we see it was an ego thing — Ben killed *his* father, and everyone knows it. But Locke is unable to do the same thing. Now Ben takes him up to see Jacob, once again to humiliate Locke, to show him that yes, he might have healed quickly on the island, but he can't hear or see Jacob the way Ben can. When he finds out that Locke *does* hear Jacob (and see him, although Locke never reveals that to Ben), Ben snaps, shoots Locke, and leaves him for dead. Why doesn't Ben actually kill him? Maybe this is the ultimate test: if Locke really can rise from the pit of death, then maybe even Ben will accept Locke as a prophet.

Ben has lived a difficult life. He never knew his mother, and his father was a horrible man who reminded him that his birthday is in honor of the day he killed his mother in childbirth. As a boy, he's quiet and introspective, and the only people he seems to gravitate to are a little girl named Annie, and Horace Goodspeed, the man who brought them all to the island. Horace is an interesting character. We don't see much of him in this episode — here's hoping he'll make a return engagement in a future Ben flashback — but in the few moments we see him with Ben, he seems more fatherly and loving to Ben than Roger ever was. Ben kills his own father without blinking. But when he returns to the camp and sees Horace's body, he steps forward to close Horace's eyes, as if Horace's may have been the only death he regretted.

This episode illuminated the power structure inside the Others. Young Ben goes out into the jungle looking for his dead mother, who he swears he's seen and spoken to (it's yet another case of island inhabitants seeing things in the jungle that are important to them — Kate and the horse, Hurley and Dave, Jack and his father). He encounters Richard, who until now has been understood to be Ben's inferior, and Richard tells him that some day, if he's patient, maybe he can come and be with them. The next thing we see is the Purge — the complete slaughter of the entire Dharma Initiative that Mikhail talked about in "Enter 77" — with young Ben at the helm. It's as if the Others make him their leader because he actually had the courage to kill his father.

Until Locke comes along. Ben needs to show them that unlike himself, Locke can't actually kill his father. But Richard isn't convinced. Perhaps after the surgery, Ben's lack of rapid recovery has made Richard see Ben as a charlatan, and Locke as the real deal. When Locke suggests in this episode that maybe Richard could take him to see Jacob if Ben couldn't, Ben says in an exasperated voice, "Why would *Richard* take you?" Ben's starting to see his empire crumble. Later, when Mikhail shows up — and there's apparently no love lost between him and Ben — and Locke begins beating him, Ben pleads with Richard and Tom to do something, but they just stand there. Ben knows the tides are beginning to turn.

So he takes Locke to see Jacob. The scene at Jacob's cabin is easily the most memorable, most mysterious, and most frightening scene of the season. When Ben begins talking to an empty chair, the audience is right there with Locke, wondering when Ben went off the deep end, and how deep his psychosis runs. (Michael Emerson is simply brilliant in this scene, maintaining a complete back and forth dialogue with an empty chair.) Locke storms out, angry that the answers he'd been looking for are not here. Interestingly, like Jack in season 2, Locke suddenly requires physical proof to believe in Jacob's existence. When he *does* hear Jacob say "Help me" in an unearthly voice, the entire scene changes. And then . . . we see Jacob. In a sudden flash, Jacob is sitting right there in the chair (blink and you'll miss it) and as Locke stumbles to the door, confused and terrified, the camera closes in on Jacob's mystifying bloodshot eye as it slowly turns from Ben to Locke. It's a chilling moment.

Ben's flashback served to show us how he came to the island, the circumstances of his birth and upbringing, his most and least sympathetic moments, and why he is the way he is. But there was a *lot* missing that will hopefully be picked up in future flashbacks. What changed Ben from the quiet boy to the conniving man? What happened to Annie? Did she die, and maybe her death is what triggered Ben's hostility? How did Ben find Jacob?

Almost every Locke-centric episode features a moment where he's flat on his back, whether it was on the beach after the plane crash; lying in the toy store parking lot after chasing his mother; lying on the ground after his father had pushed him out of an eight-storey window; recovering after a boar had attacked him; waking up in the jungle after the hatch explosion. But he's always gotten up and walked again. Will he be so lucky this time?

Highlight: The flash of Jacob sitting in the chair.
Timeline: Ben's birthday is December 21. He shoots Locke on December 22.
Did You Notice?:

- Ben's mother's name was Emily, which is also Locke's mother's name.
- Ben was born outside Portland, which is the city Richard tells Juliet the Dharma Initiative is based in ("Not in Portland").
- Locke never says to Ben that he killed Cooper, he only implies it.
- When Ben offers Locke some scotch, Locke just stares at it. Perhaps the last time someone offered him scotch was when Cooper poured him a glass of MacCutcheon right before throwing him out of the window.
- When Locke calls Ben a liar, Ben looks deeply offended, just as he did when Juliet accused him of lying about her sister.
- When Ben and his father first arrive on the island, there is an older man with a white beard standing on the dock, and an African-American man standing behind them (who looks a lot like the real Henry Gale we saw on the driver's license in "Lockdown") and they look as if they have just arrived. But when Ben is standing in the Dharma office waiting for his father to be assigned his position, he's watching a Dharma video hosted by Marvin Candle, and the two men walk behind Candle on the video. Later, when older Ben is talking to his father while Roger loads the van, you see the white-bearded man walk behind them again, looking the same age as he did when they arrived.
- In the previous episode, when Hurley needs to tell a trustworthy person about Naomi, he chooses Sayid. In this episode, Sawyer waits in the bushes

for someone he can trust, and also chooses Sayid.

- There seems to be a caste system on the island whereby if your father was a workman, then so will you be.
- There's no Dharma patch on Ben's uniform.
- "Shambala" is playing in the vw bus, which is the song playing when Hurley and Charlie get it going again. "Roger Workman," a.k.a. Skeletor, was Ben's father.
- Jacob seems to be a god-like figure and Ben is the prophet who brings his message to the people, but there is a definite twist on the Old Testament version of a prophet. Ben doesn't talk to Jacob with reverence, but like he's a younger brother or ailing parent that Ben condescends to. He talks back to Jacob, scolds him, and tries to put him in his place. Yet when he's away from him, he again talks about him with reverence and acts like he's in awe of him.
- Ben insisted that Locke kill Cooper with his bare hands, using a knife, yet he killed his own father with gas, and didn't touch his father. He also expected Locke to do it publicly, while he did it privately.

Interesting Facts: In a creepy bit of casting, the actress playing Ben's mother is Michael Emerson's real-life wife. She had been a fan of the show long before he was cast in the role of Henry Gale. Horace Goodspeed is played by Brian Hutchison, who was the sniveling guard in *The Green Mile*, and the villainous Tooms on *The X-Files*. Olivia Goodspeed is played by Samantha Mathis, who appeared in several movies in the 1990s, including *Pump Up the Volume* with Christian Slater. Hutchison appeared on *Party of Five* with Matthew Fox and *Millennium* with Terry O'Quinn, and Mathis was on *Harsh Realm* with O'Quinn.

Besides the obvious allusion to *The Wizard of Oz* (see page 171), this episode pays homage to *Alice's Adventures in Wonderland*, just as the season 1 episode "White Rabbit" did. Alice follows a white rabbit down the rabbit hole to Wonderland, an alternative world where things that seemed to make sense in our world suddenly become nonsense, and the nonsense of Wonderland makes perfect sense. In this episode, Ben follows a white rabbit into "Wonderland" and then he follows it down the rabbit hole (or through the sonar fence) into a world where the dead talk to him, and people don't age. The season finale will focus on Lewis Carroll's other masterpiece, *Through the Looking-Glass, and What Alice Found There* (see page 204).

Horace could have been named after the important Egyptian god Horus, who was depicted with the body of a man and the head of a falcon. The son of Osiris, he was said to be the sky, with one of his eyes the sun and the other the moon. In

Carrie Preston, Michael Emerson's wife, stars in "The Man Behind the Curtain" as his . . . mother. Apparently Freud was one of the Others. (MARY LEAHY/AGENCY PHOTOS)

a battle with Set over the throne of Egypt, the moon eye was gouged out, which the Egyptians believed explained why the moon wasn't as bright as the sun. As dynasties rose and fell, Horus became more identified as the sun god, and also became subsumed into Ra.

Nitpicks: Ben is a *really* big baby for one born two months premature. He should have been about two or three pounds, but he looks like a full-term baby. Also, it's a very long trek from the beach to Otherville, as we saw when Kate, Sayid, Rousseau, and Locke traveled across the island to get there. Hurley finds the vw bus close to the beach and is able to go back and forth between it and the beach several times in that episode. How did Ben leave the vw bus there and make it back to Otherville so quickly? Did he or someone else move the bus later?

In "Tricia Tanaka Is Dead," Hurley says the beer in the van is from *Rocky III*, maybe even *Rocky II*. That puts the Purge in the early '80s, which isn't possible. First of all, if we say Ben was 12 to 14 years old when he came to the island, and his father was in his mid-30s, and Ben is 40 now (which Jack established looking at the X-rays), then Ben and his dad arrived in the mid-1970s. When Ben kills his father, his dad looks like he's about 70. The island and hard drinking have clearly aged him quickly, so he's obviously not that old, but he's also not only eight years older than he was when he arrived, and there's no way Michael Emerson, as brilliant as he is, is playing early twenties in that scene. So Hurley's probably wrong about his assessment of the age of the beer, and the Purge happened more recently than he thinks. Or the makeup department has screwed up a lot in this episode.

4 8 15 16 23 42: When Roger comes out of the woods carrying Emily and Ben, the highway sign says "Portland, 32 miles" (reverse **23**). The code to deactivate the sonar fence is 54439. Ben checks his watch right before killing his father, and it's 4 o'clock.

It's Just a Flesh Wound: Locke beats Mikhail to a pulp. Ben shoots Locke in the stomach.

Any Questions?:

- In season 1's "Deus Ex Machina," Emily Locke tells her son that he'd been born by immaculate conception. It's later established that she's mentally ill, but was there something more to her statement than the ranting of someone whose mind is sick?
- In the season 2 episode, "Two for the Road," Ben told Locke that he had been coming for him, and that Jacob had sent him. Was he telling the truth? Had Locke already caught the attention of the Others as someone who was "special"?
- What does Ben mean when he says, "I am the last that was"? The last of the Dharma Initiative?
- If the island can cure cancer and paraplegia, why can't it cure Ben's near-sightedness?
- Were Ben and his dad drugged before they got onto the sub?
- Annie gives Ben an Apollo bar and tells him they can eat as many as they want. Was there some substance in the bars they wanted the kids to eat?
- Why does Alex give Locke the gun? Did Ben take someone else to see the wizard, and shot that person, too?
- In one flashback, Olivia Goodspeed teaches the children about volcanoes, and mentions one that erupted on the island. When did it happen? Is it significant to future episodes?
- Why does Ben see Dharma as a threat, when in fact they always seem to be defending themselves against the Others?
- Ben keeps a white rabbit as a pet. Is it the great-grandbunny of the one he painted the number 8 on, or is there a chance it's the same animal?
- Roger asks Horace for hazard pay, and says, "Don't tell me you don't have it." Did he know of the Dharma Initiative's significant financial backing from Hanso?
- Is Emily dead? Was Ben just seeing a vision of her on the island, or is this a place where dead people can come to life again? Seeing his mother definitely evokes the memory of Jack seeing his father in season 1; could Christian be roaming the island, too? Or is Smokey manipulating everyone by taking the form of their beloved dead? Notice she's wearing the same

outfit she's wearing in Ben's photo, so that's the only way he knows her. Is Jacob controlling Smokey somehow?

- Who is making the whispers in the jungle? Is it the Others, or the voices of the dead?
- When Young Ben meets Richard in the woods, Richard looks exactly the same age as he does now, but with longer hair. Do the Others not age? Notice at the beginning of the episode, Ben tells Richard it's his birthday, and then adds, "You do remember birthdays, don't you Richard?" as if Richard were ancient. When Horace referred to them as natives, just how native did he mean? Are they the first people on the island? Did they arrive on the Black Rock? Are they immortal? Are they related to the "Adam and Eve" skeletons found in the cave in season 1?
- Locke and Ben cross what appears to be a line of ash to get to the cabin (literally "crossing a line" to see him). In mythology, a circle of ash is used to keep demons away. In the case of Jacob, is the line of ash to keep other people out, or to keep him in? Was the ash from the volcano that Olivia mentioned?
- When Locke and Ben are about to enter Jacob's cabin, you hear a man scream far away in the jungle. Locke turns when he hears the sound. Who was it? What was happening?
- In Jacob's cabin there are jars of fluid and a painting of a dog. What does the painting signify? What fluids are in those jars?
- What did Jacob mean when he asked Locke to help him? Is he being held captive somehow? Ben looks completely shocked when Locke tells him that's what Jacob said. Does he think he's doing something good for Jacob, and Jacob doesn't see it that way?
- Who is in the chair? The day after this episode aired, *Lost* online forums lit up with fans speculating that it was actually Locke himself. Or Christian Shephard. Or Future Ben. Maybe it was Danny Pickett. Or Jack. Or Dennis Hopper. Or the human form of Old Smokey. Or some combination of all of the above.
- Is Jacob trapped between worlds somehow?
- Jacob knocks the kerosene lamp off the table and it shatters, spreading fire as it hits the floor. Locke runs out, then Ben comes out and hangs the lamp back, intact. Also, all the jars are back on the shelf despite Jacob hurling them across the room. What happened?
- Why doesn't Roger roll down a window or open the door to escape the gas?

vw buses don't exactly have power locks.

- Mikhail was telling the truth in "Enter 77" when he said there was a purge and all of the Dharma people were killed at once. So was he telling the truth when he said he was the last living member of the Dharma Initiative? Could he have been a Dharma member who happened to be away from the camp that day, and that's why he and Ben don't get along?

- How does the Dharma Initiative fit in to what is presently going on on the island? Is there a chance the head office has no idea what happened to their people, and think their work is still continuing? Why is the pallet drop still happening? Do the Others have any connection to Dharma besides Ben? Why was Kelvin Inman in the Swan station? If the Purge happened so long ago, and if Inman and Radzinsky were stationed after it had happened, why had they been sent? Or were they there before the Purge, and if so, did they not know what had happened? Was Kelvin wearing the yellow suit because he knew about the gas attacks? Why would he recruit Desmond if he knew the Dharma dream was over?

- Ben tells people he was born on this island. But now we know he wasn't. What does "born" mean to him?

Michael Emerson (Benjamin Linus)

"We're the good guys," Ben says to Michael at the end of season 2, and a shiver runs down our spines. We've seen him lie to our heroes for several episodes, use underhanded measures to turn them against one another, and in this scene he's kidnapping three of them. How could he be a good guy? we think to ourselves, and yet we *want* to believe him, because he's so convincing.

And therein lies the genius of Michael Emerson.

Born September 7, 1954, in a small town in Iowa, Emerson attended Drake University with a major in theater and a minor in art. He attended the Alabama Shakespeare Festival's Master of Fine Arts program in 1993 (where he met his future wife, Carrie Preston), and moved to New York, starring in several theater plays, notably the off-Broadway show *Gross Indecency: The Trials of Oscar Wilde*, where he played Wilde himself. "I thought Des Moines [Iowa] was this crazy big town. New York just knocked the wind out of me," he

Michael Emerson has won kudos for his eerie portrayal of Benjamin Linus on *Lost*. (YORAM KAHANA/SHOOTING STAR)

says. "I was looking for a big challenge and I found it."

His first Broadway play was starring opposite Kevin Spacey in *The Iceman Cometh* in 1999, which is interesting, since much of Emerson's performance in season 2 of *Lost* is similar to Spacey's in *The Usual Suspects*.

It was Emerson's turn as serial killer William Hinks in a six-episode arc on *The Practice*, however, that earned him his greatest notoriety to date. Emerson won an Emmy for the role, and continued to do character work in television, including appearances on *Law & Order: Criminal Intent*, *The X-Files*, *Without a Trace*, *Law & Order: Special Victims Unit*, and *The Inside*. In 2004 he appeared in the notorious horror film *Saw*.

Emerson's work on *The Practice* had caught the eye of the producers on *Lost*, and they contacted him. He wasn't actually a rabid fan of the series, but his wife certainly was. "It was on every Wednesday in our home because my wife is a Lostaholic, but I would watch most of them," says Emerson. "I would be doing housework and stuff passing through the living room, so I was pretty well caught up on it, but once I got the job then of course I had to cram a little bit."

Once he'd accepted the part — which was originally to be a three-episode stint — there was no time to get acclimatized to the set. "You fly to Hawaii, a place I'd never been before, get to your hotel room for the night, and the next morning, you're out in the jungle somewhere and hanging from a tree," he laughs.

After watching Emerson's work on the set, and more importantly, the way his character interacted with and set off the others, the producers rethought their initial plan, and Henry Gale was turned into Ben, a member of the cast. "I think when they saw what they had, in terms of the function of this character, whether intentional or not, they had found their right villain for the show. Their right antagonist," says Emerson.

Fans and critics loved this enigmatic villain, and even when the show was receiving criticism at the beginning of the third season for not being focused enough or not providing audiences with enough answers, Michael Emerson had a powerful presence throughout season 3 and was receiving kudos. Emerson was proud of the role, and embraced the show.

Emerson was fascinated by the way the show shifted during that critical season. "The whole thrust of the third season seems to be to thwart the audience's first impression. Some people that had our sympathy are maybe beginning to lose it a little bit. Some people that we didn't like, we are starting to rethink. Some people that we thought were bad, may not be so bad."

Near the end of the season, Ben finally got his own flashback in "The Man Behind the Curtain," and Emerson was able to share the set with one of his favorite actresses — his wife — when she played, um . . . his mother. "It was kooky and Freudian," he says. "She had actually come up with that idea months ago. She told me, 'If I'm ever on *Lost*, I think I'd like to be your mom in a flashback.' I said, 'Ha ha.' And I think we mentioned it a couple of times at cocktail parties within earshot of decision-making people, and lo and behold it happened . . . And we may not have seen the last of her."

But even as a full-fledged cast member, Emerson's not getting too comfortable. He and Preston still haven't bought a house in Hawaii. "My gypsy instincts always tell me that, you know, the next episode could be the last. Home is still New York City."

The mystery of not knowing what is coming next is one of the exciting things about the show for him. "We only know what is going on when we get the script in our hands," he says. "We don't know what is going to happen in two or three or four episodes. The writers might give you a clue, but they tease you with it. They'll say something cryptic like 'Be ready for a big change.' You get greedy to get your hands on a script, because you want to see if you live or die."

The Wonderful Wizard of Oz by L. Frank Baum (1900)

L. Frank Baum's book is one of the most beloved children's stories of all time. Yet, since 1939, more people have probably seen the MGM film based on the book than have read the novel. The two are different in several ways, but the message is the same. In the book, Dorothy lives in Kansas, a land of no color, and her Auntie Em and Uncle Henry have become as gray and bleak as the landscape. She is whisked away by a cyclone while trapped inside her house and ends up in the land of the Munchkins. She realizes her house has landed on the Witch of the East when the Munchkins begin thanking her for ending their servitude to the witch. As a gift of thanks, they give Dorothy the witch's silver slippers. They want her to stay and live with them, but Dorothy just wants to return home. The Witch of the North appears and tells her about the Wizard of Oz, and tells her to follow the road made of yellow brick to get there. She kisses her on the forehead, telling her the mark there will prevent anyone from harming her. Along the way Dorothy finds a scarecrow in a field that is stuffed with straw and has a painted-on face, who tells her all he's ever wanted is a brain. Next they find a Tin Woodman who had once been human, but had been cursed by the Wicked Witch of the West. All he wants is a heart. Finally they meet a Cowardly Lion who wants courage. Together the foursome heads for Oz.

As the journey goes on, Scarecrow makes most of the intelligent decisions, the Tin Woodman is so scared to kill a bug that he watches his every step and cries if he does accidentally squash one (forcing Dorothy to constantly oil him), and the Cowardly Lion performs most of the stunts of bravery. In other words, they all possess the very qualities they'd been going to the Wizard to get. They travel through various lands before finally reaching Oz. Once there, the people of Oz see Dorothy's silver slippers and the mark on her forehead, and they grant her access to the Wizard — but only one at a time. Each one enters the room separately and sees a different incarnation of Oz, but they all receive the same message — they will be rewarded with what they desire only if they kill the Wicked Witch of the West. The foursome leaves in search of the witch, whom they are told will capture them and make them her slaves.

As they journey, the Wicked Witch of the West can see them with her telescopic eye, and she sends one plague after another, but each one is defeated. Finally she sends the Winged Monkeys by using a Golden Cap. This cap allows her to call upon the monkeys three times to do her bidding, and this is the final time she can use it. The monkeys destroy the Tin Woodman and the Scarecrow, but they refuse to harm Dorothy and they bring the lion and Dorothy back to be enslaved. When the witch sees Dorothy's slippers, she wants them, and tricks Dorothy to get one. Dorothy is so angry that she'd been tricked that she throws a bucket of water on the witch, who melts away. Dorothy retrieves the shoe, and she and the Lion leave. They find the Tin Woodman and Scarecrow and put them back together again, and return to Oz.

The foursome enters the domain of the Wizard and tells him the witch is dead, but there is no one there, just the voice of the Wizard reverberating around the room. The Lion roars to scare the Wizard, and Toto, Dorothy's dog, rolls away in fright, pulling down a screen on one side of the room, where an elderly, bald man is sitting. They realize, to their utter disappointment, there is no Great and Powerful Oz, just a small man who admits he's a "humbug" (an archaic word meaning imposter) and he's just a ventriloquist from Omaha who can throw his voice. He worked at a circus, going up in a balloon, until one day he was carried far away and eventually landed in Oz. He tells them to come back over the next few days so he can figure out what to do with each of them. He sews bran into Scarecrow's head and tells him he now has "bran-new brains." He cuts open a hole in the Tin Woodman's chest and inserts a silken heart. He tells the Lion to drink a green liquid and tells him it's courage. And he promises Dorothy that he'll fly her back to Kansas in his balloon, but when the straps on the balloon break, he floats away, leaving Dorothy in Oz.

Dorothy tries calling on the Winged Monkeys and asks them to take her back, but they refuse, saying they are not allowed to leave their land. The Scarecrow — who is now the ruler of Oz based on his intelligence — asks a soldier in Oz what to do, and he suggests Glinda, the Witch of the South, could help them out. The foursome heads off to find her. They travel through a forest, where the Lion kills a giant spider who had been terrorizing the inhabitants, and they bow before him and call him their king. Then they come to the Hammer-Heads, a group of people with no arms but with heads that shoot out on long necks who headbutt the foursome violently. Dorothy calls on the Winged Monkeys to carry them the rest of the way. They eventually meet Glinda and give her the Golden Cap. She tells them she will use the Winged Monkeys three times — to take the Scarecrow back to Oz to rule, to carry the Tin Woodman to the Winkies in the west so he can rule over them, to take the Lion back to the forest where he can be the king — and then she will give the cap to the King of the Winged Monkeys so they will be freed. She then tells Dorothy that all Dorothy has to do is tap her silver slippers together three times and tell them to take her home, and she will be home. Dorothy gives a tearful goodbye to her companions, clicks the slippers together, and is suddenly back home in Kansas, where her aunt and uncle wonder where she's been.

The movie is very different from the book, many of the adventures are missing, yet it's far more satisfying and exciting (and has a lot more singing). We spend a longer period at the beginning in dreary Kansas, where Dorothy fights with Miss Gulch, who is constantly threatening to kill Toto; she jokes around with the three farm hands; and she eventually runs away from home only to encounter a fake psychic in a traveling caravan. She gets caught in the storm and hits her head, waking to see the house floating in the air. When she arrives in Munchkinland, Glinda is the Good Witch of the North, rather than splitting her into two different people. Dorothy follows the yellow brick road in a pair of ruby slippers. On their way to Oz, the Wicked Witch of the West (whose *sister* is the Witch of the East, a relationship that is specific to the movie) is watching them most of the way, trying to stop them by using poison poppies and other sorcery. The foursome sees Oz all together, and he tells them to bring back proof they've killed the witch by showing him her broom, and they all set off to find the Witch. The Winged Monkeys capture them and bring all four of them to the castle (rather than disposing of two of them along the way) and it's only when the Witch tries to burn the Scarecrow that Dorothy throws the water on her to put out the fire, causing the Witch to melt. The soldiers bow before Dorothy as their leader, and the foursome returns to Oz. The Wizard tries to get rid of them, until Toto trots over to a curtain and pulls it back, revealing a man who has several bells and whistles, but is a sham. He gives the Scarecrow a doctorate, the Tin Man gets a red plastic heart with a clock on it, and the Lion gets a medal of bravery. He promises to fly Dorothy back to Kansas in the balloon, but like in the book, the cables snap, leaving her behind. Glinda suddenly appears and tells Dorothy to click her heels together, saying, "There's no place like home," and when Dorothy does, she wakes up in her bed in Kansas, where Auntie Em and Uncle Henry tell her she'd bumped her head and it was all a dream.

Based on the clues that we've gotten from *Lost*, it would suggest the writers on the show were far more influenced by the movie than the book. First, in the movie Dorothy's last name is Gale, and her uncle is Henry Gale (Ben uses the alias "Henry Gale" throughout season 2, and his mother's name is Emily, like Dorothy's aunt). In the book, the family has no last name. In the movie, when Toto pulls back the curtain, the little man says, "Pay no attention to the man behind the curtain!" which Locke quotes in the episode of the same name.

However, the book illuminates many ideas that are central to the film, but not examined in depth, and are also important to *Lost*. Dorothy sums up the feelings of most of the survivors of the plane crash when she says, "No matter how dreary and gray our homes are, we people of flesh and blood would rather live there than in any other country, be it ever so beautiful. There is no place like home." Dorothy recognizes early on that her three new friends already possess the qualities they are seeking from the Wizard. Similarly, on the show, the characters don't seem to know themselves as well as everyone else does. Jack believes he's not a leader, but everyone else sees him as one. Kate thinks she has everyone fooled about who she really is, but Sawyer sees right to the heart of her.

When the Winged Monkeys see Dorothy for the first time, they refuse to carry out their orders to kill her. The king says, "We dare not harm this little girl . . . for she is protected by the Power of Good, and that is greater than the Power of Evil." The concepts of good and evil run rampant through this series, and the theme becomes central to season 3 with the Others believing they're the good guys, while the Losties see them as the ultimate bad guys.

But what both the book and movie capture well is that the Great and Powerful Oz is nothing but a con man. And *everyone* on this island seems to be a con artist in some way. The most chronic of them all is not Sawyer, but Ben. Where the other survivors refuse to let their companions in on their deepest secrets, Ben created an entirely different personality — and name — and was completely convincing in his role. He's deceived the survivors and even his own people, and no one seems to know what his real plans are. Locke hits the nail on the head when he calls Ben the man behind the curtain, but ultimately, the man pretending to be the Great and Powerful Oz wasn't an evil person at all, just a weak man. Does that mean Ben's not the bad guy everyone's made him out to be? Just as the man pretending to be Oz gave the Scarecrow, Tin Woodman, and Lion the confidence to be who they always were, will Ben ultimately serve a good purpose?

3.21   Greatest Hits

Original air date: May 16, 2007
Written by: Edward Kitsis, Adam Horowitz
Directed by: Stephen Williams
Guest cast: Sam Anderson (Bernard), L. Scott Caldwell (Rose), John Henry Canavan (Simon Pace), Andrea Gabriel (Nadia), Brian Goodman (Ryan Pryce),

Neil Hopkins (Liam), Tracy Middendorf (Bonnie), Lana Parrilla (Greta), Jeremy Shada (Young Charlie), Zack Shada (Young Liam), Joshua Hancock (Roderick)

Flashback: Charlie

Charlie embarks on a suicide mission when Desmond tells him he has to die in order to save everyone else.

The week before the finale of any show is usually an episode filled with vital development and setup that is required to get viewers ready for the big event. Having a Charlie flashback one episode before the end seemed to make about as much sense as having a Rose and Bernard one right before the end of season 2, but after seeing this episode, we realize it was an important flashback for several reasons.

In this episode, Charlie says to Desmond, "Memories — they're all that I've got." For most of the survivors, that's all *any* of them has got. If you think through all of the flashbacks, not one of them has been a happy, glorious affair. The memories these people live with are dark, unhappy, and painful. They remember the sad moments of their lives — parental issues, traumas that have dogged them, relationship problems. There are no happy endings to any of these flashbacks. Even Hurley, whose flashbacks are usually comical, doesn't think of them that way — his lottery win brought deep personal pain to him, and he's an unhappy person because of them.

Up to this point, Charlie's flashbacks ("The Moth," "Homecoming," "Fire + Water") have been about how he gave up a life of faith to become a rock star, eventually succumbed to heroin abuse, watched his band fall apart, and saw everyone abandon him. He tried to take care of everyone around him, while no one took care of him, and on the island he worries that he won't be able to take care of Claire. After his drug addict brother Liam got clean, he got his life together. But Charlie's life continued to fall apart. He lives his life stuck in his moment of stardom, unable to get past the fact he's just a failed rock star.

But for the first time, we're seeing someone who's on the brink of death, and knows it, and he's decided that if the last 90 days have been about cleaning up his body and mind, accepting responsibility for his mistakes, finding love, and becoming a parent, he's only going to take happy memories with him and leave the rest behind. He has spent his time on the island coming to terms with being a has-been, but when Naomi tells him that he's known as the dead rock star who was given a big memorial service and had a greatest hits album, it changes his view. This is the first truly positive flashback we've gotten . . . of anyone. We've seen

Charlie's father as a cruel butcher who told him he'd never amount to anything; now he's a proud papa, teaching his boy Charlie how to swim. We've seen Liam as the enabler who allowed Charlie to fall apart, and didn't help pick him back up again; now he's the older brother who cheers Charlie on, shares a unique moment with him, and gives him a special gift. We've seen Charlie as a man who conned a wealthy woman; now he's a hero saving another woman in an alleyway. We've seen his relationship with Claire go through as many ups and downs as a roller-coaster, and suffered through his arrogance toward her in season 2; now we see that meeting her was the single greatest moment of his life.

Charlie discovers in "Greatest Hits" that maybe he's not the washed-up rock star he thought he was. (ALBERT L. ORTEGA)

Meanwhile, the rest of the gang is preparing for the imminent arrival of the Others. When Karl arrives to deliver a message from Alex — that the Others are coming *now* and not the next day — they have to drastically change their plan. They decide to leave behind three of their people. (Rose and Bernard have been completely absent all season, and now they suddenly appear again? That can't be good.) The rest of the Losties head off — led by Jack — to find the radio tower that Sayid's been searching for since Day 2.

The dichotomy between the two groups — one staying behind to fight a war, the other moving forward to find rescue — brings up a very important theme in the show: Do they actually *want* to be rescued, or are they all becoming distracted by island events? In season 1, these people tried everything to get off the island. Now they've formed relationships and alliances, seen friendships form and fall apart, seen people they cared about die, encountered an enemy, been separated and reunited. It's like they all see the island as home now, and rescue seems as fictional to them as the novels Sawyer reads on the beach. So when Naomi literally drops into their midst with the hope of rescue, they instead bicker about how the four guys who found her weren't honest with everyone, turning it into a therapy session rather than a celebration. At the beginning of this episode Sayid had an important question for Jack about the satellite phone, but Jack waves him off, saying he's too busy waging his war with the Others. When Sayid shouts that he's trying to get them off the island, it's like he snaps Jack out of his sleepwalking. What will happen to these people if they ever *are* rescued?

The episode ended with Charlie fulfilling his destiny, but not with the expected finish. "Greatest Hits" managed to pack in a lot of information and action, without ever feeling busy. It reunited us with the lovable season 1 Charlie, showed that Ben is not the merciful man he's made himself out to be, separated the Losties, and created the perfect setup for the phenomenal finale that would follow.

Highlight: Charlie and Hurley exchanging love.

Timeline: The events of this episode are concurrent with the end of "The Man Behind the Curtain," and take place on December 22.

Did You Notice?:

- In "Catch-22," Brother Campbell told Desmond the story of Abram and Isaac. Now it seems as though Desmond is Abram and Charlie is Isaac, and Desmond is being tested by someone to see whether or not he will let Charlie die.

- The people who went out to see Rousseau were Jack, Juliet, Sayid, Jin and Sun, Sawyer and Kate, Hurley, Desmond, Claire, and Charlie. In other words, with the exception of Locke and Ben, everyone who had a flashback this year.

- The Drive Shaft license plate is YRE2OL. If you assign numbers to the letters, it adds up to 77, which is another major occurrence of that number.

- Charlie holds his pen in a really strange way.

- The only previous glimpse we saw of Charlie's father was from the neck down, holding a cleaver that was covered in blood while chopping up meat in a butcher shop. As he growls to Charlie that music will never get him anywhere, he grabs a doll and puts it on the chopping block, severing its head. Clearly his father was an unpleasant man, but Charlie, mercifully, has one good memory of him.

Make Your Own Kind of Music

Some characters have been associated with a very distinct type of music, which almost acts as a leitmotif in their flashbacks.

Charlie: Aside from "You All Everybody," Charlie is usually associated with '60s music. In season 2, he stood on the beach singing The Kinks' "He's Evil," and in the "Fire + Water" flashback, that same song was playing in his apartment. In the season 3 finale, we'll see his knowledge of the Beach Boys' "Good Vibrations." But mostly, Charlie is associated with Oasis' "Wonderwall." The recurring line, "Maybe, you're gonna be the one that saves me" sums up what Charlie's life has come down to by the end of the season. In the rest of the song, the singer one minute suggests that today will be the day everything good will happen, and the next says nothing good will ever happen, and Charlie's life has been a similar roller-coaster of ups and downs.

Kate: Kate is associated with female country/pop crossover singers of the early 1960s. When she walks into her mother's diner to give her the insurance policy after she's killed Wayne, we can hear Skeeter Davis' "The End of the World" playing. At the beginning of "I Do," we hear the far more upbeat "Slowly" by Ann-Margret. Kate is usually linked to Patsy Cline (the music of pain). In "Tabula Rasa," she was listening to Cline's "Leavin' On Your Mind," a song where the singer tells her man that if he's got a new woman in his life, to just hurt her with the news and get it over with so she can move on. In "Left Behind" and "What Kate Did," we hear "Walkin' After Midnight." The song is a woman singing about how she goes out walking after midnight searching for someone, and hoping that person might be out there searching for her.

Hurley: Hurley is a typical muso who loves an eclectic range of music from 1960s rock to country to modern alternative. This season he becomes associated with Three Dog Night's "Shambala" because he listened to it as a kid and it was playing in the VW van, but otherwise his musical tastes are all over the map.

Desmond: Desmond's recurring song is Mama Cass Elliott's "Make Your Own Kind of Music," which is the ultimate plea for individualism. Elliott sings that some people might try to get you down, but you have to sing your own kind of song, even if no one else joins you, and only then will you cease to be lonely and start to be happy. Desmond has always done what everyone else has told him to do, and maybe being on the island has helped change his attitude.

Juliet: Because the first time we see Juliet she's crying while listening to Petula Clark's "Downtown," it's the song she's most closely linked to. The song acknowledges that life can be difficult and lonely, but if you go downtown where there are bright lights, movie theaters, cars, and noises, you can escape from your worries and get caught up in the buzz. It's a song Juliet listens to because there is no downtown for her to go to on the island.

- Jin speaks to Sun in Korean and she responds in kind. In "Tricia Tanaka Is Dead," Sun said she wouldn't be talking to him in Korean anymore, but considering the nature of his question — wanting to know what Juliet was talking about — maybe she's realized that speaking another language helps keep secrets from others.
- When Ben returns to the Others' camp, Alex is skinning a white rabbit. Could this be one of Ben's pet bunnies?
- Liam tells Charlie he's giving him the ring because he assumes Charlie will end up with a wife and child . . . which is what Liam did instead.
- Apparently the only song Charlie knew before starting Drive Shaft was Oasis' "Wonderwall." The busking scene in this episode is *not* the same one as we see in "Flashes Before Your Eyes," despite the similarities. In that episode, Charlie was wearing a black-and-white striped shirt, but in this episode, he's wearing a red one.
- When it begins to rain and Charlie is putting away his guitar, you can see a sticker on the instrument that says, "I was here moments ago."
- The woman Charlie saves from the mugging is Nadia, which now links her to Charlie, Sayid (he was in love with her and still searches for her), and Locke (he conducted her house inspection).
- When Hurley asks Claire if she needs help with Aaron, he looks sad. He knows Desmond is probably taking Charlie to his death.
- The Looking Glass station's logo is a white rabbit with a watch, indicating the Lewis Carroll reference (even though the White Rabbit doesn't appear in *Through the Looking-Glass* but rather in *Alice's Adventures in Wonderland*).

Interesting Facts: Charlie tells Naomi that his band got their start at the Night & Day Bar on Oldham Street in Manchester. This is a real bar that features live music every night. You can check out their site at www.nightnday.org. Charlie learns to swim at Butlin's. Butlin's Holiday Camps were created to provide holidays for U.K. families at low prices. There were nine camps built, which provided week-long holidays with full service within an enclosed area — food, entertainment, swimming pools, theaters, etc. Billy Butlin sold the franchise in the late '60s, and the camps soon after fell out of favor, and were sold off to other companies.

Nitpicks: It seems like a big waste of ammo — and a pointless personal risk — for Danielle to spend all that time lugging dynamite and wiring it just to blow it up for show. Not to mention, it risked giving up their plan to the Others, who might have seen or heard the explosion.

Also, it's unlikely that Drive Shaft would have had another album released the way Naomi said they did (although it's cool to think it could have happened). First, by the sounds of it, they only would have had a Greatest *Hit* album. Second, for argument's sake, let's say it took about two weeks to determine that everyone on the plane was dead, then Liam would have been in mourning, then the record company would have contacted him, then he and the other two members of the band would have chosen the tracks, the record company would have gotten all the requisite permissions from everyone and worked out a contract for the album, then put it together, pressed it, packaged it, marketed it, and *then* got it out on shelves. It's likely it would have hit shelves just before Naomi crashed, but she acts like it happened ages ago.

In the third flashback, we see Charlie in bed with two women, sleeping off a hangover, and this is before the drug problem (Liam mentions he's the only drug-free rock star in the business). Yet in "The Moth," we were led to believe that he stayed alcohol- and groupie-free, until Liam introduced him to drugs.

When Ben says they're going to go to the beach a day early, Richard tells him Juliet might not be ready yet. But in the previous episode, Ben discovered his tape recorder was missing. So wouldn't they assume that Juliet never received his instructions at all, since he's lost the tape recorder? How would she know to mark the tents? Also, there were several men who the Losties could trust to wield a gun for the ambush; why choose two men with family ties? Finally, Desmond agrees to take Charlie's place only because he can't bear to send Charlie to his death, but if Charlie had simply insisted, Desmond would have no doubt backed down. It was quite unnecessary to clock him hard with the oar, knocking him unconscious, leaving him to roast in the hot sun for hours, with the risk of the boat being overturned by the cable being pulled, which would have caused Desmond to drown. It was a wee bit drastic.

Oops: There's an inconsistency with people reporting how far away Naomi's freighter is. In "The Brig," Naomi says the boat is 80 nautical miles offshore (at least, the closed captioning says that's what she says, but it sounds more like she says 18). Kate, relaying the message, tells Jack it's 80 miles offshore. When Mikhail tells Ben that Naomi has arrived, he says her boat is 170 clicks offshore. In this episode, Sayid says "only 18 miles offshore." Which is it? And when Sayid lays the schematics map out, you can see "Looking Glass Hatch" written at the top. It should say Station, since that's how Dharma referred to them. The only reason the Losties refer to the stations as hatches is because all Locke had originally found was a hatch (which is a door). Also, when Charlie first jumps into the water, he's swimming down with the weight belt held behind him, instead of in front of him, suggesting there aren't really any weights on the prop. Only later does he hold his arm straight out and let the belt pull him down. (Also, Charlie seems to miss the point of a weight *belt*. It should have been around his waist, giving him two arms to swim down faster.) Finally, every time the camera zooms in on Charlie's greatest hits letter, the lines we saw him write previously are written differently, meaning the letters were actually five different props, and not one consistent one.

4 8 15 16 23 42: On the Looking Glass station schematics, at the top it says GVS: 199288472982. The numbers add up to 69 (**42** + **23** + **4**). Charlie says he can hold his breath for **4** minutes. Charlie tells Nadia the last time he was in a fight was when he was **8** years old.

It's Just a Flesh Wound: Sayid tackles Karl. Charlie hits Desmond in the head with an oar.

Any Questions?:

- On Day 6, a crash survivor named Joanna died when she was out swimming and got pulled out by a current. Charlie stood on the beach, completely helpless as Jack and Boone swam out to save her, saying over and over, "I don't swim!" (interestingly, he doesn't say he *can't* swim, but that he doesn't). In this episode, he seemed to be able to swim down to that rig underwater pretty naturally, and we saw at an early age his father taught him how to swim. While I'm assuming he wasn't really the Junior Champion swimmer that he tells Jack he is (he needs to say it to convince Jack to let him go) it appears he really can swim. So . . . did the writers forget what happened at the beginning of season 1, or was Charlie a coward who didn't try to save a woman when he could have? Why doesn't Jack remember Charlie saying he didn't swim?
- Where did Sayid get the schematics for the Looking Glass station?
- Where have Rose and Bernard been all season long? It seems very contrived to bring them in for the final two episodes only, and that suddenly they're a major, important part of the group, when they've been completely absent the rest of the season.
- Was the mugger in Charlie's flashback anyone significant? His hat is pulled down low, but some fans thought it might be Liam, while others pointed to Roderick, another Drive Shaft member (the one sitting in the driver's seat in the first flashback, flipping radio stations).

- Rose tells Bernard that shooting at dynamite is different than pheasant hunting in Montgomery County, which is in Ohio. Since they met and both lived in Michigan, were either of them from Ohio originally?
- Who are the two women in the Looking Glass station? How long have they been there? Was Ben lying when he said it was inoperable? Could one of the women be Ben's Annie?

Music/Bands: When Charlie is learning to swim, you can hear The Hollies' "Carrie Anne," originally from their album *Evolution*, but available on any greatest hits collection.

3.22, 3.23   Through the Looking Glass, Parts 1 & 2

Original air date: May 23, 2007
Written by: Damon Lindelof, Carlton Cuse
Directed by: Jack Bender
Guest cast: Malcolm David Kelley (Walt), Sam Anderson (Bernard), Julie Bowen (Sarah), L. Scott Caldwell (Rose), Roxanne Day (Diane), Nigel Gibbs (Funeral Director), Brian Goodman (Ryan Pryce), James Lesure (Rob Hamill), Tracy Middendorf (Bonnie), Lana Parrilla (Greta), Sonya Walger (Pen), Larry Clarke (Customer), Kate Connor (ER Doctor), Kathleen M. Darcy (Flight Attendant), Loreni Delgado (Pharmacist), Ariston Green (Jason), Joah Buley (Luke), Dustin Geiger (Matthew)

Flash: Jack

As Sayid, Bernard, and Jin stay on the beach to ambush the Others, and Charlie and Desmond try to turn off the switch in the Looking Glass station, Jack takes the rest of the survivors to the other side of the island with Rousseau and Naomi to find rescue. Ben is determined to stop them.

Wow. Now *that* is a season finale. When I first heard that this episode was going to feature a Jack flashback, I was less than impressed. What more could we possibly need to know about Jack's daddy issues and refusal to just "let it go," I thought? But the writers had a surprise in store for all of us. For the flashback we saw wasn't a flashback at all — it was a flash*forward*. What a brilliant concept!

What more could we learn from *any* character flashbacks at this point? Jack's

Locke is put to the ultimate test in this episode when the thing he fears the most happens. (MARIO PEREZ/© ABC/COURTESY EVERETT COLLECTION)

past has been played out. Locke's major issue is his father, and he's been dealt with. The second bird killed with that stone was Sawyer, the man who had haunted James his entire life, so his flashbacks have been finished off. Claire's background was about becoming a mother, and this season we found out she had a tense relationship with *her* mother, now resolved because she's become one herself. Kate's past has been about "what she did" and now that we know what it was, how it affected her, and that her mother won't forgive her for it, there's not much else to say. Sun and Jin's pasts are tied up in her father and what Jin did for a living, but now we know Sun knew everything, we know how Jin ended up the pawn of Paik, and that the affair with Jae Lee did *not* produce the child she's now carrying. Hurley's flashbacks focused on the numbers and his curse, but he's broken it and now believes that he makes his own luck. Desmond has always run away from relationships, but now he realizes he can commit to Penny. Sayid's past has been about his life as a torturer, but with the Amira flashback we saw that he's been deeply affected by what he's done, and will no longer torture others. Even Juliet, who's only had two flashbacks, has been fleshed out, and we know why she went to the island and how much she wants to leave.

Of all of those, I'd still like to know why Desmond ended up in prison and what he did that was so dishonorable. Juliet mentioned Basra to Sayid a couple of episodes ago, so there's clearly more to his story than what we've seen. Flashbacks are still essential for Ben, and hopefully Alex, Rousseau, Richard, and Jacob. But for the most part, the survivors' stories have been told, and now it's time to move forward. This episode showed exactly how they might do that. Most television series eventually come to an end, leaving us to wonder what will happen to the characters. Some shows — like *Six Feet Under* — give viewers an epilogue describing the future so they'll know. But *Lost* has come up with something new. If the next three seasons show what the future could hold, we will know where the show is heading. For a show that's so obsessed with timelines and fate and what the future holds, the idea is genius.

The key to this episode was the title itself. It refers to one of Lewis Carroll's two *Alice* books, *Through the Looking-Glass, and What Alice Found There*. In that book, Alice steps through the mirror into the looking-glass world, where everything is the opposite of what it should be (see page 204). The same goes for this episode. We thought we were watching a flashback until we realized we weren't (unless, like several fans, you picked up on the fact that Jack was using a 2006 cell phone in the flashbacks, or saw the date of the newspaper at the very beginning). Of course, the trick that was played on us suggests that other things we saw weren't as they seemed. Maybe they *won't* really get rescued. That probably wasn't the real live Walt standing by Locke. Mikhail almost certainly isn't really dead (what is *up* with that guy?).

This episode was primarily about Jack. From the beginning, he was billed as the reluctant leader, and we discover that one day he'll be the reluctant hero. This season he's been kidnapped, forced to do surgery, and more insultingly, been told that they had to use trickery to get him to do the surgery because they knew that Jack wouldn't do it willingly, calling into question his dedication to his job. He saw Kate choose Sawyer, he became part of the Others for a short time, and was promised passage off the island, only to have that thwarted. He's apparently chosen Juliet over Kate, and when he returned to the beach, he raised suspicions everywhere. He's trusted by neither the Others nor the survivors, yet the latter will still follow him out of habit. He's lived up to what Isabel said his tattoos meant — "He walks amongst us, but he is not one of us." From Day 1 on the island, he's had immense pressure on him. Long ago he learned to count to five to let the fear in before shutting it out, and now he doesn't let it in at all. He was angry and felt betrayed before he came to the island, and nothing's changed for him while he's been here.

"Check me out! You cannot kill me! *And* . . . I have two eyes!" As Mikhail, Andrew Divoff puts the "wha?" into this season of *Lost.* (ALBERT L. ORTEGA)

In his flashforward, Jack has turned into his father, the very man he loves and despises: he's drunk, belligerent, insisting on doing his own job while others know he's unfit. Except that, while Christian was able to keep it together so only his son knew just how bad off he was, Jack's had too much pain in his life to put up a good front. He's falling apart, and everyone knows it. His future will be no better than his past or his present; he will regret decisions, feel guilt, and want to go back to "fix" things that can't be fixed. The moment he makes contact with Naomi's boat, we see Jack more elated than we've probably ever seen him throughout the series, but putting that happiness in the context of the flashforward, we know it will be fleeting.

In this finale, Kate is torn between Jack and Sawyer. She's been part of this love triangle since the first season, but in this season things have gone way beyond flirtation. She's slept with Sawyer, and some part of her now knows that the Others put them up to it to find out if she'd get pregnant. Jack tells her he loves her, and that the only reason he told her not to come back for him was to protect her. Is he lying? If not, that admission is the one thing Kate needed to hear. She's been beating herself up for a week thinking that he didn't want her to come back because he wanted to save himself, and while she squandered his rescue attempt, she knows he doesn't hate her for it. She goes into season 4 taking responsibility for her actions in the past, but not offering any apologies for them. Unlike Jack, Kate knows how to move on.

Then there's Charlie. Dear Charlie. In season 1, he was a lovable hobbit with a dark secret, but he got past his addiction and seemed poised to move forward with Claire. By season 2, Locke was putting doubts in everyone's head, and Charlie was keeping his newfound heroin close by, almost as self-punishment.

Locke humiliated Charlie in front of everyone, and Charlie slowly became a morose, unlikable, and often vicious character. His tenderness with Claire turned into constant guilt-tripping, as he reminded her all the time that she was going to give up Aaron, that she's not watching him closely enough, that Aaron's hungry and needs her attention. He kidnapped Sun and hurt her just to help Sawyer disgrace Locke. But in season 3, his revenge against Locke has been had, and he's moved on. He's a loving surrogate father to Aaron, and cares deeply about Claire. He still has moments where he succumbs to his season 1 worries — that he won't be able to take care of the two of them — such as when Desmond saved Claire from drowning and Charlie kept trying to push him away so he could help her instead. But in the midst of returning to his previous likable self, he was told that he was going to die. At first he didn't believe that he could die, and figured as long as he stayed close to Desmond, he'd be safe from harm. But eventually the religious side of Charlie came out, and he believed that God had a purpose for him, and that purpose was to die in the Looking Glass station so that Claire and the others would be rescued.

Throughout the episode, Charlie cracks jokes at Bonnie and Greta (driving Bonnie bonkers), sings, and is generally upbeat, as if he's accepted his role and is here to play it. He shoots his mouth off about Juliet and Ben, because he believes that nothing they can do at this point can stop him. He is destined to turn off the switch, which will lead to rescue, and they can't do anything. Watch how Bonnie is instantly disarmed after she asks him what he'll do when the place floods and he calmly says, "I die." He's accepted his fate. However, there's a moment near the end when there's a small part of Charlie that believes maybe he *won't* have to die, and maybe he will receive a reprieve, and maybe all of this was just to test him, as God did to Abram. But the moment he sees his final act begin to play out, he doesn't hesitate. Charlie dies a hero, not only in allowing himself to drown, but in writing one final urgent message to Desmond, ensuring that Des will do what he can to save the others.

What does season 4 hold for Desmond? He's seen a glimpse of Penny on the monitor, and now knows she's never stopped looking for him. But he also knows that he needs to warn the others about Naomi. He'll have to get out of that hatch and back to the beach and radio Jack using Hurley's walkie, but will it be too late? Like Charlie, he believes in fate, and while he's clearly saddened by Charlie's demise, he stands at the portal and accepts it reluctantly, as if he wishes there were another way. If Naomi doesn't rescue them, will Desmond worry that he counseled Charlie the wrong way, and that Charlie's death wasn't necessary? Or will he simply move on with the hope of one day being reunited with Pen?

Ben plays a huge role in this episode. He tells Richard that he needs to keep Jack and everyone else on the island because Jacob told him to, but doesn't give any explanation beyond that. We know that he's only just discovered Naomi's existence, and at the beginning of this episode finds out for the first time that Naomi has a sat phone. Yet by the time he gets to Jack, he's begging and pleading with him not to go, insisting that Naomi is a bad person. Can Jacob talk to him when he's not in his presence, and has told him this news about Naomi, or is he simply making it all up just to keep everyone there?

Ben has been losing the faith of his followers through the latter half of the season. First, he didn't immediately heal after the surgery. Then he promised Jack a way off the island, but the sub was gone. Juliet went to the beach in the guise of working for Ben, but she's really working against him, and he now knows that. Ben has made everyone believe in Jacob, the way the Old Testament prophets made everyone believe in God. Yet when anyone has asked to see Jacob, he refuses to take them. A couple of days previous to this episode, he took Locke, an outsider, and many of the Others now resent Ben for that, including, it seems Tom and Richard. Alex hates Ben for what he's become, and prays he isn't really her father. Everyone he's sent to the beach has been killed by the Losties. Ben's perfect plan that has been working all along now seems to be floundering, and the rest of the Others don't know who to trust anymore. Is there really a Jacob, they must be wondering, or have they been believing a charlatan?

If Mikhail survived holding the hand grenade underwater, will he ever trust Ben again? He believes in Jacob, but he only knows Jacob through what Ben has told him. If he no longer trusts Ben, will he lose faith in Jacob?

The one person who may still end up with Ben could be Locke. Sure, Ben tried to kill him, but in "The Man Behind the Curtain," he shot Locke and left him there, when he could have finished him off. It's like he wanted to see if Locke would rise, Christ-like, from the pit. And Locke did. The look on Ben's face when Locke suddenly shows up speaks volumes. Perhaps now he'll finally see Locke as the Messiah the rest of the Others believe him to be. Maybe Locke will become Jacob's new voice.

Locke's faith has been tested, tried, destroyed, and reaffirmed throughout the series. This episode brilliantly captures his single lowest and highest moments on the island, all within the same minute. As mentioned earlier, Locke has fallen again and again, and the first thing he always checks are his legs. This time, they fail him. The island was supposed to be his salvation. The outside world holds nothing for him except loneliness, depression, and paralysis, while the island is full of hope, potential, and meaning. But when he loses his legs, the island becomes nothing more to him than the outside world ever was, and in his lowest moment, he grabs a gun and holds it to his head as a single tear runs down his cheek. But the island has bigger plans for John Locke. When a vision of Walt suddenly appears above him and says, "You can move your legs. Now get out of the ditch, John . . . you have work to do," it's like the same moment of revelation he had in "Walkabout," when he saw the white light in the jungle and knew that he'd found his purpose. For the first

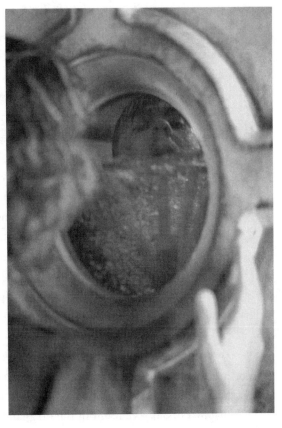

Charlie: The definition of a hero. (MARIO PEREZ/© ABC/ COURTESY EVERETT COLLECTION)

time all season, we see a genuine smile come over Locke's face. His faith has been renewed, he can walk again, and the island has once again chosen him as its disciple. He won't be leaving with the other survivors.

Another person who won't be leaving is Rousseau. Ever since we heard Tom call out to someone named Alex in "The Hunting Party," fans have been waiting for the reunion between Rousseau and her long-lost daughter. And what a reunion it is. Their first act as a mother-and-daughter team is to tie up Ben. Was there ever a more touching mother/daughter moment? Rousseau knows where her place is, and it's not in the outside world. She refuses to leave — she's lived on the island for 16 years, and it's the only home her daughter knows. Now that Alex has been brought together with Rousseau, they have a lot of catching up to do, but it'll be interesting to see what happens. Despite Alex's animosity toward her adoptive father, the Others are the only family she knows. Will she try to take Rousseau to them? Is there a chance Rousseau has already *been* a part of them?

One of the highlights of this episode is Hurley finally becoming a bona fide hero. His character has come full circle, where he believed the numbers had cursed him to forever be miserable, but this season he's realized, through the memory of his father, that his choices do matter. After Charlie turns him away (for his own good), and Sawyer does the same (probably also for his own good, though both of them sadly blame his weight on the fact he can't accompany them), Hurley takes matters into his own hands, and shows everyone just what he's made of. Not satisfied with simply *killing* the Others, Hurley then gloats to the rest of them by sending out a broadcast message warning them to keep away. Hurley reassures Claire that Charlie will be coming back, but the look on Hurley's face from the moment Charlie leaves the beach with Desmond tells us that he knows he won't be. Hurley immediately steps in as the new surrogate dad, holding Aaron and being there to help Claire. He goes into season 4 as full of hope and confidence as he was broken and disheartened at the end of the last season.

Claire will have to deal with the loss of Charlie in season 4, and how that will affect her is unclear. She's made her peace with him, and in the ongoing get-out-of-my-tent/stay-in-my-tent game she plays with him, she has tended toward the latter. Similarly, Jin and Sun will have to deal with the baby and what could happen to Sun as a result of the pregnancy (if they *don't* actually get rescued). But what if there is a sort of rescue attempt, and only a few people will be allowed to go? Would the rest of them allow these three to get onto the helicopter?

Not a lot has happened with Sayid's character this season. He hasn't had any major revelations that he didn't already have last season. We've seen a mellowing in him, where he's announced he's no longer torturing people, though that hasn't stopped him from seeing himself as Juliet's Grand Inquisitor. He makes it clear to Jack in this episode that rescue means everything to him, and he'd give his life if it means the rest of them will get away (meanwhile, Charlie was doing just that). By the end of this episode, torturer or not, Sayid once again proves he's not someone to mess with, as he kills a man by just using his legs. Don't mess with Sayid.

The other guy no one will want to mess with come next season is Sawyer. When he killed Cooper in "The Brig," his behavior afterward didn't seem to change, and it seems that, despite what happened at the end of that episode, he was going to be largely unaffected by what he'd done. But he's not. He's gone back to being dark Sawyer, the man who can look another man in the eye and shoot him in cold blood. He's withdrawn from Kate, telling her he doesn't want her with him and snarling at her that he hopes she isn't pregnant. He's killed "Sawyer," but realizes the Sawyer inside him lives on, and he's going to go back to being that person. Who will be able to pull him back from the brink next season?

Both Sayid and Sawyer distrust Juliet, and there's definitely a look of fear on her face when Sawyer shoots Tom. But in going back to the beach with Sawyer, grabbing the gun away from Tom, and telling everyone about their plan in the first place, she's done everything she can do to earn their trust. Will it be enough?

The big question for all of the characters is, are they really about to be rescued? Jack's flashforward suggests that there *was* a rescue, but because his flash happens over two years in the future, perhaps this seeming rescue isn't the one that gets them off the island. Next season could be a new fight with a new enemy, with Naomi's people waging a more serious war on the Losties than the Others ever did. Is Naomi really a bad person? Pen tells Charlie that she doesn't know who she is, but in "The Brig," Naomi simply says her company was hired by Penelope to find Desmond. So there's a good chance Pen doesn't know who Naomi is, because she's hired a company, not a person. Charlie first asks Penny about Naomi, then mentions a boat, and it's all so fast that maybe Pen didn't know what he was on about, but that doesn't mean Naomi isn't legit. Or . . . maybe Ben was right. Maybe Naomi was hired by *Mr.* Widmore, and is here to get rid of Desmond once and for all before Pen can actually find him and be reunited with him. Either way, these people *will* be rescued; the question is *when*.

But one wonders why some characters even want to get rescued. Rousseau makes it clear she's staying put, as is Locke. Kate's on the run from the law, so a rescue would get her arrested again. Jack's father is dead, his wife has left him, he's falling apart, and his mother probably blames him for his father's death, so there's not much waiting for him. Rose has cancer, and last season convinced Bernard that it's gone because of the island, and she doesn't want to leave. Sun and Jin would have to be on the run from Paik, and there's no telling what would happen to her magical baby.

Other characters *would* benefit from rescue. Hurley's still a millionaire, unless his parents went and blew all his money or gave it away like his father suggested, and now he believes he's broken the curse. Sayid has said that he thinks Nadia is dead, but there's something about him that makes us think he doesn't really believe that, and is still looking for her. Claire could certainly benefit from diapers and baby clothes and medical help should anything happen to Aaron.

"Through the Looking Glass" has a shocking ending –
what will it mean for the future of Jack and Kate?

Desmond could be reunited with Pen, though he would be in danger of Widmore's revenge. Juliet could see her sister and nephew again.

In the case of a rescue, what would happen to the survivors when they had to explain all the deaths? Michael and Walt are missing, Nikki and Paulo are dead (yay!), as are Ana Lucia, Libby, Eko, Nathan, Marshal Mars, Joanna, Charlie, Boone, Shannon, Arzt, and Steve (though the survivors will say it was Scott). They can't blame those deaths on the plane crash, since most of them are buried on the beach. What about the survivors who are now part of the Others, like Cindy and the children and the 11 other people from the tail section? What about Dharma and the Others? They'd be exposed to the media. The Dharma Purge would go public. What about the mystical elements of the island, like Old Smokey and Jacob? Would officials ever be able to find their way back to the island to investigate further, or would the survivors tell their story and never be able to verify it?

Several moments in the episode got fans talking, mostly those in the flashforward. The most talked-about one was: Whose obituary does Jack read about on the plane? The most complete transcription available online is the following: "The body of John Lantham of New York was found shortly after 4 a.m. in the 4300 block of Grand Avenue. Ted Worden, a doorman at the Tower Lofts complex, heard loud noises coming from the victim's loft. Concerned for tenants' safety, he entered the loft and found the body hanging from a beam in the living room. According to Jaime Ortiz, a police spokesman, the incident was deemed a suicide after medical tests. Latham [sic] is survived by one teenaged son. Memorial services will be held at the Hoffs-Drawlar Funeral Home tomorrow evening." Of course, this transcription has caused a big stir on the Internet, mostly because most of what is transcribed online cannot be seen in the prop obit, so either it was leaked by someone in the prop department, or a fan is just taking a wild stab at it, filling in the blanks between areas they actually can see.

What we do know is this: The death of the person affects Jack deeply, and it's someone both he and Kate know. This person has no family or friends who attended the funeral. The person is from New York (that we definitely do see on the obit), but was living in Los Angeles. Kate isn't especially close to the person, and seems surprised when Jack asks why she wasn't at the funeral. Of the name we can see Jo__ at the beginning, and __antham at the end. (At first, fans speculated that the name was Jeremy Bentham, the name of an eighteenth-century philosopher who was a contemporary of Locke and Rousseau, but the 'o' and the 'a' are too noticeable for that to be correct.) Could it be Locke? He has no friends or family, both Kate and Jack know him, and he would be someone whose funeral Kate probably wouldn't attend since we last saw him threatening to shoot Jack. Or could it be Sawyer? Does he end up withdrawing from her so much or treating her so badly that she'll have nothing to do with him? He, too, has no friends or family in the area.

If the full transcription is to be believed, the most likely possibility (if this is a character we've already seen and not one that is yet to come) is Michael. He betrayed all of them to get a ticket off the island, so Kate would feel no compulsion to go to his funeral. He is from New York. He has a teenage son (or will by the time the flashforward takes place). His death would affect Jack because, like Jack, he wanted to get off the island by any means necessary. But maybe, like Jack, he realized that life off the island wasn't what he thought it would be, and he took his own life because of it. Because Jack has hit rock bottom, he could see himself in Michael, and be affected by what he sees as his own future.

We only see two of the characters at the very end, and what Jack says to Kate raises even more questions. He tells her he flies out of town every Friday night, hoping the plane will crash. He says, "I don't care about anybody else on board." Does he take comfort in the fact that he doesn't care about these people, or does he *want* to care about these people so much that he hopes the plane will crash, so he'll have more things to fix, more people to bond with, more adventures to experience? Jack's purpose on the island is so much greater than it is at home, and maybe he needs to reclaim that.

Or maybe he just wants to get back to the same place. He says he goes to Tokyo, Singapore, and Sydney, so he seems to be trying to get back to that same

Fate vs. Free Will

One of the running themes of *Lost* is the question of fate and destiny versus free will and choice. The faith-based characters — Locke, Eko, Desmond, and Charlie — believe in fate, as do the Others. Many remaining characters — Kate, Jack, Sayid, and Sawyer — believe it is not destiny, but our choices that determine our futures. This season saw Hurley jump from one camp to the other, as he went from believing he was cursed no matter what he did, to making his own luck.

- At the beginning of "A Tale of Two Cities," Juliet quips she thought free will still existed on the island.
- In "Outlaws," Christian tells Sawyer that some people are destined to suffer, and that's why the Red Sox will never win the World Series. He believed in destiny and fate, and that no matter what that team does, they'll never win. He passed this belief on to Jack, who unconsciously bought it, but when Ben rolls out the television in "The Glass Ballerina," you see Jack's face fall when he realizes his father was wrong, and the Sox had changed their luck.
- In "Further Instructions," Locke explains that a sweat lodge tells a person what they are fated to do with the rest of their lives. He then says he's supposed to go to the bear cave.
- When "Yemi" asks Eko to confess in "The Cost of Living," Eko offers no apologies, saying he was given a certain life and he lived it as best he could. He comes closest to straddling both sides of the argument: on the one hand, he believes that his life was destined, but he also believes that he made certain choices that allowed his life to turn out the way it did.
- In that same episode, Ben tells Jack that he found out he had a spinal tumor, and two days later a spinal surgeon fell from the sky, proving to him that God existed and Jack was fated to crash there.
- In "Flashes Before Your Eyes," Penelope tells Desmond that they should celebrate that fate has spared him having to work for her father. Ms. Hawking tells Desmond that there is no free will, and if we try to change our fate, destiny will simply "course-correct" in order to get back on track. She says he'll push a button for three years, and "you don't do it because you choose to, Desmond, you do it because you're *supposed* to." Desmond accepts what she says, and tells Penny they're not supposed to be together.
- In "Stranger in a Strange Land," Achara says she can see into the heart of people, as if we cannot change who we are. She marks them with a tattoo saying what they are, after which they are fated to live the destiny that is painted on their skin.
- Hurley has always believed that the numbers have cursed him, and that everything bad that happens around him is due to the curse, not to the choices those other people have made. In "Tricia Tanaka Is Dead," he decides to test his theory, and realizes that by making his own luck, he can change the course of his life.
- In that same episode, Sayid mocks Locke for thinking that he was fated to go north "because of the way the sunlight hit Mr. Eko's stick."

- In "Enter 77," Sayid says that Mikhail is his prisoner and he will decide his fate — again, he's mocking the idea, because Mikhail's "fate" will depend on the choices Sayid makes.
- In "One of Us," Richard tells Juliet that she had created life where life wasn't supposed to be. It's as if the Others are fascinated by Juliet because she can change a person's destiny.
- In "Catch-22," Desmond says they have to go into the jungle all together because "that's the way it's supposed to happen." When Charlie refuses to go, Desmond delays his departure because he doesn't want to change fate. Interestingly, while Desmond believes in fate, he also clearly believes that our choices can alter that fate. In that same episode, Desmond tells Ruth that he knew he couldn't marry her because he had another calling, but Brother Campbell tells Desmond he wasn't supposed to be a monk.
- In "The Brig," Richard tells Locke he wants him to find his own purpose, as if he believes in destiny.
- In "Greatest Hits," Desmond tells Charlie that he must die in order for the rescue flash he saw to come true.
- In "Through the Looking Glass," Charlie willingly dies because he believes he's fated to do so. In the same episode, Locke tells Jack, "You're not supposed to do this." In the final flashforward, Jack tells Kate, "We were not supposed to leave," as if he now believes in fate and destiny.

island in the Pacific. He adds that he's sick of lying. What is he lying about? Is it possible that only he and Kate got off the island? Did they leave other survivors behind? Was there a war, a bloodbath where Jack was forced to sacrifice people the way he thought he'd sacrificed Sayid, Jin, and Bernard, and he did so to get himself and Kate off the island? Dr. Hamill calls Jack a hero, "twice over," obviously referring to the recent car rescue, but also getting off the island (though at that point in the episode we think he's talking about the mother and son). Every time Jack's called a hero, he balks and leaves. Whatever he did to get off the island, the public doesn't have the full story, and Jack can't live with the guilt of what he knows. There's a scene on the island where Jack tells Kate that Ben killed Jin, Sayid, and Bernard, and Jack let it happen, but he tells Kate, he *had to* let it happen. Did he *have to* do something much worse?

And yet the rescue was clearly publicized. People are calling Jack the big hero because of the island rescue, and Oceanic had to pony up with Golden Tickets for everyone. This is not something he and Kate did quietly. So why is Kate a free woman? If they did end up in the media, she should be in prison or on trial, but instead she's driving an expensive car and looks like she's doing well for herself. She's with someone — maybe Sawyer, maybe Kevin, maybe someone new — and feels no guilt for what happened. Did she sell her story and make millions? Was she granted immunity? Or was her rescue hush-hush and Oceanic paid her off to keep her quiet?

Jack mentions his father a few times in the episode as if Christian is still alive. Is he alive or dead? Jack could have kept a copy of his prescription pad, which would explain why he didn't want the pharmacist to call his dead father. Or Christian could be alive and Jack faked his signature and doesn't want the pharmacist to find out. When Jack tells Hamill to get his father downstairs and find out who is drunker, it seems as if he's talking about someone who's on another floor of the hospital. Or he could be speaking metaphorically, as if telling him to get his father down from Heaven and find out who's drunker. He follows up the line by telling Hamill not to look at him with pity, as if saying that he *knows* his father is dead, but he'll always haunt him.

Will season 4 feature flashforwards? Will the flashbacks be scrapped altogether or will they be kept for some characters? Will each one be a guessing game where we have to decide which way they're going?

More importantly, are these flashforwards set in stone? The entire series so far has been about fate versus free will. Characters either believe in destiny — that things are *supposed* to happen a certain way — or they believe their choices will determine their future. So are these flashforwards necessarily what is going to happen, or is there a chance Jack can make choices that will prevent it from happening? Could we end up seeing various scenarios as the seasons go on, with a happy scenario, followed by a depressing one? The possibilities are endless. Even Nikki and Paulo could end up being alive again (though if that's the case, Jack won't be the only person jumping off a bridge).

"Through the Looking Glass" was an extraordinary episode, one that will keep fans guessing about the show's upcoming format, hashing out new theories, and wondering what will happen to the characters. The writers did answer one huge question, though — our heroes *will* get rescued. But it won't be what any of us expected.

Highlight: There were several: Charlie singing "You All Everybody" in a falsetto to distract the women from hearing Desmond in the station; Rose telling Jack that if he says "live together, die alone," she's going to punch him in the face; Sawyer asking Juliet if she's screwing Jack yet, and her reply, "No, are you?"; Hurley the hero; Rousseau cracking Ben in the face to shut him up.

Timeline: Everyone sets off on December 22, the same day Charlie heads down into the station. The ambush at the beach happens that night. The rest of the episode happens on December 23.

Did You Notice?:

- Now we know that "Greatest Hits" was an obituary for Charlie.
- Jack getting drunk on the plane echoed what he was doing when Flight 815 crashed (the difference is, Cindy the flight attendant gave him more drinks in the original crash).
- When Jack is on the plane and picks up that day's newspaper, the date on it is April 5, 2007, giving us the exact date of his flashforward.
- Ben admits to Mikhail that he lied. Except for telling Jack at the beginning of the season that he'd lied to him about being Henry Gale (which was rather obvious) this is the only time Ben's ever admitted to lying.
- Mikhail tells Ben that he'll be able to get to the beach by dawn, which means Desmond lay in that boat all night, and Charlie's been gone from the camp for 24 hours before he turns off the switch.
- Sarah was supportive of Christian when he had the drinking problem, but she's accusatory with Jack during his crisis.
- Both Kate and Sarah say, "Goodbye, Jack," with a tone of finality.
- Ryan says, "Sayonara," to Jin before he's about to shoot him, which is Japanese, not Korean.
- Alex tells Ben that she's going with him, and he agrees without a fight. The last time we saw him agree to something that readily was when his father suggested they hang out in the van and drink beer, and we saw how *that* turned out.
- Sawyer tells Kate that for her, there's always someone to go back for, and he's right. While Marshal Mars told her she'd never stop running, Kate always comes back. She returned to her childhood sweetheart Tom in "Born to Run" (and got him killed), she came back to see her mother twice, despite her mother's hatred, and it's disastrous both times. When she returns to get Jack, she thwarts his chances of leaving. She runs away from circumstance, but returns to the people she loves (usually inadvertently hurting them).
- When Desmond is hiding in the locker, he looks like he's in a confessional.
- Ben tells Mikhail that he needs his help to "clean up this mess that I've made." In "Further Instructions," the vision of Boone tells Locke to clean up his own mess.

- Malcolm David Kelley's voice is changing. By the time the series ends in 2010, the actor will be 19, so the writers will have to figure out how (or if) Walt can continue to be a recurring character. Perhaps he will appear in flashforwards.
- The name of the funeral home is Hoffs/Drawlar, which is an anagram for flashforward.
- Bonnie tells Mikhail that she followed orders by jamming the frequency, and adds, "The minute I start questioning orders this whole thing falls apart." She has the same blind faith that Desmond, Eko, and Locke had while pressing the button.
- Of all the things the Others have done to Kate, Jack, and Sawyer, Sawyer shoots Tom for taking Walt from them, which is what he believes is the instigating event of all of this.
- In the scene where Dr. Hamill confronts Jack about how he got to the bridge so fast, Jack immediately counters with, "Do you have any idea what I've been through?" and lays a guilt trip on Hamill for having the audacity to question his problems. Christian did exactly the same thing to Jack in the season 1 episode, "All the Best Cowboys Have Daddy Issues."
- The iteration number on Rousseau's distress signal is very close to being right. When they last heard it on day 2, it was at iteration 17294533, and it's now at 17550445. That means the message has repeated 255912 times since they've last been there, and since it plays roughly 2880 times a day, it's been playing for 89 days. Ninety-one days have passed since they last heard it, but the number is probably off because the message isn't exactly 30 seconds long.
- Locke says to Jack, "I will kill you if I have to," resolutely, but then drops the gun and walks away. It's as if he knows he doesn't have to kill Jack, because Jack's going to do it himself.
- The man who answers Jack's call is named Minkowski, which is another Polish name (Kelvin's Swan station mate was Radzinsky).

Interesting Facts: None of the cast members except for Evangeline and Matthew had any idea how the season was going to end, because if they weren't in the final scene, their last script page was blank. The rest of the cast had to tune in to see what was going to happen just like the rest of us. Despite the secrecy, however, and the fact that only a handful of production people had the final pages of the script, it was somehow leaked, and an Internet site posted the whole plot as a spoiler a week before the show aired.

In an interview with Michael Emerson after the finale aired, *NY Mag* asked him if he thinks Ben is bluffing or if Naomi is really bad, and surprisingly, his response was, "She's a messenger from the dark side. I think we can take Ben at his word. Whoever is on the boat that they just called mean them no good. As soon as we're in season 4, I think we're gonna discover that everyone is in deep trouble."

Naomi asks Jack what he used to be before he was Moses. It's an apt description of him. Moses led his people out of Egypt, and went through many trials along the way, including wandering the desert for 40 years. When he and his people finally arrived at the promised land, Moses and his brother Aaron (Jack's nephew is named Aaron) were not allowed to enter. Along the way Moses was supposed to speak to a stone so that God would bring forth water from it, but instead Moses hit the rock twice with his rod. God said he was making it look as though he, not God, had brought forth the water from the stone, and therefore Moses was not being allowed to enter the land to which he had led the people (Numbers 20), thus punishing him for having his own God complex, another thing viewers have criticized Jack for.

Dr. Hamill says "Gary Nadler" will be doing the surgery on the woman. Nadler is Bernard's last name (it's never mentioned on the show, but is in the scripts).

On Ben's map, you can see an area marked "Pascal Flats." It was probably named after Blaise Pascal, a seventeenth-century French mathematician, physicist, and philosopher. He was famous for his ideas on the probability theory, but suffered from various illnesses that caused him to lose the use of his legs. When he was 31 he had a near-death experience, and after awakening from a coma, had a religious vision, which caused him to write the words, "Fire. God of Abraham, God of Isaac, God of Jacob, not of the philosophers and the scholars. . . ." The area on Ben's map isn't so named by coincidence.

Oxycodone is the generic name for OxyContin, or "hillbilly heroin," a highly addictive painkiller prescribed for serious pain treatment. The drug is very effective, but patients also develop a fast tolerance to it, forcing them to constantly increase the dosage to maintain the drug's effectiveness. Because of its fast high, it's become a popular street drug, sold illegally in most countries due to high regulation standards.

In *The Prisoner* (see page 81), Number Six tells Number Two that he will escape, come back, and obliterate the entire village, which is similar to Jack telling Tom that he'll kill him for what he did. Also, in one escape attempt, Six gets all the way back to his apartment in London, only to realize the life he's returning to isn't worth living, just as Jack seems to discover in this finale.

Nitpicks: They're lucky that Naomi's phone worked at all by the time they got to the radio tower. Throughout the episode, it seems every time we see Naomi, she's got that phone turned on and is checking it. The battery on a satellite phone is pretty limited, and you'd think she would have been smarter than that. Also, Desmond said in "Catch-22" that the pieces of his flash have to go together to work, but Charlie puts it in jeopardy when he alerts the women to Juliet's back-stabbing — which caused them to call Ben, who might have stopped the ambush on the beach if Ryan's walkie had been on, and who ended up heading off Jack and everyone at the pass. Charlie did it again when Mikhail showed up at the underwater station and he told him everything about why he was there, causing Mikhail to also call Ben. Finally, in one of Jack's flashforwards, he's at the pharmacy and a man in line tells the pharmacist to "give him what he needs" because he's a hero. Right. Because heroes can just get whatever drugs they need. What a stupid thing to say.

Oops: When the gang leaves the beach, the water is to their right, but in the next scene, they're walking along the rocks and the water is to their left, as if they're going in the opposite direction. When Charlie spits up blood and says, "Let's call Ben," there's no mark on his right cheek. In the next shot, he has a gash on his cheek that is bleeding. It's gone again in the next scene. (He finally incurs the gash when Bonnie hits him for singing "You All Everybody.") In the previous episode, you couldn't see the beach when Charlie dived down into the water. In this episode, the boat is suddenly so close to shore Mikhail is able to shoot at it.

Later in the episode, you can see Aaron's head sticking out of Claire's carrier, and he has a full head of hair. At the end of the episode, he just has peach fuzz on his head again. Charlie writes on his hand and shows Desmond the message, and it's faded, but when Desmond puts his hand up against Charlie's, the message is suddenly strong and clear, but it's faded again in the next scene. Finally, Charlie crossed himself with his left hand, which is a no-no in the Catholic Church.

4 8 15 16 23 42: When Ben is drawing the line on the map with the ruler, the line is **15** inches long. Jack saved a **40**-year-old woman and her **8**-year-old son. When Jack meets Dr. Hamill the first time and tells him he wants to do the surgery, the clock behind him reads **4:48**. The number Jack's trying to call in front of the funeral home is 310-555-0**148** (the first three numbers add up to **4**; the next three add up to **15**). When Juliet and Sawyer get to the beach, Sawyer notices they have three guys and **4** guns. In the final flashback, Jack's license plate is 2SAQ321. The numbers add up to **8**, and if you assign numbers to the letters, it adds up to 44 (**4** & **4**). Kate's is 4QKD695. Numbers and letters add up to 56 (**16 + 16 + 16 + 8**).

It's Just a Flesh Wound: Charlie is beat up by Bonnie. Five Others are killed by dynamite, two others when Jin shoots them. Sayid, Bernard, and Jin are beaten by the Others. Mikhail shoots Greta and kills her, then shoots Bonnie in the back, and she eventually dies also. Desmond shoots Mikhail with a spear gun. Jack tackles Ben and punches him in the face nine times. Jack's knuckles are scraped. Hurley kills Ryan with the vw bus. Sayid snaps Jason's neck with his legs. Sawyer shoots Tom in the chest, killing him. Mikhail sets off a hand grenade in his own hand, killing Charlie. Locke kills Naomi with a knife plunged into her back. Rousseau elbows Ben in the face.

Lost in Translation: In an early scene, we see Ben writing in a journal. A screen capture of the page he's writing says this (whenever a word isn't clear, I've used a square bracket; rounded parentheses are Ben's): "An important meeting tonight with (R) and (M) regarding the developing situation. We are now in day 3 of our exodus from the village and I am, I fear, at the limit of my tactical resources. (J)'s agenda, which I don't question, is however a [narrow] and difficult one and I could well wish we'd had time to prepare, not merely for the military strike, but for a [?] campaign in the bush. We are short on provisions (seasonal) and, more importantly, the long-awaited re-supply of camp gear having been missed (and so necessary!) and just as our water supply routes have been cut off. We look like a very sad sort of [?] army. Morale, I have to say, is as low as the circumstances [?] [?] Yet, for all that, I feel apprehensive . . ."

Any Questions?:

- What made Sayid think Jin was an excellent shot? We've never seen him handle a gun before, and he's clearly a lousy shot. Speaking of which, if the dynamite is so unstable that Arzt was blown into tiny pieces just by moving it too quickly, why didn't it blow up with the force of Jin's bullets landing mere inches from it?

- Sarah is pregnant when she comes to see Jack in the hospital (Julie Bowen was pregnant at the time, and had her baby a couple of weeks after filming the scene). Who is the father of the baby? Why did she say it would be inappropriate to give Jack a ride? Is there a possibility they had an affair when he returned? Could he be the father of the baby?

- Ben tells Richard to proceed to the temple. What is the temple? Does it have anything to do with the four-toed statue?
- When Kate worried she might be pregnant, and Sawyer said, "Let's hope you're not," did he mean it to sound like he really didn't want a baby with Kate, or is he worried about Kate dying if she stays on the island?
- Who is the woman that Jack saved? Does she have any connection to the island? Could her son be Zack, from the tail section?
- Have Juliet and Jack kissed before?
- Was Walt astrally projecting himself to Locke, or was Smokey taking on the guise of Walt, the same way it presumably made Yemi appear to Eko and Emily appear to Ben?
- Ben says that he recently made a decision that took the lives of over 40 people in a single day. Was the Purge his idea? Is he referring to a different incident?
- Is Christian alive?
- Ben warns Jack, "If you phone that boat, every single living person on this island will be killed." Why did he add the word "living" in there? Isn't it presumed that only living people can be killed? Is there a suggestion some of the people *aren't* living? Who?
- Bonnie says the code set to "Good Vibrations" was programmed by a musician. Is it possible, if the time travel theorists are correct, that it was somehow programmed by Charlie? How else to explain the fact he nailed it on his first try, even though the numbers didn't seem to exactly correspond to notes on a piano?
- How did Penny just happen to be sitting there the moment the signal went clear? Does she have an alarm set to tell her when the signal is suddenly clear and it's okay to transmit? Does she really not know Naomi, or is she just confused about what Charlie is saying?
- Is Mikhail dead now that he's set off a grenade in his hand? How did he survive a spear-gun shot? Ben tells him earlier that if he'd instructed Bonnie and Greta to kill him, he'd already be dead, so Ben clearly doesn't think Mikhail is immortal.
- Will Claire ever see Charlie's note?
- What did Ben mean when he said if Jack makes that call, it will be the beginning of the end? He knows how badly Jacob wants to keep them on the island; does he know what Jacob will do if they leave?

- Is Naomi's rescue what Desmond saw in his flash, or did he see another one?
- Who is the "he" that Kate mentions is waiting for her in the final flashforward?
- What happened to put Jack and Kate into their future positions? What have they been lying about?

Ashes to Ashes: Charlie Pace is best known as the brains and talent behind the one-hit-wonder band, Drive Shaft. Their hit, "You All Everybody," rocketed the band to stardom, before drug addiction, alcoholism, and a mediocre sophomore album brought them back down to earth. Charlie is survived by his brother Liam, his sister-in-law Karen, his niece Megan, his girlfriend Claire, and his surrogate son Aaron.

Greta and Bonnie were assigned the post of working at the underwater station, the Looking Glass, when the Swan station detonated. Their job was to jam all frequencies trying to transmit off the island. They did their job loyally, without ever asking questions. They were killed by Mikhail.

Ryan, Jason, Luke, Matthew, Diane, Ivan, and three other Others were loyal soldiers to Ben who were killed in the line of duty while fulfilling Ben's orders to take the women from the beach and kill anyone who gets in their way. Ryan Pryce was a brutish man who wasn't kind to anyone, and Jason was his sidekick (and a lousy shot). Five — including Diane and Ivan — were killed by dynamite, Matthew and Luke were shot by Jin, Jason was killed by Sayid, and Ryan was mowed down by a vw bus.

Tom, a.k.a. Mr. Friendly, a.k.a. Zeke, was also a loyal soldier until recently, when he began to question Ben's methods. Nevertheless, he, too, was following orders when he died by Sawyer's hand. He was probably gay.

Mikhail Bakunin . . . actually, I'll save this one for when I have proof. (See "Par Avion.")

Music/Bands: When Jack is driving to the funeral home, he's listening to Nirvana's "Scentless Apprentice" (*In Utero*). The song is based on the 1985 novel *Perfume*, which was one of Cobain's favorites. The novel is about a man who doesn't fit in, and he murders 25 women to try to make himself "normal." Could the song be saying something about Jack? The song programmed in the Looking Glass station's computer is "Good Vibrations" by the Beach Boys (*Smiley Smile*). The song is Brian Wilson's masterpiece, and it's an interesting choice, considering it was the Swan station's not-so-good vibrations that caused Greta and Bonnie to be underwater in the first place.

Through the Looking-Glass, and What Alice Found There by Lewis Carroll (1871)

Often read as the sequel to *Alice's Adventures in Wonderland* (even though Alice never refers back to those adventures in this book), *Through the Looking-Glass* is yet another nonsensical trip through a strange world that could be read as Victorian satire. On a wintry afternoon, Alice is playing with a kitten in her living room when she wonders aloud what it would be like to climb through the mirror above the fireplace and into the "Looking-Glass House." She imagines everything would be the opposite on the other side, and when she climbs up onto the mantle to get a better look, the mirror turns to mist and she steps through. In the other room she finds chess pieces scattered on the floor, but they're moving about of their own accord, and the White Queen is fretting about her daughter Lily. Alice grabs the White Queen and White King and lifts them up onto the table much to the shock and horror of the chess pieces. Amused at the expressions on their faces, Alice notices a book lying on the table called "Jabberwocky," which she is only able to read when holding it up to the mirror. The book tells a story that she can follow somewhat, but is filled with nonsense words that don't make any sense to her:

'Twas brillig, and the slithy toves
Did gyre and gimble in the wabe:
All mimsy were the borogoves,
And the mome raths outgrabe.

Determined to see what is beyond the house's door, Alice leaves the house and enters the Looking-Glass world.

At first Alice encounters the Garden of Live Flowers, where the flowers argue with each other and insult Alice's intelligence. Alice spots the Red Queen, now life-size, who shows her that the countryside consists of squares like a chess board. Alice muses that she'd love to be a queen, and the Red Queen tells her she can be, if she starts off as a pawn and moves to the other side of the board. From this point on, the book becomes an actual chess game, with Alice encountering other pieces and making the right moves to get to the other side of the board and be crowned queen. Throughout, all of the white pieces she meets are kind and sweet (if a little foolish), while the red pieces are unlikable and haughty.

As Alice travels through the Looking-Glass world, she discovers that everything is done the opposite way she's used to. When she's thirsty, the Red Queen gives her a dry biscuit to quench her thirst. The Red Queen tells her to keep moving quickly just to stay in one place, a comment on how the rest of the chess game is moving around her and that she needs to be aware of the other pieces.

One of the book's major themes is the impact of semantics and language on our society. Alice encounters problems with labels: she forgets her name, finds out names of other creatures, and becomes involved in absurd discussions about language.

Alice next encounters Tweedledee and Tweedledum in one of the funniest chapters of the book. They point out the Red King taking a nap nearby, and tell her that everything that is happening to her is actually part of his dream, and that she only exists as part of that dream. Tweedledee recites the brilliant poem, "The Walrus and the Carpenter," and afterward argues for the merits of the poem on the basis of logic and semantics.

Next Alice encounters the White Queen, who tells her that in the Looking-Glass world things move forward and backward all the time (the same way chess pieces can move either way) and that their memories exist the same way, between the past and the future. The Queen transforms into a sheep sitting in a shop, and the shop becomes a boat on a river.

The most interesting person Alice encounters is Humpty Dumpty, an egg-like man sitting on a wall who is also the central figure in teaching Alice about language. He interprets the first verse of "Jabberwocky" for her, explaining what the nonsense words mean, and while his explanation initially comes off as a load of bunk, it actually makes perfect sense from a semantics perspective, as he identifies nouns and verbs and what they could mean from an onomatopoeic perspective. As she leaves him she hears a huge crash, and is suddenly caught in an onslaught of all the king's horses and all the king's men.

Alice next meets the Lion and the Unicorn before seeing the White Queen go flying past (in a chess game, the queens can move from one side of the board to another, so in this world they would always appear to be rushing past at a high speed).

Just as Alice is beginning to feel completely disoriented and alone, she encounters the White Knight. Of the two *Alice* books, the White Knight is the only truly kind and sympathetic character to appear. The Cheshire Cat helps

Alice in the first book, but he's not exactly friendly. The White Knight, on the other hand, is a clumsy man constantly falling off his horse when it jolts in a funny direction (if you think how a knight would move on the chess board, it moves one square and then a sudden diagonal, explaining why the Knight can't seem to stay in the saddle). He helps Alice get to the edge of where she needs to be in order to be crowned queen. She sees him off, jumps into the eighth square, and is made a queen.

The White Queen and Red Queen appear on either side of her, and Alice ends up at a party, thrown, apparently, by Alice herself. As the food gets up and leaves, and guests jump into the tureens, and the Red Queen continues to lecture and criticize her, Alice decides she's had enough, and yanks the tablecloth off the table, spilling things everywhere. She grabs the Red Queen, suddenly no bigger than a doll, and begins to shake her, and the Red Queen turns into Alice's kitten. Alice realizes she's back in the living room with the kitten sleeping nearby, and she'd been dreaming. Or maybe . . . she was just part of the Red King's dream.

Alice's Adventures in Wonderland is referenced in passing in various *Lost* episodes, including "White Rabbit," where Jack chases a vision of his father throughout the jungle, and "The Man Behind the Curtain," where Ben follows his rabbit into a strange world indeed. The idea of being lost in a world that doesn't make any sense speaks to what the survivors are going through on this island. Just as Alice is lectured on her knowledge — or ignorance — of language, math, Victorian customs, and nursery rhymes, so does the island seem to be rife with theories of religion, philosophy, physics, and the coexistence of all three.

Through the Looking-Glass is the more apt book to reference in season 3. Just as the White Queen tells Alice they move backward and forward on the chess board and thus have memories of before and after, so does Desmond seem to have knowledge of his future. More importantly, the use of the game of chess ties it to this season. The Losties play mental games of chess with the Others, and Ben tries to stay one step ahead of them at all times, but is often thwarted. When Jack thinks he's about to trump the Others and win, he, too, is disappointed.

Alice always seems to pass through these worlds relatively unscathed and is not traumatized by their nightmarish quality, but the characters on *Lost* are more deeply affected. The Others are like the otherworldly creatures in both the books, preaching to the survivors, playing with their minds, and making them question everything they've ever believed. But where Alice is definitely dreaming in both books, the survivors aren't quite as lucky.

The Others

Season 3 has been about getting to know the Others and seeing them as more than the unnamed "Hostiles" that Rousseau and Kelvin warned against in the first two seasons. We've seen their camp and their laboratory island, and we have a better sense of why they are doing what they're doing. We don't know where they've originally come from or what their ultimate motivations are, but throughout this season we've gotten to know a lot of them, even if many were massacred in the finale. The following is a list of the named Others we've seen (there are dozens more in the background).

Benjamin Linus: The leader of the group, he answers only to one higher being — Jacob — but he makes the rules and the others follow. He was originally part of the Dharma Initiative, but when he helped orchestrate a purge that killed them all, he was granted leadership of the Others.

Richard Alpert: He moves back and forth between the United States and the island, and seems to have Ben's trust. He recruited Juliet to the island, and filmed her sister playing with her nephew Julian to prove Ben wasn't lying. He was the first Other who Ben met, and he doesn't seem to have aged since Ben first met him, making us wonder if he's immortal. By the end of season 3, he's starting to have his doubts about Ben, and helps Locke behind Ben's back.

Juliet Burke: She was recruited into the group, and has never been a fully active member. She participates in their schemes, but only to gain Brownie points so she can leave the island and get back to her sister. She was brought to the island because of her groundbreaking research in female fertility, but on the island her research has not lived up to its promise. She has seemingly defected to the Losties, and hates Ben.

Ethan Rom: He was the surgeon for the Others, and was the one Ben sent to the beach where the fuselage had landed to pose as a survivor and collect "lists." He had accompanied Juliet to the island and helped Richard recruit her. We first saw him as one of the presumed survivors in "Solitary." He administers needles to Claire during her pregnancy, and when Hurley discovers Ethan wasn't on the plane, Ethan kidnaps Claire and attempts to kill Charlie. He acts as Claire's ob/gyn while he has her, but when he tries to follow her after she escapes, he's shot and killed by Charlie.

Goodwin: He was sent to the beach where the tail section landed. He had assisted in Ethan's surgeries to save the pregnant women who were dying, and was in an intimate relationship with Juliet (it's not clear how close she was to him, though, because she doesn't seem broken up over his death at all). When Ana Lucia realizes he's making lists in "The Other 48 Days," she kills him by impaling him on a spear.

Alex: According to Rousseau, two weeks after she gave birth to her daughter, Alex, the Others took her, raised her, and she has been living with them ever since. She knows only Ben as her father, but like Richard, no longer trusts him. We first see her in "Maternity Leave" when she helps Claire escape, and she is not a willing member of the Others. In the finale, she is reunited with her mother and appears to be leaving the Others. Her boyfriend is Karl.

Tom: He is a loyal soldier to Ben, and in the beginning appeared to be the leader. We first saw him in "Exodus, Part 2" when he kidnapped Walt off the raft, and we saw him a second time in "The Hunting Party," when the script was referring to him as Mr. Friendly and Sawyer was calling him Zeke. Since then, he's become a fan favorite (the actor, M.C. Gainey, somehow makes us like him while he's kidnapping people and remaining loyal to the Others). He is killed by Sawyer.

Danny Pickett: Another loyal soldier, and a brutal one. We first see him in the fake Others camp when he comes to take Michael's blood. He was married to Colleen, and formed a particular hatred for Sawyer, threatening to kill him. When Kate and Sawyer got out of the cages, he hunted all over the island for them, and would have killed them if Juliet hadn't shot him first.

Bea Klugh: We first see "Miss Klugh" when she interrogates Michael in "Three Minutes." By her actions in that episode she seems to be a willing member of the group. We know she's put Walt through a series of tests, and she convinces Michael to bring Jack, Kate, Sawyer, and Hurley to the dock. We see her again at Juliet's book club, and when we see her one last time at the Flame station with Mikhail, she's shot by Mikhail — at her own urging.

Ryan Pryce: Also a loyal soldier to Ben, Ryan replaces Danny as the brutal one. He heads up the expedition of ten Others to the beach to retrieve the pregnant women and bring them back to Ben. Ryan first becomes prominent when he's the guy guarding Sayid in Otherville, as Sayid is handcuffed to the swing set. He's harsh to Alex, as if he sees her as a kid who's in the way. Ryan is killed during the ambush on the beach when Hurley mows him down with the vw van.

Colleen: Married to Danny, Colleen is another loyal Other who comes off as a harsh person. She looks at Juliet with some disdain as if she doesn't trust her, and goes on an expedition to get Desmond's boat in "The Glass Ballerina." She's shot by Sun in a confrontation on the boat, and dies the next day.

Mikhail Bakunin: One of the strangest of these strange people, Mikhail lives alone in the Flame station where he is in charge of communications. When the plane went down, Mikhail studied satellite footage of the news broadcasts announcing the missing flight, and he was in charge of collecting files on every survivor, which helped Ben determine who to kidnap. We first encounter him in "Enter 77," where he's still living in the Flame station, but communications have been wiped out since the electromagnetic surge. Locke seemingly kills him, but he shows up again six episodes later. There is distrust between him and Ben, which grows more hostile by the finale, when Mikhail realizes Ben has been lying to him about why the communications aren't working. Mikhail remains loyal however, and kills two Others and Charlie, after surviving a spear through his chest administered by Desmond. It's unclear if he's dead or alive, since the last we saw of him he was letting off a grenade in his own hand.

Karl: Alex's boyfriend meets her vengeful father, Ben, when he puts Karl into Room 23, a horrific psychological torture chamber designed to brainwash him from ever wanting to touch Alex again. (Some dads brandish baseball bats, some have psychedelic brainwashing rooms.) We first see Karl in "A Tale of Two Cities," when he's in the cage beside Sawyer and warns him against pushing the button three times. After Karl is rescued from the room and escapes to the other island, he seeks out Alex, who hides him from Ben until she hears Ben is going to kill the Losties. He goes ahead to warn them, and seems to have defected from the Others along with Alex.

Isabel: While she only appears in one episode — "Stranger in a Strange Land" — she's referred to as "The Sheriff," and she rules over a trial to determine if Juliet should be executed for killing Danny. She translates Jack's tattoos and is a confident, mysterious person.

Bonnie and Greta: Ben assigned them to the Looking Glass station after the electromagnetic surge so they could jam all incoming and outgoing signals, but he told the rest of the Others the two women were on assignment in Canada. Bonnie is the more violent of the two of them, has unquestioning loyalty to Ben, and believes that if she begins to ask questions, everything will fall apart. Both are killed when Mikhail shoots them, though Bonnie is able to help out Charlie before she dies.

Aldo: A guard who we only see during "Not in Portland," when he's guarding Room 23, where Karl's being held. He's reading a copy of *A Brief History of Time*, and is highlighting the section of the book where Stephen Hawking is talking about future and past light cones.

Ivan: Ivan is an African-American soldier who is present during Ben's surgery (he's the one Jack knocks out) and is the one Juliet sends out to get Danny out of the cage. He's killed on the beach by one of the two dynamite explosions in the finale.

Jason: Another soldier with few lines, Jason appears throughout season 3 as a guard and soldier, usually accompanying Ryan or Danny. He sports a shaved head, and we see him chasing Kate and Sawyer when they're on the run in "Not in Portland," and shooting wildly at them, missing them every time. He is killed in the beach ambush when Sayid snaps his neck using his legs. Ouch.

Luke: A guard also accompanying the soldiers, Luke is seen at the quarry when Sawyer and Kate are breaking and hauling rocks, and Sawyer elbows him in the face when he enters his cage. He's killed in one of the dynamite explosions on the beach.

Matthew: Another Other named after the Gospels, Matthew is mostly a background character, though we see him in "Every Man for Himself" when he's injecting a large needle into Sawyer's chest, and is very nervous about it. He's shot by Jin during the beach raid.

Adam: A belligerent coot, it's not clear what role he plays in the military side of the Others, but we see him only in "A Tale of Two Cities" when he comes to Juliet's book club and attacks her choice of *Carrie*, calling it "popcorn" and "by the numbers religious hokum-pokum." His main objection to the book seems to be that Ben wouldn't like it, which shows his loyalty to him.

Amelia: She's the older woman attending the book club, and it's also unclear what her purpose in the group is or if she's an unwilling or willing member. She seems infinitely amused when Juliet attacks Adam back during the book club argument.

Diane: A soldier sent on the beach mission, she gives Ryan the all-clear to go onto the beach, and while the others are holding guns, she's holding a needle of some kind in her hand, presumably a sedative. She's killed by one of the dynamite explosions.

Sabine: We never actually see this Other while she's still alive, but in Juliet's flashback in "One of Us," Sabine is the dead woman on the operating table who died because she was pregnant. Ben tells Juliet that Sabine knew what she was getting into, and wanted to get pregnant anyway.

Cindy Chandler: She was the flight attendant on Oceanic Flight 815 who was in the tail section of the plane when it crashed. She was kidnapped by the Others in "The Other 48 Days," but when we next see her in "Stranger in a Strange Land," she's been assimilated into their group. When Locke talks to her in "The Brig," she's a happy and willing member.

Emma and Zack: Two of the children in the tail section of the plane who were kidnapped at night, they are also part of the Others now because they are with Cindy, but it's unclear if they are willing members.

Sources

Adalian, Joseph. "*Lost* Set for Three More Years." *Variety*. May 6, 2007.

Armstrong, Jennifer. "The Tailie's End." *Entertainment Weekly*. November 10, 2006.

"The Art of Playing God — Lessons from UMMO." *Brainsturbator*. Online. Accessed June 1, 2007.

Ausiello, Michael. "Exclusive! *Lost* Snags 'Brazilian Tom Cruise'!" *TV Guide Online*. July 25, 2006.

—. "My Top 10 of 2006!" *TV Guide Online*. December 28, 2006.

Basgen, Brian. "Mikhail Bakunin: A Biography." Marxists Internet Archive. Online. Accessed June 5, 2007.

Baum, L. Frank. *The Wonderful Wizard of Oz*. New York: Sterling, 2005. [Original published 1900.]

Brevet, Brad. "Rodrigo Santoro on *300*: The God-King Speaks!" *Rope of Silicon*. Online. Accessed March 6, 2007.

Butlin's Memories. www.butlinsmemories.com. Online. Accessed May 24, 2007.

Carreau, Isabelle. "Kiele Sanchez — In the Limelight." *TV Squad*. Online. March 20, 2007.

Carroll, Lewis. *The Annotated Alice*. Ed. Martin Gardner. New York: Penguin, 1987.

Crook, John. "Michael Emerson." Zap2it.com. Online. March 18, 2007.

Dickens, Charles. *Four Novels: Oliver Twist, A Tale of Two Cities, Great Expectations, A Christmas Carol*. New York: Barnes and Noble Books, 1992.

Doorly, Sean. "The Castaways and the Crew of *Lost* Come Clean." *TV Tattler*. Online. September 5, 2006.

"Feast of the Ascension." *Catholic Encyclopedia*. Online. Accessed June 5, 2007.

"Feast of the Ascension." LovetoKnow1911. Online. Accessed June 5, 2007.

"Feast of the Ascension of Our Lord and Savior Jesus Christ." *Greek Orthodox Archdiocese of America*. Online. Accessed June 5, 2007.

Fernandez, Maria Elena. "*Lost*'s Mr. Eko Says Goodbye." *LA Times*. November 3, 2006.

Gilchrist, Todd. "Interview: Michael Emerson." *IGN*. Online. August 23, 2006.

"The Hatch Is History, Stars of *Lost* Reveal." Associated Press. August 16, 2006.

Hawking, Stephen. *A Brief History of Time: From the Big Bang to Black Holes*. New York: Bantam, 1990. [Original published 1988.]

Heller, Joseph. *Catch-22*. New York: Simon & Schuster, 2004. [Original published 1955.]

Internet Movie Database. imdb.com. Online.

"Interview: Carlton Cuse Season 3 Details and Info." *IGN*. Online. Accessed August 21, 2006.

Juba, Scott. "Elizabeth Mitchell — Lost with the Others." *The Trades*. Online. February 6, 2007.

—. "Michael Emerson: A Romantic 'Other.'" *The Trades*. Online. March 21, 2007.

—. "Michael Emerson: The *Other* Illustrator." *The Trades*. Online. June 14, 2006.

—. "Yunjin Kim: Across Continents." *The Trades*. Online. June 28, 2006.

Keck, William. "Happy to Be in Hawaii." *USA Today*. August 25, 2006.

—. "Santoro Leaves Fame in Brazil to Find 'Lost'." *USA Today*. November 1, 2006.

—. "The *Lost* Cast Answers Your Questions." *USA Today*. August 16, 2006.

—. "The Shadowy Others Take Charge on *Lost*." *USA Today*. October 4, 2006.

"Kiele Sanchez." Tvnz.co.nz. Online. Accessed June 14, 2007.

King, Stephen. *Carrie*. New York: Pocket Books, 1999. [Original published 1974.]

—. *On Writing: A Memoir*. New York: New English Library, 2001.

Lachonis, Jon. "*Lost* to Deliver the Goods in March." Buddy TV. Online. March 6, 2007.

Lee, Harper. *To Kill a Mockingbird*. New York: HarperCollins, 1999. [Original published 1960.]

Lost. TV Series. Exec. Prod. Carlton Cuse, Damon Lindelof. ABC. 2004–

"*Lost* Boss Explains Last Night's Double Demise." *TV Guide Online*. March 29, 2007.

"Mikhail Bakunin." flag.blackened.net. Online. Accessed June 10, 2007.

Morrison, Mike. "A Perfect 10." infoplease.com. Online. Accessed June 5, 2007.

Nichols, Katherine. "'Lost' Actress Feels at Home." *Honolulu Star-Bulletin.* February 9, 2007.

Night & Day Café. www.nightnday.org. Online. Accessed May 24, 2007.

Pearlman, Cindy. "Santoro Finds 'Lost'." *Chicago Sun-Times.* March 11, 2007.

Porter, Rick. "*Lost*'s Long 'Day Break.'" Zap2it. Online. July 18, 2006.

The Prisoner — Complete Series (40th Anniversary Edition). DVD. A&E Home Video. 2006.

Ramati, Phillip. "Interview with *Lost*'s Michael Emerson." The TV Guy. Blog. May 4, 2007.

Ravitz, Justin. "'Lost': What Can Ben Tell Us about Season Four?" *NY Mag.* Online. May 25, 2007.

Renaud, Jeff. "Gale Force." *Geek.* March 2007.

"Saints and Angels." *Catholic Online.* Online. Accessed June 5–8, 2007.

"Sanchez Boards *Lost* Season 3." *Variety.* August 6, 2006.

Sells, Mark. "Michael Emerson." The Reel Deal. Online. March 2007.

Snierson, Dan. "Elizabeth Mitchell." *Entertainment Weekly.* November 3, 2006.

"Something Really Big." *Honolulu Advertiser.* August 16, 2006.

Song, Jaymes. "Actor Emerson Takes Charge of the Others." Associated Press. September 27, 2006.

"St. Anne." *Catholic Encyclopedia (1913).* Wikisource. Online. Accessed June 8, 2007.

Steinbeck, John. *Of Mice and Men: Steinbeck Centennial Edition.* New York: Penguin, 2002. [Original pubished 1937.]

"Where Did He Come From?" *The Star Online eCentral.* Online. June 7, 2007.

Wikipedia. wikipedia.org. Online.

Yuan, Jada. "The 'Lost' Finale: Character Deaths, a Secret Ending, and a Blank Page." *NY Mag.* Online. Accessed May 23, 2007.

The essential companion to the first two seasons of **LOST**

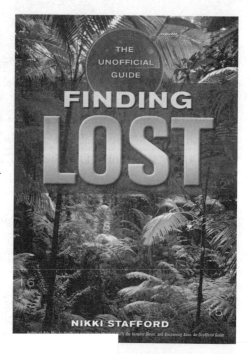

"If you're a fan of the popular TV show *Lost*, you can't be without this unofficial guide."
— *California Bookwatch*

"Stafford has a gift for writing about television and this book is an interesting read and definitely a must for any *Lost* fan."
— The Medium Online

"[A]fter ... an in... for th... ...hree armed with ...uch better feel ...est guides to a ...

- an in-depth episode guide and bios of all of the major actors on the show
- chapters on the real John Locke and Jean-Jacques Rousseau (and how they compare to the fictional ones), fan conspiracy theories, the blast door map, the Dharma symbol, and B.F. Skinner
- sidebars chronicling trivia such as Sawyer's nicknames for people; what Hurley's numbers could mean; Vincent's mysterious appearances and disappearances; the redemption of the characters
- summaries of the show's literary references, including *Lord of the Flies*, *The Third Policeman*, *Our Mutual Friend*, *Watership Down*, and many more

Finding Lost: The Unofficial Guide
ISBN-13: 978-1-55022-743-7 / $19.95 Cdn, $17.95 U.S.

Throughout season 4, check out Nikki Stafford's regular *Lost* updates and episode guides at her blog at Nik at Nite

http://nikkistafford.blogspot.com